COLONIAL AFRICA

CROOM HELM HISTORICAL GEOGRAPHY SERIES
Edited by R. A. Butlin, University of Loughborough

Colonial Africa

A.J. Christopher

CROOM HELM
London & Canberra

BARNES & NOBLE BOOKS
Totowa, New Jersey

© 1984 A.J. Christopher
Croom Helm Ltd, Provident House, Burrell Row,
Beckenham, Kent BR3 1AT

Croom Helm Australia Pty Ltd,
28 Kembla Street, Fyshwick,
ACT 2609, Australia

British Library Cataloguing in Publication Data

Christopher, A.J.
    Colonial Africa.—(Croom Helm
    historical geography series)
    1. Africa—Historical geography
    I. Title.
    911'.6DT4

ISBN 0-7099-0368-5

First published in the USA 1984 by
BARNES & NOBLE BOOKS
81 Adams Drive
Totowa, New Jersey, 07512

ISBN: 0-389-20452-8

Printed and bound in Great Britain

CONTENTS

For the Great Aunts
who went to Australia instead

LIST OF FIGURES

PREFACE

Over 20 years have passed since the formal ending of the colonial era for most of the African continent. Some degree of objectivity can now be brought to bear upon what was for much of Africa, a short but important episode in its history, and an assessment of the European impact weighed. This stage has been reached in the discipline of History where the Cambridge and UNESCO series of volumes offer some degree of synthesis and perspective on the African experience. In Geography this stage has not yet been reached. Comparatively little has been written in the field of historical geography and the colonial impress has been a neglected area of research. The present work can be no more than a brief introduction to one aspect of the colonial period, namely the impact of the colonisers upon the landscape of the continent. It is to be hoped that others will follow to increase our understanding of the era.

I should like to thank the staffs of the many universities, institutes, libraries and government departments, as well as individuals in Africa, America and Europe, who have assisted me. Financial assistance towards the costs of research from the Human Sciences Research Council and the University of Port Elizabeth is gratefully acknowledged. My thanks are also due to Columbia University, New York, where I spent sabbatical leave availing myself of its excellent research facilities. I express my gratitude to Catherine Lawrence for her expertise in preparing the diagrams and to Mrs Anna Bouwer and her typing pool for their skill in typing from the manuscript text. Not least I wish to record my appreciation of the substantial contribution made by my wife, Anne, to both the field-work and editing and for lightening the task considerably.

A.J. Christopher
Port Elizabeth

INTRODUCTION

'The past is another country: they do things differently there.'
The Go-Between

There have been few more remarkable events in the past 100 years than the European colonisation and decolonisation of Africa. Often within a single lifespan countries were conquered, reorganised, settled and then granted independence. For most of the continent the experience was of such short duration, although parts had been subject to European control since the fifteenth century. The economic and political expansion of the European powers influenced the development and underdevelopment of Africa over a far longer period than that of formal colonial control, as the various societies of the continent were integrated into the world economy.

During most of the period of contact between Europe and Africa, political and military control by the former was limited, often to no more than a few forts and trading posts on the coast. African polities remained intact and operated independently of Europe. With the exception of Southern Africa this remained the pattern from the Portuguese capture of Ceuta in 1415 until the French intervention in North Africa in 1830. Only in the 1880s, symbolised by the rules adopted at the Berlin Conference of 1884-5, were the coastal enclaves expanded to encompass virtually the whole of Africa by the time of the First World War. Clearly the more than four centuries of coastal contact were of a different nature from the later-nineteenth- and twentieth-century Imperial intervention, and the two need to be treated as distinct phases.

It may be asked why this intervention took place at all? In simplistic terms the initial Portuguese thrust into Africa in the fifteenth century provides an answer which was as valid for later periods (Boxer, 1969, pp. 17 – 25). The Portuguese entered Africa with five basic goals. The first was scientific; the need to explore the continent with the objective of finding a sea route to India. The second was commercial; seeking to open trade within the continent and beyond. The third goal was military; to assess the strength of the Moslem enemy and the fourth was to link up with any Christian powers to be found. Finally, missionary activity was to be directed to the saving of souls. Although these aims remained throughout the colonial period, if in modified form, it was the aspect of commercial gain which came to dominate the enterprise and guide most other European powers which became involved in the continent. Once involved, disengagement usually proved to be impossible. Further, the distinctions between trade, industry, civilisation and Christianity were at times somewhat blurred.

It was the later Imperial phase which witnessed the greatest transformation of Africa. New states were established and boundaries demarcated. New towns were founded and old ones selectively expanded or abandoned. The communication patterns of the continent were enlarged and realigned. New forms of communication were introduced, more especially the railway. European colonisation was encouraged both in the rural and urban areas, producing enclaves of European society in an African setting. The major lineaments of the colonial era were drawn in the 30 years between 1884 and 1914. Thereafter the continent was more the scene of neglect as the metropolitan powers sought to solve their own internal problems. Attention was only redirected to Africa briefly in the 1950s and 1960s as decolonisation took place.

In attempting to organise the subject, the basic Turnerian frontier thesis with its elaborations as Webb's (1952) Great Frontier and Wallerstein's (1974, 1976) Modern World System appear to offer some perspective. An examination of the imprint of the various groups of Europeans interacting with Africans and with the African environment, offers a means of disentangling the complex changes which took place in the geography of Africa in the colonial period. It must be remembered that Africa was peripheral to European interests and that the numbers involved were small compared with those engaged in penetrating the other continents on the Great Frontier. Furthermore, many of the social and political ideas associated with the Turner thesis, such as the growth of democracy and private enterprise, did not apply in an environment where state control was so pervasive (Billington, 1961). In this Africa followed the Latin American, not the Anglo-American prototype, unfettered by the laws and representative assemblies which characterised the metropoles (Hennessy, 1978). It was the distinctive colonial state which emerged, not a developed frontier state. However, this does not detract from the approach of examining the imprint of the various colonisers (Gann and Duignan, 1969).

The landscape of Africa was partially transformed in the colonial period by the various groups within the colonisation movement.

Each contributed elements to the landscape reflecting not only their function but also national style. The European penetration of the continent was not one monolithic movement but made up of several different nationalities who were usually in competition with one another. Eleven European countries established bases on the African continent, while seven took part in the final scramble of the 1880s and 1890s. Each sought to place its own impress upon Africa, with its own ideas and organisation, adding to the diversity of African societies and landscapes in the reproduction of European diversity on the continent. The evolution of the African landscape under colonialism therefore offers insights into both Meinig's (1982) geographical analysis of imperial expansion, and because of the high degree of state invervention, Whittlesey's (1935) impress of central authority paradigms.

Despite their divergent national origins, the various groups involved in the colonisation process each acted with some degree of international cohesion. The politicians, most of whom never visited Africa, drew the boundaries of the new colonies, which are one of the greatest collective inheritances received by the post-Independence African states. The soldiers carried out the conquest of the continent and frequently chose the posts from which to control the population. The military often formed the first colonial governments and coercion was an essential part of the maintenance of colonial administration (Gann and Duignan, 1979a). Indeed the demarcation between soldier and administrator in the colonies was rarely defined. The administrators determined the pattern of urban settlement by selecting the administrative posts and deciding upon the nature of the administrative regime. European priorities differed from African and it was the administrator who was faced with reconciling these divergent ideals.

The traders constitute another major group who influenced the landscape of Africa, whether at the scale of one of the major chartered trading companies such as the Dutch East India Company or the Royal Niger Company, or at the scale of individual traders who established trading stores at considerable distances from the wholesale centres (Moodie and Lehr, 1981). Trading required posts, but it also required transportation and the carriers constitute a group who redirected trade along new routes linked to the rest of the world, often with little regard for neighbouring colonies or pre-colonial trading systems. Hence there was created the entrepôt, the overwhelmingly important coastal link between the ocean trade and the inland trade routes. Trade at times was little more than a matter of hunting and gathering the human, animal and vegetable resources of the continent, although in the latter phase it evolved into plantation work. The continent was also viewed as a field for explorers, who drew the map and filled in the blank spaces, whether it was the coastal outline in the fifteenth and sixteenth centuries, topographical detail in the nineteenth or geological in the twentieth. The influence of the missionaries also should not be forgotten as providing respectability and a *raison d'être* for colonisation, although their impact upon the landscape was comparatively small in itself. Individuals, or indeed groups, often possessed more than one function, and saw their work in one field as being complementary to their work in another. Missionaries acted as traders, and traders as administrators. Few clear distinctions were visable, so that a framework based on function must in some measure be arbitrary.

The groups so far referred to were small, itinerant, and few were likely to make Africa their permanent home. However, two further groups introduced a completely different aspect to the colonial experience: the miners and the settlers. Permanent intercontinental settlers, usually initially agricultural, left Europe in substantial numbers from the sixteenth century onwards. Few came to Africa owing to the political and medical obstacles to settlement. However, at the two extremities of the continent and in a few favoured localities in between, the natural environment was physically akin to the other lands of mid-latitude settlement. The result was an attempt to establish permanent European colonies of settlement on the continent. The settlers, as in the Americas and Australia, transformed the landscape by creating a new one as close to their image of Europe as possible. Agricultural settlement, with its attendant urban elements was a slow process in Africa. It was the influx of miners into Southern Africa, with their demands, which enabled a precarious settlement to be converted into a major industrial power and a sub-core of the world economy, even during the colonial era. In North Africa it was the direct intervention of the state which fostered the development of colonisation, but with a consequently heavy dependence upon the political decisions taken in the metropole. The mixed heritage of these groups still hangs over Africa, posing the question as to whether the colonial era has ended? Although settlers were present in many parts of the continent, White African nations were few. The Afrikaners of South Africa achieved the most complete identity as a separate nation but others in Southern Africa, such as the English settlers even of the Rhodesia of the 1965 – 79 era, were too attached to the metropole in Europe to create a new identity. The French colonists in Algeria in the late nineteenth century began the same process but fell back on metropolitan France for both economic and military support, to an extent that Algeria was conceived of as an extension of France overseas.

As in the elaboration of the Turnerian frontier thesis so the number of characters in the colonisation of Africa can be increased. Gautier (1930) in his study of Algeria noted the significance of the intellectual in the development of overseas communities and the acculturation of the African population to European civilisation. He also recognised the significance of the indigenous population in providing the mass of labour needed to effect the various schemes of the colonial period, one of the major departures from Turnerian theory. The majority of the colonial armies and police forces were manned by Africans. In the First World War, Africans under British and French command fought other Africans officered by Germans. In administration the majority of positions were held by the indigenous population. Much of the early colonial trading activity, and indeed in large parts of the continent trade in general, remained in African hands, with the exception of the coastal whole-sale trade. The major construction, agricultural, and industrial works of the colonial era relied upon the employment of large numbers of labourers, who were recruited by force or enticement. Slaves, indentured labourers, and free men physically built the railways, cleared the forests, planted and harvested the crops on European owned farms, and laboured in the mines and towns to build up the colonial economy; and finally paid taxes to maintain the administration. For much of the colonial period labour even provided the main form of African merchandise, through the iniquitous trans-Atlantic slave trade.

The African contribution to the colonial era has been the subject of much recent writing as changes in historiography have reflected the ending of the colonial relationship. An Afrocentric history of Africa has become the norm and inevitably new priorities in research have arisen (Curtin, 1981). In addition to the rediscovery of the pre-colonial period, historians have proceeded with the re-interpretation of African perspectives, concentrating upon two major aspects of the colonial era, namely, underdevelopment and class formation. The inevitability, even the necessity for African underdevelopment for the functioning of the colonial state has been proposed. It has been suggested that without the impoverishment of the African sector of the economy the European colonial powers would have been unable to profit from their colonies (Rodney, 1972).

In radical historiography, the impoverishment of the indigenous population thus became the unstated policy of the colonial administrations (Temu and Swai, 1982). This is in contradiction with the liberal approach to African history which sought to explain the disruption of African societies in terms of cultural constraints and the problems for the indigenous population in rapidly adapting to the changing circumstances of colonial rule (Wright, 1977). The idea that given the opportunities, the indigenous peoples could gradually adapt to the perceived favourable openings offered by the world market economy, was fundamental to much liberal writing in the colonial period and immediately afterwards. Research, however, also revealed a picture of rapid indigenous adjustment to changing economic conditions. Indeed African successes in agricultural adaptation in the southern and central regions of the continent have been well documented (Palmer and Parsons, 1977). Whether this reveals the taking up of spare capacity within the traditional agricultural and social systems or a radical rearrangement of social and economic relationships is still a matter of fundamental dispute. However, to create a cheap labour supply for expanding colonial industry and agriculture, the destruction of the emergent African peasantry was essential and it was only through determined government action that this could be achieved (Samuel, 1981). Whether the colonial governments acted in such a manner, or whether the seeds of destruction were to be found in the survival of elements of traditional society also remains a subject for resolution. Proletarianisation thus became a major theme in African history in the 1970s and the broader aspects of People's History offers a perspective for further investigation in the 1980s (Cooper, 1981).

The impact of urban class formation and its effects upon the development of the colonial city have been most intensively studied for the Witwatersrand (Van Onselen, 1982). It was in the South African gold mining complex that the first truly industrial society emerged on the continent. As such it is of vital importance for an understanding of the rapid succession of changes which overtook the population drawn or pushed towards the expanding urban agglomeration. As yet the geographical implications of these changes for the spatial organisation of the industrial cities have been little explored (Beavon and Rogerson, 1980). Republican and colonial administrations in the Transvaal attempted to avoid the worst features visible in European and American industrialisation for the settler population, through state intervention. No such humane concern was expressed for the African population which was reduced to a migratory cheap labour force by rural impoverishment and the increasing demands of the colonial state. Clearly such developments over a short period of time, sometimes within a single working life, were of profound significance for the indigenous population, and for the continuing image of the colonial period.

The African role in the colonial era was of fundamental significance. However, owing to the restrictions placed upon the author by the length of the work, a necessarily abbreviated view must be pursued against such a vast background. The focus of this volume will therefore be directed towards certain aspects of European control and the impact of the colonialists upon the landscape of Africa. The African contribution requires extended treatment which it is hoped may be forthcoming in a later volume.

Each of the aforementioned European groups influenced the form of the landscape, but within the colonies of settlement the changes were more radical, and these will be examined more extensively than those areas where it was largely the economic influences of colonialism which were at work. The basic psychology of the colonial era also needs to be understood. To return to the quotation from the *Go-Between*, prefacing the Introduction, the colonial period is indeed another country. The colonial powers and peoples did things differently, often with little regard for the contemporary ideas of legality in Europe or regard for the rights of their African compatriots. The title of a recent political study of Zimbabwe in the colonial period, *The Past is Another Country: Rhodesia 1890-1979*, illustrates the point that Rhodesia and Zimbabwe are two different countries (Meredith, 1979). Similarly settler Rhodesians and indigenous Zimbabweans did things differently, and this is reflected in the landscapes of the single geographical entity they occupied. There is a warning in this observation. Historical Geography, as Moodie and Lehr (1976) have emphasised, is not 'old geography'. The geographies of the continent written in the colonial era (Bernard, 1937a; Maurette, 1938; Stamp, 1953), or immediately after independence (Hance, 1964) therefore have not become historical geographies. Geographers also did things differently. A comparison of studies such as Hardy's *Géographie et colonisation* (1933) and Isnard's *Géographie et décolonisation* (1971) reflect the changing perspectives. The emulation of the chairs of Colonial Geography established in France, was sought in England as late as 1948 (Harrison-Church, 1948). However, once the colonial period had ended, colonial geography disappeared with political control. Few works in African historical geography were published in the 1960s and 1970s (Dickson, 1969, 1972; Christopher, 1976a). Now after a space of more than 20 years it may be possible to examine the colonial period in Africa in terms of contemporary historical geography, independent of colonial geography.

1 THE FORERUNNERS

Those who for a long period from the fifteenth to the nineteenth century established and maintained the coastal enclaves of Europe upon the African continent, and sought a better understanding of the interior, may be regarded as the forerunners. During a period of 400 years the European link was territorially small and the numbers involved were limited, but because of the very persistence of European control, the impact was highly significant for the nineteenth and twentieth century development of colonialism. Three elements of geographical concern in this period will be examined, namely the importance of the explorers, the traders and soldiers, and the evangelists and settlers. The larger scale colonisation of the Cape of Good Hope is reserved for a later chapter.

The Explorers

The classical understanding of the geography of Africa was continuously revised in the North by reports of voyages in the Mediterranean; but of the regions beyond these shores, European knowledge in 1400 was no more advanced than it had been a 1,000 years before. The first priority of European contact was therefore the exploration and mapping of Africa. This fell into at least three stages. The first was the charting of the coast and the exploration of the sea route from Europe to India around the continent. The second was the mapping of the interior through the linking of the main rivers and the determination of the positions of towns and other features. The third phase was the exploration of other aspects of the geography of the continent, whereby the surveyor, botanist, zoologist, geologist and anthropologist all contributed to the compilation of a body of knowledge superseding the image of the 'Dark Continent'.

The exploration of the coast was achieved by the Portuguese in the course of the fifteenth century, culminating in Vasco da Gama's voyage to India in 1499 (Boxer, 1969). The capture of Ceuta in 1415 was the first stage in securing a series of bases along the African coast. Exploration was directed towards the extension of the known coastline, more especially beyond Cape Bojador, which was believed to hide an awesome green boiling ocean of darkness. This was rounded in 1434 and the achievement was a major psychological breakthrough in addition to being a remarkable scientific and technological advance. Subsequently the fishing grounds off the Guinea coast were explored as were the offshore islands of the Azores, Cape Verde Islands, Fernando Poo, Sao Tomé and Principe. In 1482 the Congo mouth was reached and in 1488 the Cape of Good Hope was rounded by Bartholomeu Dias. Finally the route to India was opened by Vasco da Gama, as a result of which the Portuguese entered the Indian Ocean trading system, replacing the previous carriers and gaining their knowledge of the coastline. At each stage the Portuguese advance was marked by a stone cross (padrao) indicating the extent of discovery . These were erected as far as Malindi, from where da Gama sailed for India.

European knowledge of the interior of the African continent depended upon Arabic and other traditions, many of them highly fanciful. In addition there was much wishful and inaccurate thinking. The courses of the Niger and the Nile were open to speculation, while the sources of the gold supplies in West and East Africa similarly excited much controversy. Yet legends such as the wealth of Timbuktu or the power of the Christian kingdom of Prester John allowed the optimism of the Renaissance map makers to fill the gaps with highly imaginative interpretations of the known and the unknown. Reality was slow to dawn. Successive 'Prester Johns' were discovered but the final contact between Portugal and Ethiopia in the mid-sixteenth century revealed that it was Ethiopia which needed assistance against its Moslem neighbours and thus was unable to assist Portugal in its original aims. The legend of Timbuktu survived the conquest of the Songhay Empire by Morocco in 1591 as information exchange tended to be limited between Moslem and Christian powers and indeed between one European power and another.

Active exploration of the interior was limited by the disease element and an often inhospitable reception accorded lone explorers who attempted to force their way across the continent. The origins of the gold supplies were closely guarded secrets not open to European travellers, who were viewed with suspicion in their vicinity. In Moslem areas Christian explorers were regarded as infidels and spies from hostile powers and treated accordingly. It is thus scarcely surprising that Jonathan Swift penned his well-known lines in the eighteenth century – after 300 years of exploration:

So geographers in Afric maps,
With savage pictures fill their gaps,
And o'er inhabitable downs,
Place elephants for want of towns.

Nevertheless, even as Swift wrote, maps were becoming more factual, following Guillaume De l'Isle's map of Africa in 1700 which removed the mythical and unsubstantiated material from the continent, leaving most of the interior blank. It took a further 200 years of exploration to fill in the gaps.

The explorers who spearheaded the European penetration of Africa in the sixteenth and seventeenth centuries had largely been defeated by disease in the central part of the continent, and by religious suspicions in the north. Only in the south had exploratory parties in the seventeenth and eighteenth centuries made much headway, and that not particularly encouraging as extensive aridity was the major finding (Forbes, 1965; Raven-Hart, 1967). Few attempted to penetrate north of the Orange River until the nineteenth century.

A reawakening of exploratory activity occurred in the late eighteenth and early nineteenth centuries, in the age of scientific enlightenment, when the gaps in the map of Africa appeared particularly challenging to the spirit of enquiry (Cameron, 1980). In 1788 the African Association was established in London to explore the continent. This merged in 1831 with the (Royal) Geographical Society, founded in 1830, which was but one of a number of societies established at the time to promote geographical knowledge. The Paris Society of Geography, founded in 1821, and the Berlin Geographical Society, founded in 1828, promoted exploration by offering prizes for unravelling particular objectives and by employing explorers. In the course of the century most countries in Europe and the United States of America established such organisations with the aim of exploring the African continent.

In all their journeys the explorers were heavily dependent upon the indigenous population, for information, guides, interpreters, and as the nineteenth century progressed, porters. The explorers generally travelled on well-known paths, whether the trans-Saharan caravan routes or the Zanzibari trade routes of East Africa. Many of the major discoveries were the result of information offered to the explorers to guide them to phenomena which the local inhabitants either thought curious or worthy of admiration. Thus David Livingstone was shown the Victoria Falls in 1855 by a friendly chief, while John Speke was told of Lake Victoria in 1858, (where a Zanzibari trader maintained a trading base), only in casual conversation. Despite the truism that all places were known to somebody, the main point of European exploration was to piece the information together and produce a map of the whole.

Although most explorers received a great deal of assistance, there were considerable problems. In particular suspicion and hostility had to be overcome. This was particularly prevalent in the Moslem areas where religious fundamentalism viewed Christian travellers, with some justification, as spies for hostile countries. This also applied to non-Islamic states where the arrival of armed strangers was the subject of mixed emotions. The confrontation between Samuel Baker and Kamurasi of Bunyoro in 1864 illustrates the problems involved for both the explorer and the local ruler. Baker's request to visit Lake Albert, about which he had heard as a source of the Nile, was met with delays and problems. Oral tradition records 'Kamurasi knew that the stranger was speaking lies, for no man would leave his own country and people, and face danger and fatigue merely to look at water' (Rotberg, 1970, p. 161). In this Kamurasi was overly suspicious of the individual, although Baker at the time was in the employ of the Egyptian government, with the purpose of establishing the province of Equatoria in the East African Lake region. Explorers were the forerunners of others to come, who sought to undermine society through conversion to Christianity, trade at disadvantageous conversion rates, and finally conquest in order to impose alien colonial rule.

The Niger route became one of the first areas of exploratory activity, when the African Association sent Mungo Park on two expeditions. The first from Gambia reached the Niger and the second, on which all were killed, followed the river to a point 1,000 km below Timbuktu, but the explorers failed to see the city itself. In 1824 the Geographical Society of Paris offered 2,000 frs. as a prize for the first man to reach Timbuktu. Four years later René Caillié accomplished the journey from Senegal, returning across the Sahara Desert. The accounts which Caillié gave were sufficient to dispel many of the ideas of the riches in the interior of the Sudan, as James Bruce's explorations had done for Ethiopia at the end of the eighteenth century.

The course of the lower Niger was finally solved by the journey of the Landers brothers in 1830, who showed it to emerge between the

Bights of Benin and Biafra, and thus not connected to either the Nile or Congo systems. The West African interior was explored by Heinrich Barth and Gerhard Rohlfs as well as a host of French explorers who opened the way for military conquest. In general the direction of approach was from the north and the interior of West Africa was viewed in North African terms.

Attention was directed towards East and Central Africa in the mid-nineteenth century. A series of major explorations took place in the 1850s with the object of solving many of the remaining problems of the geography of the continent, more particularly the drainage systems. David Livingstone explored south-central Africa, crossing from coast to coast between 1853 and 1856, and later from 1858 to 1863 exploring the Lake Nyasa region. His last journeyings from 1866 to 1873 could more properly be described as wanderings, but it was his concern as a missionary first and foremost that inspired his explorations and indeed for which he was later to receive acknowledgement in Europe. He stirred an awareness of Africa and its problems and so inspired a sense of moral duty to improve the social and economic state of the continent among influential groups in England.

Richard Burton and John Speke explored the lake systems of East Africa in 1857-8 and finally (1861-2) solved the mystery of the sources of the Nile. Samuel Baker virtually completed this exploration in the mid-1860s, while Henry Stanley examined the Congo basin. Thus the broad outlines of the geography of Africa were known by the 1870s. Individual exploration of smaller areas continued into the colonial period as the gaps were filled in. Often the detailed mapping only followed the partition of Africa which ensued, but Africa was not an unknown continent when European states began the 'scramble'; although the imperfections of that knowledge were particularly serious in matters of boundary definition and the granting of concessions.

The last major blanks upon European maps were in the Sahara, where the combination of aridity and indigenous hostility was particularly difficult to overcome (Ettinger *et al.*, 1973). Individual explorers had attached themselves to caravans crossing the Sahara, as Caillié had done, but systematic survey was impossible in such circumstances, and the death-rate among explorers was exceptionally high. The impetus to exploration came finally from the French, who, after sustained army losses in Southern Algeria, launched a major expedition under the experienced Fernand

Foureau in 1898-9, which crossed the Desert from Algeria to Niger. In the early twentieth century military exploration was pursued by Henri Laperrine, who built up the fort system in southern Algeria, mapping the previously unknown Desert. In 1920 and 1922 a new age was introduced by the first flight over the Sahara, and the Citroen tracked vehicles which successfully crossed the desert landscape.

The Soldiers and Traders

Military penetration of Africa was pursued immediately after exploration in the fifteenth and sixteenth centuries, but thereafter slackened as interest in Africa declined and the Portuguese and other nations failed to find the wealth and power they sought. Attention was directed to other parts of the world and the military visions of the early stages of contact faded. The conquest of the coastal regions may be divided into the systems evolved on the North, West and East coasts. The southern coast was regarded by the explorers as too inhospitable for settlement until the mid-seventeenth century.

The European conquest of North Africa was strictly limited in extent, if the initial aim had been grandiose. The Portuguese, joined later by the Spanish, attempted to extend the reconquest of the Iberian peninsula across the Mediterranean to the heart of Morocco and the Maghreb (Braudel, 1976). However, they never successfully reached beyond the capture of the coastal fortresses. The advance was checked and after the disastrous battle of Alcazarquivir in 1578, Portuguese ambitions in North Africa were terminated. Nevertheless they retained their last three coastal cities for some time: Ceuta passed to the Spanish in 1640; Tangier was ceded to England in 1661, but abandoned in 1684 owing to the excessive expenses of maintaining the garrison; and Mazagan, which was only abandoned in 1769, again for reasons of economy (Ricard, 1936). Spanish intervention was initiated in 1502 with the capture of Melilla. In the following 40 years the Spanish crusade resulted in the capture of a chain of towns from Melilla to Tripoli. However, the failure of the Emperor Charles V's expedition to subdue the city of Algiers in 1541 dashed hopes of converting North Africa into an Iberian Christian province. Although the Spanish have remained in North Africa until the present, the towns slowly slipped from their control, leaving only Ceuta and Melilla in Spanish hands by the end of 1791. This line of intervention collapsed through lack of funds and manpower. The North African enterprise has been cited as the last of the political and religious expansions controlled by the nobility, as opposed to the essentially mercantile aims of the remainder of Portuguese and Spanish overseas ventures (Wallerstein, 1974, p. 47).

The Portuguese and other powers trading on the West coast of Africa built, over a period of 300 years, more than 60 castles, forts and lodges along a stretch of coast less than 500 km in length. Most of these were concentrated in the comparatively short distance of the Gold Coast. In Van Dantzig's (1980, p. 1) words 'the whole chain of buildings . . . could be seen as a collective historical monument unique in the world: the ancient "shopping street of West Africa" '. They are also significant in that they were largely built with the consent and often at the request of the local African rulers. There were misgivings however, as witness the local ruler at Elmina in 1482 who perceptively claimed that a permanent European settlement would not be conducive to good relations (Boxer, 1969, p. 32). Until the nineteenth century the Europeans had no territorial jurisdiction and even the forts and castles were built on land rented from the local African rulers. Indeed although the first of these were erected with strong landward defences, the Portuguese soon realised that the real threat to their security came from other European vessels and it was the sea defences which needed to be strengthened.

The major castles housed the headquarters of the trading countries (Lawrence, 1963). The first was established at Arguim off the Mauritanian coast in the period of 1445 – 55 in an attempt to tap the trans-Saharan gold trade of the western Sudan. It became the prototype of the fortified post which the Portuguese built along their routes to the East Indies. Castilian interference with Portuguese trade in the 1470s prompted the construction of the most important castle at Elmina in 1482. The stone structure was built according to the latest principles of fortification developed in Italy, to serve as a military base, trading post and as a centre for evangelism. The commercial object of the castle was to attract the gold trade to the south and thus bypass North Africa. In this they were successful as the mines lay close to the castles and satisfactory trade relations were established. Similarly the Portuguese initiated the slave trade, at first directed towards Portugal and later towards the

Atlantic islands, such as the Cape Verde Islands and more especially Sao Tomé. Early in the sixteenth century direct exportation to Brazil began.

The Portuguese elaborated their system on the west coast with a chain of forts and castles from North Africa to Angola. In the first half of the seventeenth century these came under increasing pressure from the Dutch, followed by the British and French; effectively ousting the Portuguese from virtually the entire coast apart from Angola and the islands. The Portuguese West African headquarters at Elmina were captured by the Dutch in 1637 and became the headquarters of the Dutch West India Company. They in turn were followed by Sweden, Denmark, Brandenburg, and Courland (now in Latvia) (Blusse and Gaastra, 1981). The result was a massive building programme. On the Gold Coast alone in the course of the seventeenth century two further major castles, Christianborg (1661) and Cape Coast (1665) were built by the Danes and English respectively. In addition a further 24 forts and a large number of semi-fortified and unfortified posts were constructed, the remains of which have only partially survived. During this period, competition for possession and control of the trade routes was fierce. The wars in Europe were replicated on the West African coast and this resulted in the transfer of the forts belonging to Brandenburg, Sweden and Courland to their competitors soon after their foundation. The French based at St Louis and Gorée similarly built forts which were particularly susceptible to British attack in the eighteenth century. Fort building continued on the Gold Coast until the completion of the Danish Fort Augustaborg at Teki in 1787. Later trading posts such as those constructed by the French in the Ivory Coast in the 1840s abandoned the medieval castle design and were more akin to the trading post of the late colonial era (Atger, 1960).

The forts were viewed primarily as trading posts, and trade was carried on by the factors who represented the Company or the Crown, living in the forts. The middlemen lived in the adjacent towns and villages, which although usually purely indigenous in origin were subject to increasing organisation by the Europeans, especially in the eighteenth century. Greater numbers of Europeans now came to the West Coast, although they were numbered in tens rather than thousands. The French established towns at both St Louis and on the island of Gorée. At Gorée the plan of straight streets was controlled by the limited space between the two forts and the landing beach. Squares were laid out and the churches, governor's palace, hospital, barracks and parade ground were incorporated into the plan. Stone houses, usually double storied, gave an urban character to the settlement. However, even at the end of the eighteenth century the population was little more than 2,000, of whom half were slaves (Delcourt, 1981, p. 19).

As the number of interested countries increased so the number of forts increased, with the various trading routes tapped by several coastal outlets. The local rulers tended to encourage the rivalry of the forts as competition obviously worked to their trading advantage. Thus forts were established within a few kilometres of one another enabling the African traders a choice of outlet. In Dahomey the European traders were carefully regulated until the mid-nineteenth century and military installations were banned. It was soon realised that competition hurt the European trading companies and attempts were made by some to monopolise sectors of the economy. The Swedes in 1654 established the inland Fort Ruychover close to the goldfields, with a view to obtaining a monopoly, but the fort was destroyed five years later and the venture was not repeated. The French were more successful with their chain of ports on the Senegal River, which by 1719 had reached Fort Mediné some 650 km from St Louis.

The business of the forts prior to the early nineteenth century was directed towards the slave trade. This originated in the use of African slaves in Portugal under the Moors and its continuation thereafter. Thus the first West African post at Arguim was engaged in slaving from its inception, and reports suggest that in the late fifteenth century over 1,000 slaves a year were passing through Arguim on their way to Portugal. The slave trade expanded as plantation agriculture was developed on the West Coast islands, more especially Sao Tomé, and then the demand came from Brazil and the West Indies. The trade became increasingly organised as the forts were modified with holding prisons for the slaves, and trading routes were extended into the interior of the continent. By the 1780s long distances were traversed by the slavers, so that the area of capture for the posts at the Congo mouth extended to the lower Ubangi, while the Angola traders penetrated far into the plateau region.

The number of slaves exported from the continent has been the subject of an extensive debate since Curtin's (1969) pioneering attempt to produce a census. The figure of 11,300,000 persons imported into the Americas suggested by Rawley (1981) appears to be the most accurate. The calculation of the number exported is more problematical and possibly a figure of approximately 13,000,000 would allow for the death-rate on the middle passage (Curtin *et al.*, 1976; Inikori, 1978). The trade was not uniform in either time or origin. There was a build-up in activity from the mid-fifteenth century to the eighteenth century when the trade reached its peak. It then tailed off, ending fairly abruptly around 1870. Some 60 per cent of all slaves delivered to the New World were transported in the 100-year period 1721–1820. In part the increasing numbers reflected not only a rise in demand, particularly on the sugar plantations, but also greater efficiency of collection in the interior. This aspect of the trade was in African hands and supply reflected more the position of the African state economies and the results of warfare than fluctuations in demand.

Significantly no coastal region exported slaves at a consistently high rate. Senegambia attained an export peak in the 1710s, Sierra Leone in the 1740s and the Gold Coast in the 1780s. The Bight of Benin, after decline in the early eighteenth century experienced a sudden surge in the 1780s, while the Angolan coast exported its greatest numbers only in the nineteenth century as a result of the contraction of trade north of the equator and the anti-slavery patrols. The abolition of the slave trade by Denmark in 1792 followed by Great Britain and the United States in 1807 did not bring the trade to an end, although it did effectively cease at the forts under the control of those powers. The Spanish and Portuguese trade continued into the 1860s but was subject to increasing harassment by the Royal Navy anti-slavery patrols. The illegal trade was only suppressed when the demand for slaves was satisfied by a flow of indentured labourers, who were legally transported and nominally free. The number of such workers originating from Africa was small.

The termination of the slave trade resulted in a crisis in the West Coast settlements. Their *raison d'être* was removed and a substitute, 'legitimate', trade was difficult to find. Limited quantities of ivory, palm oil and groundnuts partially replaced the slave trade, but the forts became unprofitable. Denmark sold its possessions to Great Britain in 1850 and the Netherlands followed suit in 1872 (Norregard, 1966). In both 1828 and 1865 recommendations were made to Parliament in London that the West African settlements be abandoned. They were not accepted, and the West African settlements remained in the economic doldrums until the revival of trade associated with the development of agricultural export commodities in the last quarter of the nineteenth century, and the conquest of the interior by the European powers at the same time.

The Portuguese penetration of the East African coast was of a different nature from that of the West Coast, as they invaded the existing well-established urban system of the Swahili towns, which were linked by trade to the Middle East, India and, at times, China (Strandes, 1961). Politically though, the system constituted a group of often mutually hostile city states with little control beyond their immediate vicinity. The states were Moslem in faith with a blend of African and Islamic culture distinguishing them from other parts of the continent. Through a common religion they were on occasion able to call upon Moslem powers to come to their aid. Thus the Turks and the Omanis became embroiled in the complex struggle for control of the East African coast. The period of Portuguese supremacy was challenged both by Islamic powers and other European countries, making the history of the European penetration of the East African coast one of conquest, warfare, slaughter and destruction.

The result was the construction of a series of major forts whose purpose was not so much trade as the maintenance of control over the cities. Some replaced pre-existing Swahili forts such as at Moçambique where the mainland fort at Caciebera was abandoned in favour of the island site. Similarly further north the mainland site at Malindi was supplemented by the selection of Mombasa. On these islands two of the major military structures of the continent were built at the end of the sixteenth century to protect the natural harbours: San Sebastian on Moçambique and Fort Jesus on Mombasa (Kirkman, 1975). In addition a series of smaller forts and trading posts were established along the entire East African coast. Only Mogadishu successfully resisted Portuguese control. Politically the rise of the Omani Sultanate in the late seventeenth century resulted in the displacement of the Portuguese from their possessions north of the Rovuma River, with the fall of Mombasa after the siege of 1696-8.

The East Coast cities varied in their response to the Portuguese in terms of acculturation and the imprint of Portuguese powers. Many possessed little more than a trading post with a few Portuguese based there to run it. Thus Malindi was not fortified and the post operated through the generally pro-Portuguese attitude of the rulers of the town. Others including Shela and Faza only occasionally accommodated Europeans and their urban fabric remained entirely Swahili, as indeed did some of the towns which prospered in the colonial era, such as Lamu (Ghaidan, 1976). Yet others were destroyed or bypassed in the search for secure positions in the age of conflict which the Portuguese arrival in the Indian Ocean heralded.

It was the two main settlements at Mombasa and Moçambique which received the greatest imprint prior to the late nineteenth century, although they differed in basic organisation. At Mombasa, Fort Jesus had been constructed some 700 metres south of the Swahili town. The Portuguese settlers were then housed along a street built from the fort entrance to the old town. By 1606 there were some 70 dwellings in the district housing perhaps only 50 Portuguese settlers but a substantial number of Eurafricans and Eurasians (Strandes, 1961, pp. 151-2). The chequered history of Mombasa resulted in the repeated destruction of the European town until the final Omani occupation (Boxer and De Azevedo, 1960). At Moçambique the Portuguese town was built adjacent to the fort and parade ground (Lobato, 1967). It grew gradually and with little planning over the 470-year period of Portuguese rule (Figure 1.1). The organisation evident in Gorée or indeed in later colonial cities was absent, except for the individual embellishments of the public buildings and gardens. The settlement received a considerable boost in the mid-eighteenth century when Moçambique was separated from control from Goa, and municipal government was established. Grand eighteenth-century edifices for the Governor-General's palace, town hall, customs house and hospital were added to the houses and churches of the earlier and contemporary periods. The stone and plaster Portuguese town contrasted markedly with the adjacent indigenous settlement of timber and thatch. This was continuously displaced as the Portuguese-inhabited area expanded, until by the end of the colonial period the entire island was occupied. Thus a twofold division recognisable in later colonial cities was already evident on the east coast in the sixteenth century. The European and indigenous towns were constituted as recognisably separate entities. As on the west coast, the European populations remained small and the death rates were high. In the period 1528-58 some 30,000 men died at Moçambique (Boxer, 1969, p. 218). It is thus hardly surprising that few permanent settlers were attracted to East Africa.

The East Coast economy differed little from that of the West. The

Figure 1.1: Moçambique island

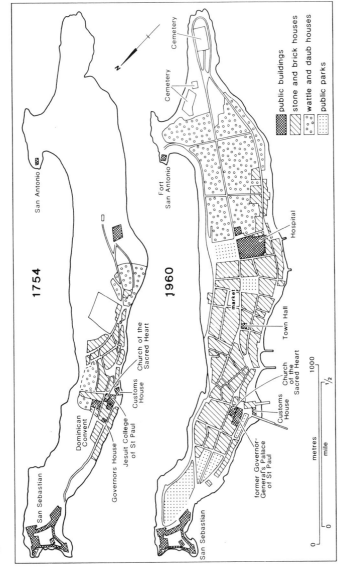

1754

San Sebastian

San Antonio

Dominican Convent

Governors House

Jesuit College of St Paul

Customs House

Church of the Sacred Heart

N

1960

San Sebastian

Cemetery

Cemetery

Cemetery

Fort San Antonio

Hospital

market

Town Hall

former Governor-General's Palace of St Paul

Church of the Sacred Heart

Customs House

public buildings

stone and brick houses

wattle and daub houses

public parks

metres   0   1000

mile   0   ½

Portuguese sought the gold of the interior and hence Sofala became a key post. They also sought to control the Indian Ocean trading system, which was largely achieved for a century until the Dutch penetration of the East Indies. The system brought considerable wealth, as contemporary structures bore witness. The various Portuguese ports operated therefore in a similar manner to the previous Swahili system and it was only in the eighteenth century that Portuguese settlements lost many of their significant functions as they were replaced by other carriers. Later the Moçambiquan ports gained a part in the slave trade, especially after its suppression in the North Atlantic. This was an offshoot of the Angola to Brazil trade which lasted into the second half of the nineteenth century. However, the East African interior proved to be poorer than the West African interior and substitutes for gold, ivory and slaves were not forthcoming to boost the economy of the coastal settlements as these commodities declined in volume.

The Evangelists and Settlers

One of the motives for Portuguese intervention in Africa had been the evangelisation of the indigenous population. The zeal of sixteenth-century missionary activity was only to be met once more in the nineteenth century. Churches and missions were established wherever a response could be found. The greatest success, although a temporary one, was in the Congo kingdom, where Christianity was accepted and an attempt was made to create a Christian kingdom administered on Portuguese tenets (Vansina, 1966). The result was disastrous for Congo society as the strains which rapid Europeanisation caused were too great for its survival. The unequal relationship between the Portuguese and Congolese allowed Portuguese plunder and extortion to continue unhindered, offering little example for the Christian and European ways of life. Many Europeans, including the clergy, became more interested in the slave trade than in saving souls. Civil wars and a lack of Portuguese assistance led to the collapse of the kingdom and the missions in the seventeenth century, symbolised by the transfer of the episcopal see of the Congolese capital, Sao Salvador, to the Portuguese town of Luanda in 1676. Similar attempts to convert the Monomotapa Empire ended in failure and military disaster in 1572. Intermittent missionary activity continued but the Portuguese concentration upon the more attractive field in Brazil spelt the demise of the African enterprise.

Portuguese settlement was limited at first to the islands off the west coast. The sound economics of slave-worked plantations had been demonstrated in Sicily and developed by the Portuguese in the course of the fifteenth century (Tenreiro, 1953). The colonisation of Sao Tomé in the late fifteenth century represented but one step in a chain of colonial enterprises extending from the Algarve in southern Portugal to Brazil. Portuguese settlers obtained land grants from the Crown and then imported labourers from Europe, but predominantly slaves from the African mainland. Thus by the mid-sixteenth century some 8,000 people lived on the island, which had been uninhabited at the time of discovery. The sugar industry by the mid-sixteenth century was organised around some 60 estates and factories which achieved a peak production of over 2,000 tons per annum (Tenreiro, 1961). However, prosperity was of limited duration as later in the century the development of the Brazilian sugar plantations and the depredations of fugitive slaves effectively ruined the economy of the island. Revival only took place in the nineteenth century when coffee and cocoa were introduced.

The Portuguese also attempted direct colonisation on the mainland of the continent in the sixteenth and seventeenth century with the foundation of the *prazos* on the Zambezi River (Issacman, 1972). These were estates granted to a wide variety of individuals from nobles to freed convicts, including clergy. The areas were large, often of several square kilometres and including a number of villages. Indeed, the concept was more akin to the Medieval fief where the lord could support himself from the estate and offer military assistance to the Crown in time of trouble. The commercial aspects of the prazo system tended to be lost as time went by and the prazo holder became integrated into African society. The prazos acted as farming and trading enterprises which maintained a nominal Portuguese presence in central Africa until the twentieth century when direct administration was introduced.

One of the important aspects of the prazo for the later colonial age was in creating the idea of Luso–tropicalism (see p. 135), fashionable under the Portuguese New State of 1928-74 (Bender, 1978). The length of the Portuguese presence on the Zambezi and the supposedly high degree of racial intermingling, suggested to twentieth century colonial thinkers that there was a special ability in Portuguese colonialism to integrate Africans into European society. This encouraged later settlement and the idea of a mission to civilise Africa on the basis of racial integration. The theory had little opportunity for success however, as prior to the twentieth century the number of Portuguese living in Moçambique had been numbered in hundreds. Portugal was demographically too weak to sustain an African empire of settlement.

The termination of the slave trade and the operations relating to its suppression led to a further colonisation attempt, in the establishment of settlements for freed slaves (Curtin, 1964). Liberia was founded as a refuge for slaves returning from the United States. Sierra Leone accommodated other freed slaves from North America who had taken the British side in the American War of Independence, but found their first place of refuge, Nova Scotia, an inhospitable environment in which to live. To these returnees were added those released by the vessels of the anti-slave trade patrol who were landed in Freetown, Sierra Leone and at other posts along the coast. From the 1840s Libreville in Gabon served a similar purpose for the remaining South Atlantic trade. The freed slaves joined the inhabitants of the villages and towns adjacent to the forts as an increasingly Europeanised elite who were to provide a substantial manpower for the administration of the future colonies of West Africa. The towns developed a townscape of European-style housing modified to the local climate and culture. Significantly there was little attempt to create viable agricultural colonies on the coast and the populations were directed towards trade and industry.

Parallel with these settlements went British attempts to create colonies on the West coast to compensate for the loss of the North American colonies. Hence there was the need to find an outlet for both convicts and free settlers. The use of the West African coastal forts was unsuccessful. In 1782 some 350 convicts were sent out to the Gold Coast but three years later only seven were alive and fit for work. Experiments in Gambia met a similar fate, while exploration of the coastline between Portuguese Angola and the Dutch colony at the Cape of Good Hope revealed a landscape too barren even for a convict colony, and Australia was chosen for the purpose instead.

Free settlement was pursued more actively (Akpan, 1978). In 1787 the Province of Freedom in Sierra Leone was founded for poor Africans but it proved to be unworkable on the basis of Utopian Socialism. In 1790 the Sierra Leone Company was chartered and there began a series of colonisation experiments. The Company gathered settlers from an unsuccessful English colony in the

Gambia, from Nova Scotia, Jamaica and direct from Europe. Settlers were offered 8 ha of land per male settler plus 4 ha for his wife and 2 ha per child. As in so many schemes, however, the Company had been over-optimistic in its assessment of the extent of the land available and in practice holdings only averaged 2 ha per family, ranging from 1 to 5 ha in extent. The strict regulations on clearance and cultivation, and high quitrents led to conflict. By 1800 only 180 of the 300 heads of families were engaged in any agricultural pursuit at all and then only to the extent of 1½ ha of cropland per family. Only one third grew an export crop as proposed by the Company, so that the agricultural development of Sierra Leone was not judged to be a commercial proposition.

The lack of success was due to the nature of the environment which discouraged the permanent settlement of Europeans, whether in the forts or on agricultural colonies. Africa gained the image of 'The White Man's Grave' as a result of the high mortality which Europeans experienced on the West Coast of Africa (Curtin, 1961). In the eighteenth century mortality rates in any group of European newcomers reached 300 – 700 per cent in their first year, with a subsequent annual mortality rate of 80 – 120 per cent for the survivors. The reasons for this are now well known and are related to yellow fever, bilharzia, sleeping sickness, and above all to malaria. The high death-rates were suffered by all, with African children under five years of age experiencing a particularly heavy toll. Even those engaged in trade were affected. In the late eighteenth century death-rates for sailors engaged in the slave trade were 21.9 per cent compared with 4.1 per cent on the East India trade and 2.3 per cent on the West India trade (Curtin, 1964, pp. 282-5). The reputation was carried into the sea shanty:

Beware and take care; Of the Bight of Benin;
For one that comes out; There are forty go in.

The causes of the diseases were not realised, but by experience they were thought to be related to climate and topography. The result was the study of medical topography which sought to aid the siting of settlements, trading posts and barracks. This had its uses in that certain islands such as Gorée were perceived to be sufficiently far from the coast not to be affected by disease to the same extent. Similarly the mountains were safer than the lowlands, but little else was known for certain. The West African interior was effectively closed to Europeans by the African governments, and they were thus confined to the coast for the entire year. The coastal settlements remained unhealthy places until the development of quinine in the second half of the nineteenth century. Curtin (1964) noted that the image of Africa held in Europe until recent times was in fact the image of West Africa which had become ingrained by the early nineteenth century. The image persisted thereafter as later writers wrote what they thought their readers expected to read. With such a perception of the continent the lack of agricultural settlers is scarcely surprising (Ross, 1982).

2 POLITICIANS, SOLDIERS AND ADMINISTRATORS

In the second, Imperial stage of the colonial era the European powers partitioned the continent between them and established a series of formal colonies. The process was controlled by the politicians of the European governments, who regulated the partition both diplomatically and through their agents, the soldiers and the administrators, who converted the paper partition into effective and ordered government. The three groups of politicians, soldiers and administrators as the representatives of the Imperial powers thus had a direct bearing upon the evolving geography of Africa.

The Politicians

The partition of Africa between the various European nations was a rapid affair (Fage, 1978). In 1880 comparatively little of the continent was under direct European control, despite over 450 years of contact (Figure 2.1). By 1914 only Liberia and Ethiopia remained as independent states, and most of the transformation occurred in the brief period 1885-1900 (Figure 2.2). The partition is closely linked to the diplomatic history of Europe, and was undertaken with comparatively little regard for the intrinsic value of the African continent. Those who decided upon the new boundary lines and the main guidelines of the policies to be pursued, worked in the capitals of Europe. Statesmen such as Gladstone, Ferry, Bismarck and Salisbury never visited Africa and their views of the continent were derived from the accumulated knowledge gained from official and other reports. Yet their influence was immense. They followed rather then led the metropolitan demand for a more active African policy and the securing of economic spheres of influence. They viewed their actions within the framework of European politics so that local demands for a forward policy would be rejected if they did not conform to the perceived needs of Imperial policies. Areas occupied by the nationals of one country were traded for other lands and concessions, sometimes in other continents, as the European powers manipulated their global relationships (Lucas, 1922).

Politicians were faced with the problem of achieving the best conditions for their countrymen in Africa, either by protecting

Figure 2.1: Africa 1880

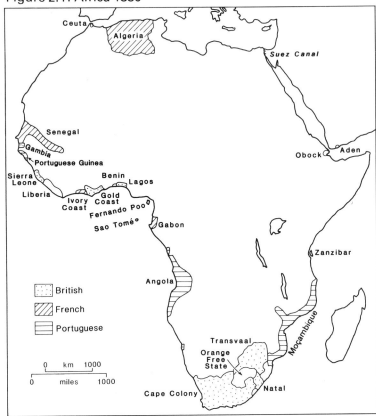

existing claims or promoting new ones. The results, however, often revealed more about the relative positions of the protagonists in terms of political power in Europe, than interest in Africa. Thus the Portuguese claims to extensive tracts of Africa linking the Angolan and Moçambiquan coastlines possessed long pedigrees, but little effective control was apparent upon the ground. Such general claims were rejected by later, but stronger, interlopers. Germany was effectively able to undermine established British positions of influence and so secure extensive tracts of territory through skilful diplomatic manoeuvring, particularly at a time when the Liberal government in London was opposed to colonial expansion.

The penetration of Africa by other groups of the European colonial population resulted in the formulation of political

Figure 2.2: Africa 1914

demands. Traders demanded protection and often exclusive trading areas. Missionaries demanded official annexation as a part of the civilising process of creating a new Christian society. The military required security for existing bases and territory as an ever expanding argument. The navy needed new bases and sources of supply concomitant with developing technology. Local settlers developed their own local imperialisms demanding additional land for future expansion. In Europe industrial demands for new products and increasing volumes of existing products led to pressure for land and minerals. Increasingly the political element entered European reasoning, linking production with colonial control rather than continued African independence. Some Europeans viewed the relative weakness of African polities as an invitation to supersede them with stronger, seemingly more stable administrations, where trade and industry could be secure and be expanded.

The involved diplomatic and military developments of the seventeenth and eighteenth centuries were concluded by the settlement after the Napoleonic Wars in 1814-15. In Africa the majority of the coastal bases were returned to the power which possessed them in 1789. Thus France regained St Louis and Góree, but the Netherlands formally surrendered the Cape of Good Hope to Great Britain. Thereafter for a century no serious fighting took place on the African continent between European forces until the First World War. Potential points of conflict highlighted by the Fashoda incident or the Moroccan crisis were resolved by diplomatic means. The politicians thus exercised a high degree of control over the evolving Map of Africa and the emergent state system. Areas annexed by local officials were on occasion repudiated when the advances did not coincide with metropolitan policy. Hence Queen Adelaide Province established on the eastern Cape colonial frontier in the 1830s was abandoned by Great Britain against the advice of the Cape government. In general Great Britain, the dominant naval power on the African coast, was hesitant to extend its authority over the interior so long as the principle of free trade was maintained and interference with the indigenous states was on a limited scale. British governments were content to police the informal empire by means of punitive expeditionary forces which were capable of exerting a powerful influence over African rulers (Mbaeyi, 1978). The Ethiopian and Ashanti expeditions for example achieved their limited aims and were withdrawn. No permanent conquest was desired.

Until the 1880s the problems of conflicting claims were not serious and thus the gradual advance from the coastal bases, whether by the French from Senegal and Algeria or by the British in the Gold Coast or southern Africa, did not impinge upon the rights of other countries. The situtation was changed by the French annexation of Tunisia in 1881 in a zone perceived to be an Italian sphere of interest, and by the British occupation of Egypt the following year in an area regarded as being of prime importance to France. Conflict between the European powers over African territory now appeared very real. Disagreement such as that between Portugal, Leopold II of the Belgians and de Brazza of France over rights in the Congo basin proved though to be the issue which prompted a major conference on the African situation, and so precipitated the 'scramble' itself.

The Berlin Conference of 1884-5 sought to draw up guidelines for the orderly partition of the continent (Hertslet, 1909). The conference decisions were of considerable importance in forcing the abandonment of the extensive claims of Portugal to the Congo basin and of Great Britain to the general supervisory position on the coasts, which had been assumed at the end of the Napoleonic Wars and reinforced by the anti-slavery patrols. The principles of free trade written into the conference documents appeared to secure British interests. The conference was nevertheless mainly concerned with territory. In order to regulate territorial claims it was agreed by the major powers that countries must notify one another of their claims and that they must be supported by evidence of occupation. As it was recognised that occupation in the sense of the presence of settlers, traders, missionaries, etc. might not be immediately effective, 'spheres of influence' would be recognised in the interim. Thus claims could be staked out but effective occupation had to ensue to guarantee the negotiated title.

The scramble for Africa which had led to the Berlin conference continued unabated through the remainder of the 1880s and 1890s. British reticence resulted in the loss of its position of pre-eminence particularly on the West Coast where Germany and France were able to circumscribe British possessions. In the south the British government was unwilling to endorse the Cape of Good Hope's request for the annexation of the territory between the Orange River and Angola. Only a small area around Walvis Bay had been annexed in 1878 leaving the remainder to be claimed six years later by Germany, which had previously shown little interest in colonial ventures. Other German annexations were equally problematical. That in the Cameroons overlapped the British sphere of influence and the Baptist mission station at Victoria was declared British territory after the German annexation. The anomaly was only removed by the German purchase of the station in 1887. On the Guinea coast British islands and bases were surrounded by French territory. The Los Islands, off Conakry, were isolated by French occupation of the adjacent coastline in the 1880s and were finally ceded to France in return for an extension to Sierra Leone in 1904. Not all attempts at simplifying the map were successful. Schemes to hand over Gambia to France came to nothing as a result of the opposition to the move by the missionaries and traders in Gambia (McIntyre, 1967). In general colonial possessions were extended inland from the coastal bases until a political barrier was met. This is best illustrated in West Africa where the French established themselves across the interior Sudan and so limited other powers which ventured into the Sudan region.

The situation in East Africa was of a somewhat different nature as three indigenous powers held, or at least claimed, extensive areas. Egypt had extended its power in the nineteenth century into the Sudan and then southwards along the Nile towards the Great Lakes. By the 1870s the Egyptian province of Equatoria extended almost to the Equator. Egyptian control was also extended along the Red Sea coast and over the Somali coast. However this was shattered by the Mahdist revolt in the Sudan in the early 1880s when not only was the Sudan lost to Egypt but the outlying possessions had to be abandoned; leading to moves to fill the gaps left behind. The Italians, established in Assab in 1882, took Massawa in 1885 and proceeded to organise the colony of Eritrea. The French who had occupied Obock in 1862 enlarged their area of control in 1884. At the same time the British entered into agreements with Somali rulers on the coast as a means of protecting British Indian possessions at Aden. It was only in 1898 that Anglo-Egyptian forces conquered the Sudan and established a condominium, which effectively operated as a British colony.

A similar partition took place with the Zanzibari possessions in East Africa. Zanzibar had been within the British Indian sphere of influence since the 1820s. No protectorate had been proclaimed and indeed in 1862 an Anglo-French convention had guaranteed the independence of the Sultanate. Attached to the islands was a portion of the East African mainland extending from Moçambique in the south to the Horn of Africa in the north. Although there was general agreement that the coast and the coastal towns were part of Zanzibar, the inland extent was uncertain. In 1884 the Germans began making treaties and obtaining trading and other concessions from rulers in the interior who denied Zanzibari sovereignty. Subsequently, through a further series of treaties the coastal zone, and with it the interior, was partitioned between Great Britian and Germany, while the Italians gained the zone North-east of the Juba River. In 1890 Great Britain was recognised as the protecting power for the islands which still remained to Zanzibar, in return for which Heligoland at the mouth of the River Elbe was ceded to Germany and the French protectorate over Madagascar was recognised.

The third indigenous power, Ethiopia, reacted to European intervention in a different manner. The country was assigned to the Italian sphere of influence under the Anglo-Italian treaty of 1894. The Italian army's defeat at the hands of the Ethiopians at Adowa in 1896, however, delayed the Italian conquest for 40 years. Italian administration of Ethiopia was only to last six years as the country regained its independence in the course of the Second World War. Nevertheless as in the case of Egypt which was only under formal colonial rule for eight years (1914-22) the European influence was strong, largely because the countries undertook westernisation and industrialisation programmes.

Metropolitan politicians sought to restrain overzealous traders, missionaries and soldiers, yet make use of the territorial and other gains which they had made. Thus it was possible to repudiate advanced positions, if the European diplomatic position warranted it, and press advantages elsewhere. Compromise lines were drawn relatively simply as in the case of the French boundaries with the British and German West African colonies. The conflict between British and French interests on the lower Niger was resolved largely by the actions of the Royal Niger Company, which received little direct aid from the British government (Prescott, 1971). However, by means of diplomacy, trade and military action, the Company was able to present a substantial territorial base for diplomatic recognition. Between 1884 and 1892 the Company signed 342 treaties with indigenous rulers. The rulers sought protection and military assistance against their neighbours in return for trade concessions and an undertaking to deal exclusively with the Company in matters of trade and diplomacy. The disentangling of the British sphere of influence thus revolved around the investigation of the territorial claims of the rulers and other parties with whom the treaties had been signed. The extent of the nominal and effective territory of the Sultan of Sokoto thus became of vital concern as British and French authorities attempted to extend or contract respectively the limits of his power. Similar struggles to establish the jurisdictions of indigenous rulers occurred throughout the continent. There can be little doubt that many of the treaties were based on an imperfect appreciation of the relationship between the rulers and their supposed subjects. The boosting of Matabele claims to the whole of modern Zimbabwe is a case in point. It was easier for the British South Africa Company to deal with one ruler than with many, so that the territorial power of Lobengula, the Matabele king, was deliberately promoted by the Company to include areas not under his control.

Treaty making and the establishment of protectorates took place rapidly as a means of establishing a claim to effective control over large areas where there were few Europeans. Certain rulers signed treaties of protection with more than one colonial power. Others were abandoned as the negotiations between the powers progressed in Europe, and the often overlapping claims were sorted out only after the treaties had been signed. The Sultanate of Witu in East Africa for example signed a treaty with Germany in 1886 but was abandoned to the British four years later, thereby weakening its position *vis à vis* its neighbours which had come under British influence at an earlier date. The 'paper partition' was effected rapidly and without conflict between the partitioning powers. Indeed a high degree of co-operation is evident in their dealings with extra-European powers to smooth the process of partition and conquest.

The First and Second World Wars shattered this co-operation and created new problems. The disposition of the German colonies after the First World War was solved by assigning them to the victorious powers. In 1919 the German colonies of Cameroon and Togo were partitioned between Great Britain and France. German East Africa passed to Great Britain apart from two provinces (Ruanda and Urundi) which were assigned to Belgium. The Belgians were in turn forced to evacuate areas gained in the war which they had confidently expected to retain at the peace treaty. South West Africa was taken over by South Africa. In each case the territories were to be governed under a League of Nations mandate which implied a certain degree of protection of the indigenous populations' interests. The war also led to the redrawing of Italian colonial boundaries to provide compensatory territory for the lack of direct gains from the German colonies. Great Britain ceded areas of Egypt, Kenya and the Anglo-Egyptian Sudan to Italy, but the Franco-Italian agreement was never ratified, thus contributing to the contemporary Libya-Chad territorial dispute.

The disposal of the Italian colonies after the Second World War was more problematical as the major powers lacked the drive to acquire additional colonies by 1945 (Rossi, 1973a). The politicians were engaged in dismantling empires rather than building them up and alternatives had to be sought. Despite some elaborate plans for boundary adjustments, the Italian colonies retained their pre-1936 limits. Ethiopia regained its independence in 1942 and acquired

Eritrea in a federal arrangement in 1952. Libya, after a brief *de facto* Anglo-French partition was granted independence in its entirety in 1951. Somalia was returned to Italian administration in 1950 under United Nations trusteeship, with an agreement to prepare the territory for independence within ten years. The increasing internationalisation of the colonial involvement in Africa in the twentieth century was perhaps best illustrated by the establishment of the international status of Tangier in 1923. This enabled the administration to operate outside both French and Spanish control and through its tax-free status it was able to attract investment and European urban settlers.

After the partition metropolitan politicians were primarily concerned with the regulation of colonial affairs through local administrations and military commands. There were however two spheres where they directly influenced the political geography of Africa. These were in the fields of inter-colonial groupings and constitutional development.

The colonial powers attempted at various stages to group their colonies into convenient units. Federations and Unions were devised on an extensive scale. The attraction for colonial ministries to deal with one colony instead of several, and to group complementary colonies together for their mutual benefit were often overwhelming. Rarely were local politicians involved and the whole process was largely directed from Europe. As a result few had any lasting qualities and only the Union of South Africa formed in 1910 and the Federation of Nigeria in 1914 have survived until the present. The first major groupings were devised by France in the 1890s to link the colonies of French West Africa and French Equatorial Africa into two federations based on Dakar and Brazzaville respectively. The advantages of common budgets, services and planning, particularly in the fields of transportation and defence were uppermost in French politicians' minds, but ultimately the political link was rejected by African rulers.

In British Africa there existed more opportunities for federations to simplify the complexity of colonial administration which emerged in the course of the partition. The first, South Africa, was designed to link together the various British territories south of the Zambezi River. Nevertheless only the four self-governing colonies of the Cape of Good Hope, Natal, Transvaal and Orange River Colony were linked in 1910. The three protectorates of Basutoland, Bechuanaland and Swaziland remained under imperial control and

resisted all attempts by the South African government to incor-
porate them until they were granted separate independence in the
1960s (Hyam, 1972). Hence the South African state contained the
anomaly of an enclave formed by Basutoland. The settler electorate
of Southern Rhodesia was offered the choice of joining South
Africa in 1923, a choice which was rejected in favour of becoming a
self-governing colony. Thus even the most successful federation
was only half completed.

Other British federations included Nigeria, where the separate
colonies of Northern and Southern Nigeria were linked. The
federation was designed for the various territories to share common
services, particularly the railway and river routes and to standardise
methods of administration. Despite the stresses, it proved to be
successful. The others were not. The East African High Commission linking the services of Kenya, Uganda and Tanganyika was
designed to act as the first stage of a federation, but the political
elements foundered on the divergent interests of the European
settlers in Kenya and the paramountcy of African interests in the
other two territories. Similarly the Federation of Rhodesia and
Nyasaland, formed in 1953, was designed to link three apparently
complementary economies into a single unit. Again the Federation
was planned in London and imposed by the British government
without regard to the opposition from local African politicians, who
were ultimately able to disband it. An even more short-lived union
was the linking in 1936 of the colonies of Eritrea, Somalia and newly
conquered Ethiopia into Italian East Africa.

Parallel with the joining of adjacent colonies into larger units was
the redrawing of inter-colonial boundaries. The establishment of
the larger groupings tended to blur the boundaries of the members.
The colonies of French West Africa were particularly volatile in this
respect as the extensive French Sudan, conquered in the 1880s and
1890s, was reorganised into progressively smaller units
(Zidouemba, 1977) (Figure 2.3). The first move in 1899 resulted in
the attachment of portions of the interior to the coastal colonies.
The renamed interior colony (Senegambia and Niger, 1899–1904;
Upper Senegal and Niger, 1904–20) was finally fragmented into
three separate colonies in 1919–20, namely the French Sudan, Niger
and Upper Volta. Financial stringency led to the disappearance of
Upper Volta in 1932 when it was attached to the Ivory Coast.
However, in 1947 Upper Volta was re-established as a reward for
the adherence of the local political leaders to the Free French cause

Figure 2.3: French West Africa 1898 – 1947

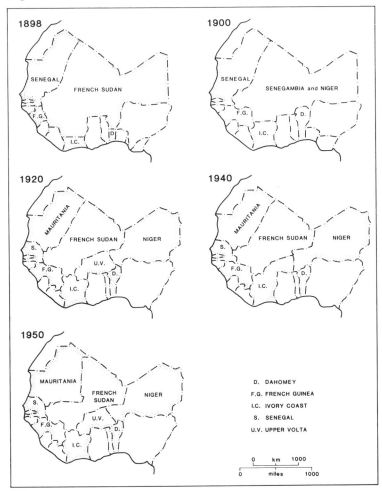

during the Second World War, when the French West African federation had adhered to the Vichy government. Mauritania was described as 'one more administrative solution created by France during her colonial venture in West Africa' when it was separated from Sengal in 1903 (Gerteiny, 1967, p. 11). Similar fragmentation of the French Congo took place between 1904 and 1920 as four successor colonies emerged, which were linked in the French Equatorial Africa federation. In British Africa small colonies were occasionally absorbed by larger neighbours, hence the annexation of British Kaffraria by the Cape of Good Hope in 1866, Zululand by Natal in 1897, and Lagos by Southern Nigeria in 1906.

Boundaries between colonies were also adjusted according to metropolitan dictates, as the original demarcations became inappropriate to changing patterns of circulation. Thus the Gabon-Middle Congo boundary was redrawn to provide the Middle Congo with a corridor to the sea for the Congo-Ocean Railway. The British East Africa (Kenya)–Uganda boundary was similarly redrawn to include the terminus of the Uganda Railway at Port Florence (Kisumu) in Kenya. These were major decisions taken in Europe and differed from the local adjustments made to colonial boundaries to facilitate the administration of the colonies.

During the colonial period local political leaders began to emerge through such activities as trade union movements, traditional African politics and the colonial civil service. These leaders reflected the scale of the new colonial state rather than the pre-colonial state, and sought to develop political activity within the colonial framework. Conflicts were inevitable not only between coloniser and colonised, but between traditional authorities and new forms of political expression and between federal and colonial authorities. The outcome of these struggles was reflected in the political map of Africa (Boateng, 1978). In the first case the indigenous struggle for greater political participation and then independence is reflected in the decolonisation movement of the post – 1945 era which gained strength, so that between 1957 and 1963 most of the continent was decolonised. The struggle between the traditional and colonial state authorities was reflected in the elaborate constitutions and decentralised powers which some British African states adopted at independence. Regions, complete with regional capitals and administrations played an important role in British decolonisation. In places traditional authorities re-asserted themselves, as witness the separate independence for Rwanda and Burundi in 1962. The federations in particular suffered at independence. French West Africa, French Equatorial Africa, Rhodesia and Nyasaland, and the East African High Commission were all dissolved as politicians with power bases in the individual colonies assumed control. The federal political links were weak and the European factors lacked the power to maintain them. Even the attempt to maintain French West Africa on a reduced scale in the form of the Mali Federation ended in dissolution, as the leaders of French Sudan and Senegal engaged in personal feuds over the ultimate control of the federal government (Foltz, 1965).

Colonial politicians thus acted within the framework of the Colonies as drawn up by the colonial powers. Few attempts to change this through federal, expansionist, or successionist movements attracted the attention of an influential element of the emergent politicians. This surprising uniformity of attitudes was reflected, in the post-independence period, in the Charter of the Organisation of African Unity (Touval, 1967; Widstrand, 1969). Those politicians with revisionist aspirations were unable to achieve them as the political structures of the colonial period proved to be remarkably sound. As Brownlie (1978, p. 9) wrote 'it is a remarkable fact that a political map of Africa in 1977 is not very different from the political map of 1914'.

Soldiers

The military played a vital role in the entire history and development of Africa during the colonial period. Colonial regimes were essentially military in basis and often in character, and the occupation of the continent was effected by force or at least the threat of force. Rebellions and civil disturbances were frequent and repression either through police action or full scale military operations involved the armed forces. The entire concept of 'pacification' so prevalent in colonial writings had a strong military emphasis. Once colonial governments were secure the military and naval officers often ceased to function as the governors of colonies, but even under civilian control, the governor was usually styled Commander-in-chief. The military played a significant role in the siting of settlements, the lines of communication, and often the initial organisation of the administration. The presence of a sizeable army and police force located in a series of strategic bases, also had a continuing influence upon the form of the colonial city. Late in the colonial period, as the independence movements began to assert themselves, so the military were drawn back into the forefront of power. The counter-insurgency wars waged in parts of Africa had a major influence upon the geography of the colonies concerned, as the army was given virtually a free hand to reorganise the landscape as part of the anti-guerrilla operations.

The initial forces sent to Africa by the colonial powers were generally naval. The links between the navy and colonial ministries

were complex and persistent. Naval bases were established around
the coast in the nineteenth century, as the need for coaling stations
arose with the transfer from wind power to steam; the bases of the
previous ages being often inadequate for the new technology. Great
Britain was most fortunate in possessing a series of stations around
the coast and on the offshore islands which were capable of adaptation with a few additions. Other powers were not so fortunate and a
scramble for such bases began, particularly related to the new route
to India through the Suez Canal, opened in 1869. The French were
especially active in seeking to emulate and challenge the British
position. Thus strategic points were acquired by the French, including Obock at the entrance to the Red Sea in 1862, the larger
harbour at Djibouti in 1884, Diégo Suarez in northern Madagascar,
and Mayotte in the Comoro Islands. Suitable harbours were also
sought by the other powers. Assab was acquired by Italy in 1882,
Luderitz (Angra Pequena) by Germany in 1884. The prizes of
Mombasa and Dar es Salaam on the East Coast were coveted later.
Changing technology also affected established bases. Thus Gorée
was abandoned for Dakar on the mainland. St Helena similarly lost
its strategic value as a possession and declined economically.

One of the problems for naval planners was the general lack of
suitable harbours. The main British base at Simonstown was
capable of adaptation through the construction of breakwaters and
quays. Similarly the French bases at Mers el Kebir in Algeria and
Bizerte in Tunisia required substantive constructional work and
differed from the European estuarine bases. In general most bases
consisted of a segregated area of the commercial harbours, as in the
case of Dakar and Durban. The naval facilities of supply, maintenance and repair of ships were supplemented by the shore base
with barracks, training grounds, extensive residential areas for the
officers, and often new trading establishments to supply the men
stationed there. At Diégo Suarez a new town largely for various
immigrant groups was established, while the agricultural supply
base was created by settlers from Réunion. To complete the Diégo
Suarez base a hill station at Joffreville was founded where sailors
could escape the heat of the coastal plain (Rossi, 1973b).

European intervention in the interior of Africa necessitated the
use of land forces, rather than naval forces. Although gun boats
which effectively controlled the coasts were used on the main rivers
and lakes as adjuncts to the foot soldier. Armies which were
stationed in Africa were at first drawn from the metropoles. The

British were stationed in South Africa between 1806 and 1914 and in Egypt between 1882 and 1956. French armies were present in North Africa from 1830 to 1962, and Spain stationed approximately 200,000 men in Morocco between 1912 and 1956 (Mikesell, 1961). At times of crisis metropolitan forces were sent to Africa whether to effect an invasion such as the British conquest of the Sudan in 1896-8 or the Italian occupation of Ethiopia in 1936. More usually it was a perceived threat to the security of the colonial administration which prompted metropolitan intervention, whether the Ashanti threat to the Gold Coast in the 1870s or the Angolan and Moçambiquan liberation armies in the 1960s and 1970s. In general, however, it was the colonial forces which maintained authority. These forces whether formal armies or paramilitary police were largely indigenous, although led by European commissioned and non-commissioned officers. In general recruitment was on a voluntary basis, although conscription was introduced by the French to supplement their own limited manpower. Coercion however was present for the support services, more particularly the large numbers of porters which colonial armies required in tropical Africa before the advent of mechanical transport.

The military effected a number of important developments at the political level. Individual army units were able to occupy large areas in advance of the expectations of their political masters, while others failed in their objectives to establish positions which the politicians had established on paper. The steady French military occupation of the Sahara at the expense of Moroccan claims in the second half of the nineteenth century effectively shifted the Moroccan-Algerian border westwards without any political authority to do so (Husson, 1960). Conversely the Italian army's failure to conquer Ethiopia in 1896 undid the political settlement negotiated by the metropolitan government.

Violent opposition to colonial rule was highly variable in intensity and duration. In North and South Africa substantial military forces were necessary to conquer and hold territory. They were employed on a large scale and for a longer period of time than in most parts of the continent, resulting in a greater military imprint upon the landscape in those areas. The first step in the colonial enterprise was often the establishment of a chain of forts to control the indigenous population. The coastal forts were obviously readily available as bases for conquest. The interior forts were established according to the military theories of the time. Major defensive structures were erected along colonial borders and at strategic points on routeways. Thus a large number of settlements were established with names such as Fort Victoria (Rhodesia), Fort Lamy (Tchad), or Forte Rocades (Angola) indicative of their origin.

The forts housed the military and often acted as centres of administration for the surrounding district. Although the choice of site might originally have been purely military, other functions often accrued to the site as a result of the security and market offered by the garrisons. Marshal Lyautey, the French Resident-General in Morocco, after the proclamation of the French protectorate in 1912, emphasised the significance of military occupation in the organisation of a new society (Scham, 1970). He considered that military posts should be chosen as permanent sites so that economic activities could be attracted to them. The forts were thus viewed as a vital element in the establishment of an urban network. The chains of forts and the roads and other lines of communication which linked them therefore formed an essential part of the framework of colonial control.

The rise and demise of forts as a part of the urban network is illustrated by one of the most persistent frontier regions in African colonial history, the eastern frontier of the Cape Colony. Between the 1770s and 1870s the boundary separating the colonists and the Xhosa to the east fluctuated with the fortunes of the eight frontier wars. A chain of major forts extending from the coast to the Stormberg mountains was built to hold each successive frontier and to act as a network of posts for the control of the areas conquered. Some forts assumed administrative and commercial functions such as Fort Beaufort and Fort Hare (Alice), while others retained nothing more than a police function as at Fort Brown. Yet others such as Fort Wiltshire were abandoned once the frontier had been moved.

Increased military presence in Africa in the late nineteenth and twentieth centuries resulted in the need for more extensive sites for barracks, officers' houses and compounds, parade and drill grounds, sports fields and stores. The old medieval style fort was superseded by the more extensive cantonment of several hundred or thousand hectares. Such large land users inevitably affected the form of the colonial city. There was little questioning of the desirability of the military demands for space as it was the army which held a dominant position in the colonial administration. Thus the extensive military base or *quartier militaire* was attached to both the major pre-colonial city such as Fez or to the purely colonial city such as Bloemfontein. In other cases cantonments were planned as an integral part of the colonial city using British India as a model. The extensive layout of the Northern Nigerian capital of Kaduna was modelled upon similar stations in India, where Sir Frederick Lugard, the first High Commissioner, had received his early training (Lock and Theis, 1967). In Kaduna the military, civil and African quarters were planned as distinct entities, each separated from the other by extensive open spaces for the race course, polo ground and parade grounds, but linked by broad ceremonial avenues.

The military also frequently provided the manpower to construct roads, defences and other basic infrastructures including drainage or irrigation canals, in frontier settlement regions. The French army in Algeria was particularly large and active, undertaking village construction and settlement as well as a more traditional role. The distinction between the army and the frontier settlers was often blurred as attempts were made to settle soldiers on the land in both North and South Africa. Military villages established on the Mitidja Plain in the 1840s under Marshal Bugeaud provided for the accommodation of the massive influx of population needed to stabilise Algeria as a colony of French settlement (Franc, 1928). Over 100,000 people migrated to Algeria between 1841 and 1851 to villages often planned, laid out, and built by the army. During the same period the French forces (not included in the foregoing statistics), increased from 63,000 men in 1840 to 140,000 men in 1845. In British Kaffraria in the 1850s a similar military settlement by the British German Legion made use of available organised manpower to colonise a frontier region.

The military reassumed an important role in the African colonies towards the end of the era. Decolonisation was on occasion as bloody an affair as the original conquest had been, and wars of independence were waged in several parts of the continent. The wars ranged from Algeria (1954-62) to Zimbabwe (1972-9) with South Africa and Namibia remaining (1983) as unresolved cases. The longest wars were those fought in the three Portuguese mainland colonies of Angola, Moçambique and Portuguese Guinea from 1961 to 1974-5. The wars epitomised the clash of the determination of the colonial powers to remain in Africa and of the indigenous peoples to become independent. The ease with which decolonisation was achieved depended largely upon the former, and thus was not consistent. France consequently decolonised with comparatively few problems, except for Algeria. Algeria was regarded in national politics as a special case – a portion of France overseas. The French stake in the country was considered to be too great to be surrendered. Furthermore there were one million French settlers in the country providing a powerful opposition to any metropolitan politicans who sought to decolonise the country. Settlers were often the key issue in delaying decolonisation. British problems in Kenya and Southern Rhodesia revolved around the settlers' ability to influence British politics. In contrast there were few Portuguese settlers in Africa in 1961, and the retaining of colonial control was viewed as a means of maintaining Portugal as a significant power. Settlers were introduced to boost that position thereby making the final withdrawal more difficult.

In each case the army, sent to solve the military problem, also sought to solve the underlying political and social problems. Officers viewed the latter as being more of an economic nature and instituted far-reaching programmes of reform and resettlement; with a view to solving both the military problem and at the same time the underlying causes, by raising standards of living. In the circumstances of the 1950s and 1960s the military problem was one of countering insurgency and guerrilla activity on the classic lines of Mao Tse-tung's maxim, 'the rebel lives in the population as the fish in the water. Remove the water and the fish dies'. The colonial military proceeded to remove the water.

Regrouping of indigenous rural settlements was not a new measure in the colonies. In Algeria villages had been established from 1848 onwards as part of the measures for exerting military control. Nomads in particular had been subjected to considerable pressure to settle in villages as a part of the quest for security. The French had undertaken similar regrouping programmes in Viet Nam in the late 1940s and early 1950s, but there appears to have been little direct transfer of ideas from Asia to Africa. New villages were established and the dispersed rural population was rehoused under supervision in an attempt to isolate them from the guerrilla forces (Cornaton, 1967; Sutton, 1981). The first villages were established in 1955 and by 1961 half the rural Moslem population of the country (3.5 million people) had been resettled or moved. Two million people were settled in some 2,400 special villages. The figure included 400,000 nomads who had not previously been fixed to the land. The regrouping was by no means uniform as the war zones were completely reorganised, while other areas experienced no resettlement at all. In 1959 buffer zones along the borders with Morocco and Tunisia were proclaimed and all villages and settlements within them were destroyed. The resettlement programme was undertaken in a hurried manner and the new villages proved inadequate as regards water supply or access to land, but it is significant that a high proportion survived after the war and were adapted to the new government's rural improvement programme (Sutton and Lawless, 1978).

A similar dilemma faced the Portuguese in Angola and Moçambique in the 1960s (Bender, 1978). The first priority was taken to be the control of the local population, making it impossible for the nationalist insurgents to reach them. This involved the concentration of the rural Africans into villages which could be supervised and guarded. Two types of settlement emerged. The first was the strategic resettlement which was located in the zones of fighting where dispersed rural Africans were grouped into villages surrounded by barbed wire and fortifications. The second type of rural settlement was not military in character or in appearance, but involved the grouping of people into villages for the purpose of supervision for rural development schemes outside the war zones. Approximately one million persons had been resettled in Angola in this manner by the end of the war. Similar programmes were undertaken by the Portuguese in Moçambique and Portuguese Guinea, and by the Rhodesian government in the 1970s. Counter to these programmes were the insurgent states which sought to reorganise settlement and society in terms of anti-colonial ideology. The insurgent states however controlled only a comparatively small population, suggesting that in large measure counter-insurgency in military terms was relatively successful (Barnard, 1982; Best, 1976; Pelissier, 1974).

Programmes were devised to improve the rural living conditions of the African population which were often seen as the root cause of dissatisfaction and therefore insurgency. Thus by extension the related far-reaching rural improvement programmes forced through under wartime conditions may be included here. In Kenya the Mau Mau insurgency resulted not only in the military operations but also the rural development schemes under the Swynnerton Plan of 1954 (Sorrenson, 1967). This provided for the reorganisation of the rural landscape of the Kikuyu areas of the country through the consolidation of holdings, the introduction of individual tenure, farm planning, the expansion of crop production, provision of rural water supplies, a livestock improvement scheme and land reclamation projects. The plan had resulted by 1962 in the enclosure and registration of 1.4 million hectares. It was made possible by the disruption of the war and the movement of the population to villages for security purposes, when new ideas were accepted as part of a rapidly changing era. Although much of the political dispute of the late colonial period revolved around the European holdings in the 'White Highlands', the African land settlement programme on the then renamed 'Scheduled Areas' only began in 1961 and its progress is a part of Kenya's post colonial development.

The Administrators

Colonial control was exercised by administrators who constituted a small but influential element in colonial society (Cohen, 1971; Gann and Duignan, 1978). The actions of the administrators in locating their operations, determining laws and their enforcement (more especially the spatial aspects of law and enforcement), were basic to an understanding of the geography of colonial Africa. The imposition of taxation, first as customs collections, later through hut and poll taxes, imposed a burden on indigenous societies which was often severe. The organisation of the taxation system was important as administrative posts had to be established to police the system. This often involved the imposition of European-style laws and the substitution of a colonial form of government for an indigenous one. The degree to which this occurred was dependent upon the political philosophy of the colonial power. In places such as the British colonies and protectorates under indirect rule, the pre-colonial settlement pattern was modified as a result of changing economic pressures rather than by administrative forces. In others such as the French and Belgian colonies administrations were modelled on their metropolitan counterparts, effectively changing patterns or reinforcing existing patterns to attain the desired, often nucleated settlement pattern. Settlement contrasts on either side of the Uganda-Zaire boundary illustrate the impact of two differing styles of administration (Kibulya and Langlands, 1967).

Effective administration assumed a pattern of operation within a hierarchy of command from the core at the capital, to progressively lesser centres responsible for clearly defined areas within each colony. The premier expression of colonial administration was the capital. Colonial capitals were largely inherited from the fore-runners of the pre-1870 era, and from the sites selected by the military for their campaigns in the occupation and conquest of the continent. Thus the majority of colonial capitals were coastal, situated at the point of contact between the metropole and the colony. Many predated any formal commitment to colonisation as such and were initially viewed as trading and supply points. The earliest capitals on the west coast were the castles at Elmina, Cape Coast and Christianborg, all now in Ghana, which acted as the headquarters for the various national trading enterprises. St Louis, Freetown, Libreville and Bathurst were established by the early nineteenth century as trading or settlement points, with no jurisdiction outside their immediate vicinities. Another group including Lagos, Algiers and Mogadishu were indigenous capitals acquired when the pre-colonial state came under European control. Pre-colonial capitals survived to only a limited extent, largely due to the differing economic and political orientations of the colonial powers. The removal of the Moroccan capital from inland Fez to coastal Rabat when the French protectorate was established, illustrates the conflicting interests of the two governments.

The selection of a capital was of considerable importance as it was here that the senior officials resided, where political advancement was to be found and where a disproportionate part of the colonial budget was spent. The coastal sites as transhipment points and therefore the headquarters of the trading companies, tended to reinforce this position of pre-eminence. This is not to suggest that colonial capitals were stable in their location. They proved to be highly volatile for a number of reasons. Owing to the perceived unhealthy character of the coast, interior sites were selected once the colonial regime was established. The British selected Nairobi as a replacement for Mombasa as the capital of British East Africa in 1906 (Morgan, 1967). The advantages of inland, upland sites with more equitable climates attracted the Italians in Eritrea to Asmara, and the Germans in South West Africa to Windhoek. In the same category was the proposal to move Angola's capital from Luanda to Nova Lisboa on the central plateau, a move which was never implemented. Summer capitals to which the administration retired from the coast, such as Simla in India, were not replicated in Africa, although the resorts of Efrane in Morocco and Swakopmund in German South West Africa fulfilled this role to a limited extent. Economic motives were paramount in the move by both the French and Belgians from the coastal capitals at Libreville and Boma respectively, to new positions above the rapids on the main section of the navigable Congo. Similarly Lourenço Marques superseded Moçambique Island as the economy of southern Moçambique overtook that of the north. On a more restricted scale, improved technology in both ocean and land transport dictated the successive moves of the Ivory Coast capital from Grand Bassam, to Bingerville, and finally to Abidjan.

The landlocked, or effectively landlocked colonies presented administrators with a rather different situation. Pre-colonial capitals including Bamako in the French Sudan, Kampala in Uganda, and Khartoum in the Anglo-Egyptian Sudan were occupied and continued to function under the new administration. Where no evident pre-colonial capital was available administrators resorted to use of the entry point, usually on a river, from where the occupation had been initiated. Thus Livingstone on the Zambezi became the first capital of Northern Rhodesia, and Bangui, on the Ubangi River the capital of Ubangi-Chari (Tchad). Naimey similarly was selected as the capital of Niger soon after its separation as an independent colony in 1922 and the military town of Zinder was abandoned in favour of a site on the Niger River (Sidikou, 1975). Two colonies, Mauritania and Bechuanaland Protectorate were administered from capitals outside the colonial territory. Mauritania shared St Louis in Senegal with the Senegalese administration until the late 1950s. Bechuanaland Protectorate was similarly administered from Mafeking situated some 25 km to the south of its territory, until the selection of a new capital at Gaberone immediately prior to independence.

Two further forms of capital need to be considered. Settler capitals in southern Africa constitute a particular group related to the needs of a settler society. They were thus located with reference to the areas of rural European colonisation rather than the criteria of metropolitan administration. The settlers were able to establish their own governments with administrative capitals as they migrated into the interior of the continent from the Cape of Good Hope. Three of these, Pietermaritzburg, Bloemfontein and Pretoria survived the political struggles which ensued to develop regular administrative headquarters. Others such as Winburg and Lydenburg in the 1840s and 1850s or Vryburg and Vryheid in the 1880s were ephemeral, as the states were incorporated into their larger and more powerful neighbours. British colonial administrators adopted the settler capitals upon annexation and also established their own ephemeral governments such as British Kaffraria. It is noticeable that the ports were shunned. Thus Pietermaritzburg was founded as the capital of Natal, not Durban its port, and similarly King Williams Town was the capital of British Kaffraria, not East London.

The other group of colonial capitals which needs to be considered is the federal capitals. These presented particular problems of balance within the federation, but because they were almost all imposed structures the usual niceties of selection did not apply. The first federation, French West Africa, was a pointer to future situations. The capital was located at Dakar in 1896 at the new major port, in preference to the Senegalese capital of St Louis. In general the capital of the most important constituent colony within the federation was chosen as the federal capital. Thus Brazzaville, Salisbury and Nairobi became the headquarters of federal authorities (Wood, 1976). South Africa chose to compromise by maintaining three of the colonial capitals as the capitals of the union constituted in 1910. The new capital solution on the model of Canberra or Ottawa was rejected.

Capital cities as the seats of government played a major role in the colonial period. The advantages of the concentration of political and economic power usually led to their growth at the expense of the other towns. Thus by the end of the colonial era there were only three countries on the continent where the capital was not the largest city and they were indicative of the exceptional circumstances prevailing, where capital and primate city were sufficiently close to operate for some purposes as a unit. It is also indicative of the small size of African cities. By 1960 only three exceeded a million inhabitants. Two of these, Cairo and Alexandria, were traditional cities and only Johannesburg was of colonial origin, and then not the capital which was situated at Pretoria some 40 km distant. Major pre-colonial cities which were not chosen as the colonial capital tended to grow less rapidly than the capital. The relative position of Ibadan and Lagos is illustrative of this (Mabogunje, 1968). In 1900 Lagos (18,000 inhabitants) was considerably smaller than the largest of the Yoruba cities, Ibadan, (210,000). By 1960 Lagos was still smaller (364,000) than Ibadan (600,000) but was catching up rapidly. Similarly Mombasa which in 1906 had been two and a half times the size of Nairobi, was by 1960 only two-thirds the size of the capital. With few exceptions the next

Figure 2.4: Plans of Four Colonial Capitals

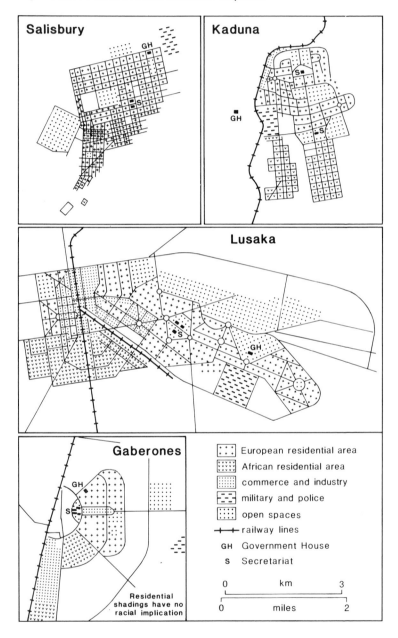

largest town in each colony was only a fraction of the size of the capital, an extreme form of primacy, reflecting the poorly developed urban systems and the concentration of functions in the capital.

Lagos was by no means unique. Growth in the capital cities was often spectacular in the colonial period (Winters, 1982). Leopoldville achieved an even faster rate of growth, increasing from a mere 5,000 in 1908 to 420,000 by the end of the colonial era. Even the capitals of poorly endowed colonies such as Dahomey and French Guinea were able to attract substantial migrations. The population of Cotonou increased from 2,000 in 1910 to 68,000 in 1960, while that of Conakry increased in size from 6,000 to 113,000 in the same period. These numbers have been overtaken by the spectacular rural-urban migrations which have affected most parts of Africa in the post-colonial era, reinforcing the dominance of the capitals in the state economies.

The colonial capital reflected not only its national origin, but also the date at which it was designed. This was nowhere more evident than in the plan. The constrained designs of the early colonial period gave way to a more generous use of space by the mid-nineteenth century, allowing for great individuality. British colonial layouts in particular changed markedly as the garden city concept in metropolitan planning and later the influence of the design of New Delhi entered colonial thought. Thus the contrast between the grid plan of Salisbury (1890) and the geometrical design of Lusaka (1934) is marked, although both reflect the same spacious orientation of Lugard's design for Kaduna (Figure 2.4) (Kay, 1967; Tanser, 1965). A significant addition in the Lusaka plan was the incorporation of an African area, although largely separated from the European area by the railway line, whereas the Salisbury plan had place only for a small location similarly situated on the other side of the railway tracks. The ultimate in metropolitan design was probably Gaberone (1963), where contemporary British town planning principles were given free rein but for a racially integrated society (Bechuanaland Protectorate, 1963; Best, 1970). In contrast French colonial capitals exhibited more uniformity in plan, based essentially upon the Parisian model, whether it was the plan of Dakar (1856) or Naimey (1930). The latter attempted from the start to integrate the African areas into the plan whereas in the former case integration was more piecemeal.

The capitals were first and foremost the centres of colonial administration. All senior officials resided in them and a high proportion of the entire civil service was housed in the capital. Thus government house, the residence of the governor or highest official, was often the finest and most impressive building in the city. It was either set in extensive grounds as was the usual British approach, or in a prominent position within the city plan as was customary in the French capitals. Thus in Dakar the setting was urban, reflecting the position of palaces in Europe, whereas in Nairobi the English country mansion served as a model (White *et al.*, 1948). Architectural design also reflected differing concepts. The dominant classical designs of French government buildings often contrasted with the Victorian Gothic and Arts and Crafts Movement designs of British government houses. Lesser officials were not so grandly housed, although a marked area of the capital was usually set aside to cater for the transitory population of bureaucrats in colonial service.

Also prominent in the townscape were the offices from which the various officials exercised control over their departments. Colonial administration prior to the 1890s was essentially simple with few officials. However, owing to the close degree of supervision which the government exercised over the activities of its colonial subjects, often in marked contrast to the limited control which the metropolitan governments exercised over their subjects, bureaucracy flourished in the later colonial period. The collection of taxes and the administration of justice became but two aspects of a highly complex civil service. Departments were established to foster production, such as agriculture, mining and industry. Control of communications through the post office, the railways and most other forms of transport resulted in another group of bureaucrats being recruited. Control over the lives of their subjects through land registration, travel restrictions and public health laws involved a host of government departments enforcing a constant stream of laws. Thus government offices were regularly being built throughout the colonial period. In scale they ranged from the all-purpose buildings, often one of the coastal forts in the early colonial period, through to the purpose-built office constructed to house several departments, and later to the multiplicity of structures each housing a separate department.

The styles and layouts of the government offices were as varied as government house itself. In general attempts were made to erect impressive buildings emphasising the power of the state. The massive Edwardian Imperial Union Buildings of Herbert Baker (1944) erected in Pretoria, and similar structures throughout the British Empire, such as the Secretariat in Nairobi, attempted to demonstrate a unity and distinctiveness which was symbolised in brick and stone. Each Imperial power sought to do the same, creating distinctively French, German or Portuguese variations of the African colonial government building. In most cases the sheer availability of space enabled the colonial architects to site buildings on larger plots than was possible in Europe. Furthermore, officials were able to plan their capitals on a scale which would have been impossible in the European environment with its accumulation of inherited structures and independent vested interests. These were missing in the colonial state, which enabled the imposition of town planning schemes with little reference to other controls and restrictions. The French, and particularly the Portuguese, exercised tight control over the day-to-day administration of their colonial empires, with the result that many officials involved with African affairs remained in Paris or Lisbon to swell the staffs of the colonial ministries, whereas their equivalents in the British Empire were based in the colonial capitals. Thus Lourenço Marques lacked many colonial offices, and pride of place in the town plan was given to the town hall, symbolic of the level of government not directly controlled from Lisbon.

In the self-governing colonies, by contrast, far more government buildings were erected, most important of which was the parliamentary edifice. Colonial councils operated in one form or another in most colonies, but the majority were nominated by the government and their importance was limited. Hence no symbolically impressive building was erected for them. In southern Africa in the nineteenth century and elsewhere in the last few years of colonial rule, elected legislatures met and the newly found freedom was manifested in colonial parliamentary buildings. The earliest were in Cape Town, completed in 1884, but complemented by the republican structures in Bloemfontein and Pretoria erected in the 1890s (Picton-Seymour, 1977). In style, British colonial, American capitol, and German municipal were taken and adapted to the circumstances of the local community. Clearly self-governing communities were willing to spend considerable sums on symbolic buildings, reflecting the prosperity of southern Africa in the late nineteenth century.

In addition to houses and offices, the governments built a number of specialised structures such as customs halls, printing works, central banks, court houses and prisons. In the majority of cases these, or at least the more important, were situated in the colonial capital. The administration of justice possibly involved the most elaborate network of structures within the colony, but the main courts were situated in the capital, as was the central prison.

When it is remembered that the capital city was usually small by contemporary standards, the administration contributed a substantial element both in terms of the population dependent upon it and in its physical layout and structure. Because of the presence of the government in the capital, beautification works in the form of gardens, parks, avenues and monuments were laid out or erected. These were often undertaken in an effort to create a European image, even in minor details, such as the rose gardens of many British colonies, or the elaborate black and white stone paved walks and squares of the Portuguese capitals. With the financial resources of the colonial budgets, administrators were able to recreate a little of Europe in the colonial capital.

Individual colonies were subdivided into smaller administrative units of provinces, districts, communes or cercles. Unlike the colonial boundaries, the subdivisions were changed frequently in the early stages of the establishment and consolidation of a government. The changes in the subdivisional boundaries of the Gold Coast prior to 1914 are a case in point. The majority of boundaries were chosen for convenience, reflecting the manpower available to the colonial government, but a number were inherited from pre-colonial entities. Within the Gold Coast, the borders of the Ashanti kingdom were retained, as were boundaries of the kingdoms in Uganda, but such occurrences were rare. Frequently boundaries were defined in terms of access from selected administrative posts, and the administrative pattern reflected the changing assessments of the strategic position of the post. Multiplication of administrative posts and therefore districts was common in the early stages of European penetration, often with a view to demonstrating effective occupation and deterring the officers of other countries. In periods of retrenchment such as the First World War or the depression of the 1930s, staff was cut and districts reduced in numbers.

Selection of administrative centres was frequently a matter of selecting a pre-existing village or town and attaching an administrative quarter to it, again creating the dual colonial town. The choice of early colonial officials was clearly vital in determining why one village grew and others did not, as there was a resultant agglomeration of governmental, ecclesiastical and commercial functions in the selected village (Bening, 1979). Only in the sparsely populated areas of the Congo basin and the semi-arid lands were new sites often chosen, and then usually with a view to the exploitation of the resources of the territory.

Once established few attempts were made to abandon administrative posts after the First World War. The initial makeshift structures were replaced by substantial edifices and the investment in infrastructure became too great to be forsaken. However, particularly unsuitable sites in the changed circumstances of the twentieth century were relegated in status. Thus Moçambique ceased to be the capital of Moçambique Colony in 1898 and then lost its status as a district capital to Nampula in 1935. The latter was more central for the administrative control of the extensive district of Moçambique and a modern city was built, contrasting markedly with the old capital on its restricted island. In general, as the administrative system became more complex, bureaucrats more numerous, and the social services performed by the government more comprehensive, particularly after 1945, so the number of administrative centres increased, each as a miniature copy of the colonial capital.

The imposition of new laws and taxation had a profound effect upon the lives of colonial subjects and the spatial aspects of society. One reminder is necessary. Government authority was not always uniformly effective through a colonial territory, so that in the remoter sections of some colonies indigenous society was not subjected to the same pressures as were exerted near the centre of power. In decentralised protectorate situations this was particularly true as authority was exercised through the indigenous rulers. Indeed European control was sometimes little more than nominal where there was little advantage to the colonial power in greater supervision (Ibrahim, 1979). A few aspects of government intervention in the geography of the colonies may be instructive.

Initial occupation and conquest necessitated the exercise of military might, and force or some form of coercion was essential for the maintenance of colonial rule. It was the local administrators who controlled the apparatus of local coercion, dealing with such matters as the police, prisons, law and taxation. Thus in some areas the first evidence of the establishment of the colonial state was the construction of the police station and the prison. Indeed as

Jorgensen (1981) has shown for Uganda, coercion was the dominant element in colonial expenditure prior to the First World War. In the ten year period 1901/2–1910/11 coercion accounted for 33.0 per cent of expenditure as opposed to 2.0 per cent for agriculture, 0.1 per cent for education, and 8.5 per cent for health services. Although expenditure on services rose, the allocation of monies only showed a marked shift towards education as a government provision in the 1950s, when it accounted for 17.4 per cent of Ugandan budgets and coercion only 11.2 per cent. Changing priorities were reflected in the structures built and maintained in the towns and countryside. Police stations and prisons symbolise the early colonial period, schools and clinics the late period.

Taxation was an essential element in the support of government. Customs duty and other minor forms of revenue provided sufficient funds in the early years of colonial rule. However, the extension of the administration necessitated a search for additional sources of taxation. Inevitably the indigenous population was viewed as a major source. This despite the fact that the burden was comparatively onerous, particularly in colonies of European settlement where the settlers attempted to use both taxation and expenditure to their own advantage. Thus in Algeria in 1919 some 60 per cent of the budget was paid by the Moslem community, although it received little in return (Smith, 1978, p. 93). Taxation was officially viewed as a means of forcing the indigenous population to work for the colonial government, or on the mines and plantations of the Europeans. Official attitudes ranged from extolling the alleged benefits of regular labour as a means of introducing civilisation, to the more blatant settler demands for cheap workers. As an example the Nyasaland government introduced regulations which doubled the head tax on all adult African males who had not spent at least one month per year working for a European employer (Pachai, 1977). This was designed to ensure a labour force for the plantations which paid very poorly. Similar devices were used elsewhere to assuage European demands for labour.

Taxation acted as a spur to increased production and indeed to commercial farming in many African areas (Morgan and Pugh, 1969; Pehaut, 1978). This process had begun with the opening of trade prior to the colonial period, whereby barter of cattle and crops had been effected for manufactured goods. The flow of crops such as groundnuts from Senegal or cotton from the Sudan began as part of a two-way trade (Suret-Canale, 1971). The impact of this two-way trade upon the landscape was considerable as the products of industrial technology enabled new areas to be cultivated (Morgan, 1959). Taxation instituted a demand for cash in indigenous society which was met by increased production. Increased production in turn resulted in a period of peasant prosperity which has been detected in a large number of countries. Nevertheless after a brief initial period, the demands of the European settlers were such as to ensure that it did not last. Without recourse to the capital market, and with the general lack of government aid, such societies were unable to overcome periods of crises. Agriculturalists or their dependents were forced on to the labour market to work for the settlers. Once initiated the burden of taxation was such that a vicious circle of impoverishment could not be broken. Other factors came into operation including disadvantageous price structures offered by traders, low wage rates by miners and settlers and lack of recourse to legal and political action. Colonial officials on occasion actively hindered African agricultural progress where other priorities of the colonial state were perceived as being of greater importance. Thus Gold Coast officials promoted British mining enterprise to the detriment of the promotion of cocoa growing and African trade (Kay, 1972).

The contrast between settler and non-settler colonies became apparent at this stage (Palmer and Parsons, 1977). The settlers viewed the development of African commercial agriculture as a threat to their own livelihood, once the need to obtain subsistence supplies had passed (Bundy, 1979). Government action was therefore invoked to aid settler enterprise and either suppress or at least not assist African agriculturalists. This was achieved by two methods. The first was the selective assistance afforded European farmers through credit, extension services and marketing arrangements. This often paralleled assistance offered to farmers in the metropole. The significant difference was that aid was not available to African farmers, either by definition, or because European farmers claimed prior attention. The second was the restriction placed on the cultivation of export crops such as coffee by African farmers and through the various Maize Control Acts in Central and East Africa.

Another sphere in which administrative action was of prime importance was in the distribution of resources between immigrant and indigene (Hailey, 1938). Mining and concessions will be examined in later chapters. However, the division of the land itself between Europeans and Africans, particularly in colonies of settlement, was of prime importance for the evolution of the colonies concerned. Conflict over land was a major theme of the colonial period and its partial resolution by conquest and occupation was completed through a policy of territorial segregation leading to the establishment of the Native Reserves.

The evolution of the Native Reserves in Africa is a highly complex issue, resulting from various motives on the part of the colonial government. These included the provision of rewards for friendly and co-operative African groups, humanitarian concern for the protection of the indigenous population from settler pressures, establishment of areas of refuge for populations displaced, maintenance of control and supervision of the population in order to secure taxes and an adequate labour force and recognition of the limitation to colonial power (Crush, 1982). The earliest reserves were established in the eastern Cape of Good Hope in the 1840s as a means of rewarding Fingo groups who had assisted the British government in the frontier wars. Demarcation of the African areas was also often a preliminary for the opening of the remainder of the land to European settlement (Christopher, 1983). The Proclamation of reserves guaranteed no security, as those which became centres of resistance to colonial rule were abolished and the population dispersed, as illustrated by the fate of the Gcaleka Reserve in the eastern Cape in 1878. Other reserves were proclaimed to protect the inhabitants from settler land hunger, such as those in Bechuanaland and Barotseland where indigenous rulers were capable diplomatically of preserving a measure of independence. Reserves in territories such as Swaziland, Zululand and Northern Rhodesia were defined to accommodate Africans displaced by declaring certain other areas available for European settlement (Crush, 1980a). Reserves in Ovamboland in South West Africa were recognised because their displacement would have involved the colonial power in excessive effort for the limited return which the land would have given. The Swazi case also illustrates the extent to which the colonial government was flexible enough to placate the indigenous rulers by the careful delimitation of reserve boundaries, thereby reducing the possibilities of active resistance (Crush, 1980b). Thus royal lands, homesteads and graves and most of the chiefly homesteads fell within the reserves, but the majority of commoners had to move.

The interaction of settler interests, colonial administrations and

Figure 2.5: The Native Reserves of Southern Rhodesia 1894-1970

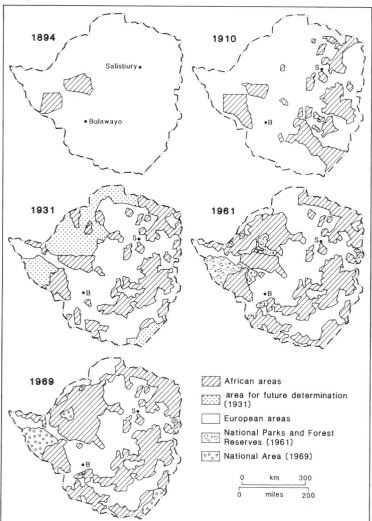

metropolitan politicians is exemplified by the definition of the Native Reserves in Southern Rhodesia (Christopher, 1971a) (Figure 2.5). The first reserves were defined in 1894 as a result of the direct intervention by the Imperial government in the affairs of the British South Africa Company (Great Britain, 1896). The political need to protect the interests of the indigenous population was seen to devolve upon the metropolitan power as settler interests were dominant in the local administration. Only 4.3 per cent of the country was set aside as reserves, but after the conflict of 1896-7 had forced a reappraisal of the land question, they were enlarged to cover some 26.0 per cent of the country. Few areas considered suitable for European settlement were allocated to the indigenous population (Mackenzie, 1974; Palmer, 1976). Successive redeterminations paralleling a rapidly expanding African population resulted in the enlargement of the reserves until the 1950s, as disease ridden and climatically and agriculturally marginal areas were included within them. By 1960 some 43.5 per cent of the colony was included in the Native Reserves. As a late dispensation related to the Rhodesian republican constitution of 1969, the reserves were defined so that European and African areas were equal in size, paralleling a potential equality of representation in parliament.

Once the lines had been drawn upon the maps and demarcated upon the ground, attempts were made to move the African population into the reserves. This applied to colonies such as Northern and Southern Rhodesia, and on a more dramatic scale to South Africa, where the process still continues (Christopher, 1982b; Lemon, 1976). The importance of the administrator in drawing the Native Reserve boundaries and then the attempt to move people from one area to another to fit the pattern, is again well illustrated in Southern Rhodesia. In 1898 the District Commissioners were given the task of defining the Native Reserves in their districts. They tackled the assignment constrained by existing European farms which could not be included and by their perception of the needs of the indigenous population. The result was a highly complex distribution where some commissioners had assigned virtually the entire district to the Reserves and others defined only small areas and sought to retain the remainder for European settlement. Hence a pattern of extreme fragmentation came into being which was only slowly consolidated in the period up to the enactment of the Land Tenure Act of 1969.

Clearly the extent of the Native Reserves depended upon the relative power of the various contending interests. Settler influence in the Orange Free State, for example, was such that by 1911 only 0.5 per cent of the territory was held by the indigenous population, who however, constituted 61.7 per cent of the population. In Southern Rhodesia some 26.0 per cent of the territory had been designated as Native Reserves, while the whole of Basutoland was proclaimed a native reserve with no areas available for European occupation. Other colonial powers also adopted the concept of the reserve. German administrators established reserves, usually as a complement to displacing the indigenous population for European plantations and farming land. In South West Africa some 3.5 per cent of the country was designated for Native Reserves by 1914, much of it covering an area of compact indigenous settlement in the north of the colony.

A number of government development schemes were undertaken by the colonial administrations. State departments were established to combat human and animal diseases and thus contribute to making new areas habitable both for men and animals. The primary concern was the formation of veterinary departments for the control of stock diseases, as this was beneficial for both European and African pastoralists. The major rinderpest outbreak which swept across Africa in the 1880s and 1890s was significant in focusing attention upon the problem at an early stage of colonial rule (Mettam, 1937). Attempts at quarantine proved to be only partially successful and it was the discovery of immunisation by the Cape Colonial veterinarian, Robert Koch, which enabled the disease to be controlled. The impact of the colonial departments was such as to lead one researcher to claim that 'veterinary work was one of the most successful developmental activities during the colonial period in many African territories' (Patterson, 1980, p. 457).

In the Gold Coast, a veterinary department was established in 1909. The aim of the officials was to control disease and assist in the development of a livestock industry in the colony, which was then a net importer of cattle. Control through quarantine at the borders and on internal movements was exercised from 1921 onwards, while a major immunisation campaign was undertaken in the 1930s. The results were spectacular. Cattle numbers rose from 76,000 in 1921 to 430,000 in 1957. Similar programmes of control were undertaken elsewhere on the continent with the object of enabling the indigenous population to increase stock numbers and thereby produce an exportable surplus (Wilson, 1979). In most cases the programmes were long term and still incomplete at the end of the colonial period. In some cases, such as Matebeleland, disease control proved to be so successful that overstocking had occurred by the 1940s (Prescott, 1961). However the political problems of attempting to destock were substantial, leading to increased resistance on the part of the indigenous population to colonial rule. Nevertheless, the stage had been reached where it was starvation induced by drought which controlled stock numbers by the 1950s in Southern Rhodesia, not disease.

Governmental development programmes were often undertaken with a view to the expansion of industry in the metropole (British East Africa, 1919). Two major examples may be taken from French West Africa and the Anglo-Egyptian Sudan, where irrigation works were undertaken with the object of promoting cotton cultivation for export to Europe. The Niger Project, in the French Sudan, envisaged the conversion of the interior Niger delta into irrigated farmlands (Vennetier, 1978). It was based on the experience of a small scheme at Soluba (1925) where 5,500 people were settled on 3,000 ha of irrigated land. The Office du Niger was established in 1932 and proceeded to plan a scheme on nearly 1,000,000 ha for an envisaged 800,000 African colonists. The dam at Sansanding was built between 1934 and 1947, providing a measure of flood control as well as water from the irrigated fields. A reassessment in 1945 suggested that the planned area and the number of colonists would have to be cut by half. By 1955 only some 44,000 ha had been irrigated and 25,000 colonists settled. Other French schemes undertaken after the Second World War by the development agency, FIDES, included the Richard-Toll project on the Senegal River, where 6,000 ha were reclaimed for rice cultivation to reduce imports. In the Anglo-Egyptian Sudan, the Gezira scheme, located between the Blue and White Niles above Khartoum, was of a similar nature (Hance, 1954). The Nile Waters agreement with Egypt in 1929 allocated a limited amount of water for Sudanese irrigation works. Approximately 750,000 ha were brought under irrigation after the construction of the Sennar Dam, although only half was cropped each year. Some 90,000 settler families had joined the scheme by Independence contributing significantly to the agricultural production of the condominium.

The majority of official development schemes were undertaken late in the colonial period. Although Joseph Chamberlain had referred to the colonial heritage and estate as early as the 1890s, the first British Colonial Development Act was only passed in 1929. Many of the schemes receiving state aid were related to traditional concerns with infrastructure rather than with agricultural and industrial development. However, after the Second World War, Great

Britain was faced with a major shortage of oils and fats, aggravated by the weakness of the currency. This meant that in the crisis climate of the late 1940s, and as a result of the government's desire to show that it was doing something to develop the Empire, a series of disastrous schemes was launched.

The largest project was the Tanganyika groundnut scheme which was proposed in 1946 and put into immediate effect. The scheme provided for the cultivation of some 1,300,000 ha of land mainly in Tanganyika, for the cultivation of groundnuts. The land was unoccupied and deemed capable of development by mechanical means both for bush clearing and planting. However the fact that the areas were unoccupied was significant as the land was of poor quality and disease ridden. The lack of inhabitants also meant that personnel had to be imported, as indeed were the stores, machines and expertise. As a later writer stated 'any benefits to the people of East Africa would be a by-product of the scheme' (Morgan, 1980 (2), p. 235). The scheme ran into problems from its inception and even a limited programme which stopped far short of the initial target had to be abandoned. The port facilities, including the railway line, at Mtwara remain as a monument to the over-ambitious project. Other rushed projects such as the Gambia egg scheme met similar fates. Development planning in the colonial period, except for basic infrastructure, was not the most enduring memorial of the administrators.

3 TRADERS, TRANSPORTERS AND MISSIONARIES

Expansion of trade between Africa and the remainder of the world took place simultaneously with the establishment of colonial rule. The two were viewed as inseparable by contemporaries and indeed governments on occasion entrusted the conquest and administration of extensive tracts of the continent to commercial ventures. Trade was a two-way movement with African primary products exchanged, however disadvantageously, for largely European industrial products. The scale varied from the major wholesale and shipping companies to the individual trader at his store. Linking them was a group of transporters who built and maintained major systems of roads, railways and shipping lines to facilitate this trade. The transport lines were laid down to promote the Europe-Africa connection with little regard for intra-Africa links, once the colonial boundaries had been drawn. A third group, the missionaries, need to be considered here as the links between Christianity and civilisation on the one hand and trade and industry on the other, were regarded by nineteenth-century Europeans as indissoluble. The missionaries effectively fostered a demand for industrial products and attempted to transform African societies into the image of industrial Europe.

The Traders

Trading activity was a significant element in the European penetration of Africa, both prior to and after the establishment of colonial rule. Indeed, the earliest contacts between Africans and Europeans were usually through trade. The course of the slave trade has already been traced, but it was through what contemporaries described as 'legitimate trade' that exchange increasingly took place. Legitimate trade broadly involved the import of European manufactured goods into Africa and the export of raw materials, amounting to an expansion of dealings initiated by the Portuguese. Although much of the pre-1800 trade was controlled by chartered companies and state monopolies, private individuals and firms often acted as interlopers and were increasingly tolerated. This became the general trend as the slave trade was abolished and the

chartered companies foundered financially. Free trade, which expanded in the eighteenth and nineteenth centuries, resulted in
increasing numbers of Europeans remaining in Africa and greater
competition with the indigenous trading system. However, it was
not until the conquest of disease that the numbers became appre-
ciable and that traders ceased to be confined to the coastal stations.
A late resurgence of the chartered companies was associated with
the partition of the continent, which ran counter to these developments, but reflects more the desire of governments to expand their
colonial empires without having to pay for it than a renewed profitability of such companies. The development of the international
economy in the second half of the nineteenth century was such that
even apparently shaky enterprises could attract metropolitan
capital (Latham, 1978). However, African enterprises represented
only a small part of the total overseas capital flow (Frankel, 1938;
Suret-Canale, 1971).

The posts and forts on the African coast provided the first bases
for European traders to market their goods and buy African
products. Prior to the early nineteenth century slaves constituted
the main item with only small quantities of products such as ivory,
gold, hides, palm-oil, gum and timber shipped on the West Coast.
On the East Coast European trade was minimal as Oman effectively
excluded European enterprise north of Moçambique. Only the
Cape of Good Hope developed the rudiments of an import-export
and internal trade system akin to mid-latitude colonies of settlement. Even in southern Africa trade was directed towards the
export of primary agricultural products from European farms such
as wine and wool, prior to the exploitation of diamonds and gold.
Trade within the colonial system thus operated according to the
early stages of Vance's (1970) model of mercantalism.

The trading penetration of the interior was associated with the
rise of European commercial firms which became strong enough to
bypass the African wholesalers on the coast. This state of affairs was
only reached in the mid-nineteenth century as the indigenous political entities weakened in the face of increasing European military
and technological dominance. This was not a sudden occurrence
and was delayed even in the most active areas of trade. On the
French Guinea coast little inland penetration took place until the
1880s when concerted action by groups of traders led to the establishment of effective colonial control over the coastal zones, and
attempts were made to establish posts in the interior in the wake of

the French army. Technological innovation enabled trade to be conducted by steam ships on the rivers and lagoons, with moored hulks serving as warehouses and depots. The charting of the navigable Niger River provided the key to the coastal traders' problem of reaching the palm-oil producers directly. Trade took the form of trading expeditions along the river, supported after 1857 by an annual display of naval power. A base at Lokoja on the Niger-Benue confluence was temporarily established in the 1850s. It was only with the formation of the United Africa Company in 1879 that the British traders grouped themselves together to remove mutual competition and to eliminate the French presence (Pedler, 1974). Its successor, the Royal Niger Company was granted a charter in 1886 which conferred the right to operate an administration to foster peaceful trade. The Company founded a series of depots and trading bases throughout the lower Niger basin, but was restricted by the French presence on the upper Niger.

Although nominally controlling an extensive territory, the Royal Niger Company was dependent upon its fleet on the navigable rivers. Its trading and government posts were riverine and no attempt was made to establish a presence in the major non-riverine cities such as Kano or Sokoto. Navigation on the Niger was possible for 960 km as far as the rapids at Bussa, while the Benue was navigable for over 1,500 km on a seasonal basis. The Company organised its first base at Akassa on the Niger delta, but later established Burutu some 20 km up the river in more favourable physical conditions (Ogundana, 1972). It was at these points that transhipment from river craft to ocean-going vessels took place, and from where the administration operated. Burutu at its height employed 1,500 workers in the dockyard, 700 on the ships and a further 100 in clerical positions. The whole was organised as a self-contained town. The vessels based there called at the trading posts and traders stationed on the rivers. It was they who dealt with African producers and wholesalers. The company, renamed the Niger Company in 1900, did not establish agencies in Kano until 1912 and it took little interest in direct retail trade or indeed in small-scale wholesale purchasing. It was the groundnut boom of 1912-13 which resulted in a change of emphasis and a more direct intervention in trading, both wholesale and retail. In that period some 18 firms were established in Kano and a network of wholesaling links was established and retail stores built to sell imported goods to the African producers.

The integration of the trading patterns in Nigeria and indeeed in most colonies was pursued in the post First World War period. This may be illustrated by the expansion of Lever Brothers which gained control of the Niger Company in 1920 (Fieldhouse, 1978). Through a number of financial moves various undertakings were grouped with Lever Brothers, who were at this stage pursuing interests in the Belgian Congo and French Equatorial Africa, as well as in British West Africa. The large multinational enterprise had to a major extent replaced the individual traders and small companies linked to specific areas of the continent. The complexities of the Unilever grouping, which emerged after a series of amalgamations in 1929 and 1930, established an organisation which controlled the entire chain of production from the plantation to the final distribution of the manufactured output. However, the distributive process was usually left in indigenous hands, rather than through the construction of a chain of retail stores.

Imperial governments resorted to the use of chartered companies to further their aims through the employment of private capital rather than public funds. Thus in the late 1880s Great Britain chartered two further companies, the Imperial British East Africa Company and the British South Africa Company to lay claims to extensive tracts of the continent in which the government had only minimal interest. The former company was to prove unequal to the task as the resources of the East African mainland were limited, while the latter was unable to pay a dividend in the entire period for which it was responsible for the administration of its territories. The Portuguese government similarly made use of chartered companies in the early 1890s to attract private and foreign capital to Moçambique (Vail, 1976). The Moçambique Company was able to foster some degree of developmental work during its 50-year period of control (1891-1941) but the Nyassa Company was unable to maintain even the minimal terms of its charter through its limited network of posts across northern Moçambique (Neil-Tomlinson, 1977).

The European trader appeared ubiquitously throughout Africa under the protection of the colonial governments. Their numbers were particularly significant in those territories where a degree of European settlement had taken place and a measure of local self-government had been gained by the settlers. The individual traders established their posts with local or colonial government approval and began to trade through an exchange of goods. The traders' role in undermining the indigenous economies has been well documented through the high prices demanded for the traders' products, low prices for African sales, and the iniquities of the credit system. In geographical terms the network of stores in the rural areas is noticeable. The threat of competition for the highly restricted African market inevitably resulted in attempts to protect business. In the Transkei, for example, no store could be established within 8 km of another, in order to reduce competition and provide a reasonably large area of business (Haines, 1933). Thus in the early 1930s there were some 650 general traders operating in the rural areas of the Transkei, or one store per 65 km² or 2,000 people. Furthermore the range of commodities offered was limited by the generally low purchasing power of the indigenous inhabitants. Trading stores thus usually earned low returns, which deterred many northern Europeans who expected a higher standard of living for the capital employed. Consequently in large parts of the continent trading was taken over by relatively poor Europeans including Greeks, Cypriots and Russian Jews, and also by Asians, particularly Indians and Lebanese. The distribution of the various groups was widespread except where legislative action was taken by local governments to exclude Asians from specific areas, particularly from parts of South Africa.

The Transporters

An effective transportation system was considered to be essential to the economic development of the continent. This took the form of both a connecting service between Africa and Europe and an internal system linking the interior to the ports, as a means of facilitating trade and consolidating colonial rule. The problems of construction and maintenance were immense. Vessels which were used for exploration in the fifteenth and sixteenth centuries were small, and only in the nineteenth century did ship sizes increase appreciably. Improved technology was reflected not only in the increased size of vessel but also its means of propulsion. The advent of steam power enabled faster, more regular, and direct sailings, together with the possibilities of penetrating the river systems (Headrick, 1981). The early steam vessels also indicated a new approach to relations between Africa and Europe in the form of the light gunboat. Conquest of the interior became possible, for the gunboat was used extensively on rivers such as the Nile, Senegal, Niger and Congo, and on the major East African lakes. Additional modes of transport were needed for much of the interior. Within tropical Africa porterage was the main pre-colonial means of transporting goods, but this was expensive even when slaves and forced labour were used. With the advent of colonial rule alternative means were demanded. The train, and later the motor vehicle overcame the problems associated with endemic animal diseases and Africa witnessed the development and elaboration of both railway and road systems. It was inevitably the former which elicited greater comment and the more grandiose schemes.

Shipping

Rapid developments in shipping in the nineteenth century resulted in a steady increase in the size of merchant vessels, and by the 1850s steamers of 1,000 to 2,000 tons were being built. In the 1890s vessels of up to 8,000 tons were under construction and by 1914, ships of 20,000 tons were in service. Furthermore the transfer from sail to steam power was rapid. In 1875 sailing ships still accounted for 72 per cent of the tonnage registered at Lloyds underwriters in London. A quarter of a century later the percentage had fallen to 25. Steam vessels thus provided greatly expanded capacities and also faster and more certain deliveries. This opened the way for the scheduled service running to a timetable. The demand for speed and regularity came first from the metropolitan and colonial post offices. Contracts to carry the mail were eagerly sought and secured a definite advantage for the contracting company. The course of such enterprises may be illustrated by the largest contract, the mail service between Cape Town and England (Murray, 1953). The first steamship, the *Enterprise* (500 tons) reached Cape Town in 1825 at the conclusion of a voyage of 58 days from Falmouth. After the resolution of a number of problems, the Union Line, later the Union-Castle line, was awarded the main mail contract in 1857. The company undertook to sail between England and the Cape in 42 days using vessels in excess of 530 tons. By 1863 the largest vessel in the service displaced 1,200 tons and thereafter tonnages increased steadily, reaching 37,000 tons in the 1950s. The sailing time was progressively reduced to 26 days in the 1870s, 16 days in the 1910s and finally 12 days in the 1960s. Because of their reliability the liner services attracted the transport of both goods and passengers, but to maintain their speed called at comparatively few ports.

The implications of these developments were substantial, leading to the construction of a number of major ports and the simplification of the port system. Although many of the port sites selected in the period prior to 1860 continued in use, others were created (Hoyle and Hilling, 1970). Major ports such as Casablanca and Dakar owe their position to choices made by colonial administrations seeking to establish facilities capable of catering for the increasing flow of men and material. Many of the island sites such as Gorée or Moçambique were unsuitable for use as mass transit points, and substitutes had to be found. Others were overshadowed by their neighbours and their hinterlands were incorporated into the latter. Thus ports such as St Louis and Rufique in Senegal suffered the effects of competition with Dakar (Pasquier, 1960). In the Gold Coast the lack of suitable natural harbours was solved by the construction of an artificial harbour at Takoradi in 1928 (Dickson, 1965). Otherwise the Gold Coast ports were surf ports, with loading and unloading undertaken by small boats plying between the ocean-going vessels and the shore. The most important surf port, Accra, still handled 600,000 tons in 1957 in this manner, as opposed to 3,000,000 tons at Takoradi. Lighterage remained an essential element in the port system throughout the colonial period. Dar es Salaam, for example, only completed its first deep water berths in 1956.

Established ports required substantial expansion as the size of vessels increased. Breakwaters and quays were built to enable vessels to moor alongside the transport, storage and processing facilities. Cape Town began a major programme of construction in 1860, Dakar in 1863 and other ports followed. In the majority of cases the expansion of facilities was accomplished by building out into the oceans, in terms of Wiese's, (1981) southern African 'any port' model. Comparatively few major ports were developed on estuarine sites where basins could be excavated. The majority required extensive reclamation schemes and the construction of enclosing breakwaters.

Parallel with the improvements in both vessel and port facilities went a revolution in shipping organisation (Porter, 1981). Steamships could now sail to a set timetable ensuring regularity in transportation. The first lines attempted to reach India with regular sailings via both Alexandria and Suez, then later through the Suez Canal and around the continent. Timetabled sailings to African ports were instituted in the 1850s and organised in the 1880s and

1890s on an international basis through a series of conference groupings. Thus in 1895 the West African Shipping Conference sought to rationalise sailings and fix rates. The British, Elder Dempster line; the German, Woermann; and the Holland West Africa line were able to co-ordinate their activities in influencing traders and administrators alike (Leubuscher, 1963). Similar conferences were formed for the South and East Africa trade, which were able to exert a powerful influence on traders and governments alike (Solomon, 1982).

Telegraphs and Posts

The communications revolution wrought by the steam vessel was paralleled by another invention, the telegraph. This required the perfection of the submarine cable as land lines were subject to delay and presented problems of construction and operation through territories not under European control (Headrick, 1981). The success of the trans-Atlantic and British Indian submarine cables in the 1860s prompted the link between Africa and Europe. In 1879 the line from Aden was extended to South Africa and by 1885 cables encircled the continent. New cables of improved manufacture were laid at intervals so that by 1900 there were for example seven cables linking France and Algeria. The almost instantaneous communication inevitably brought metropolitan government control over its subordinates in the colonies into effective day-to-day supervision, allowing fewer opportunities for independent action and concentrating decision making in the hands of officials in Europe. In commercial terms the possibilities for controlling trade and monitoring commodity prices in the metropole were of great advantage to the trading firms in the main ports, as also for inland traders and producers, for the telegraph lines were extended inland in the service of colonial advance. This development led to a greater degree of metropolitan control over trade as the major wholesale firms and banks were able to displace the smaller colonial concerns and achieve a high degree of commercial dominance in the colonies (Jones, 1978). The physical impact of the submarine telegraph was restricted to the construction of a series of cable stations on isolated islands around the continent such as Ascension and Rodriguez.

The communication system also relied upon an efficient postal system whereby information of a commercial and political nature, as well as the more personal aspects of keeping in touch with the metropole, could be rapidly transmitted in letter and parcel form.

Postal agencies were thus viewed in the period prior to the advent of inexpensive interncontinental telephone calls as vital to the maintenance and expansion of European influence. Governments appointed a range of persons, including missionaries, farmers and soldiers, to act as postal officials while attempts were made to penetrate areas not yet under direct colonial control through the overseas extension of the metropolitan postal service. Postal imperialism operated in Egypt, Ethiopia, Madagascar, Morocco and Zanzibar, where various European countries set up and conducted their own postal services independent of the indigenous government. Certain of these offices continued to function throughout the colonial period. For example, the last British post office in Morocco, at Tangier, only closed in 1957, 100 years after it had been inaugurated. The majority closed soon after another European power had established its own state service. Thus the French post office in Zanzibar, opened in 1889, closed in 1906, paralleling the history of the German service; while the British post office at Antananarivo in Madagascar closed in 1896 following the French occupation. The French postal system in North Africa, outside Algeria, was established and operated to further France's considerable economic and political stake in the region. The first office was inaugurated in Alexandria in 1837 at a time when French influence in Egypt was paramount. Other offices followed and a network from Tangier to Port Said was completed in 1880 with the opening of the Tripoli agency. Some of these were the forerunners of the colonial systems, while the others, in Tripoli and in Egypt, were closed as French interests declined in importance in states under the control or influence of other European powers.

Waterways

The waterways of Africa presented the most immediate possibilities for internal transportation in the colonial period. As early as 1832 Macgregor Laird formed the African Inland Commercial Company with the object of exploiting the resources of the Niger River for legitimate trade. The rapidly expanding demand for palm-oil for soap manufacture had focused attention upon the region. In 1814 the Niger palm-oil trade amounted to only 450 tons, but it had increased to 14,000 tons annually by the 1830s. The Niger is one of the few rivers in Africa navigable from the ocean and steamship transportation was feasible for turning the previously irregular and expensive flow of oil at the coast into a regular, cheap and profitable flow in the interior. Shipping was at first limited owing to the high death-rates encountered, but the prophylactic use of quinine on a large scale changed the situation, so that the death-rate was no longer an overwhelming factor against European activity on the River. By the 1860s a regular transportation system was in operation. The activities of the United Africa Company and its successor, the Royal Niger Company have already been mentioned. Both acted as prototypes for other transport enterprises.

Elsewhere in Africa many of the major rivers are broken by cataracts, with rapids and waterfalls preventing the passage of ocean-going vessels. The lower Zambezi, for example, was explored by David Livingstone in 1858, in the *Ma Robert*, but his progress was blocked by the Kebrabasa Rapids. However, upper reaches of rivers such as the Congo and the Nile are navigable for considerable distances. Thus internal river communication could be extensively used if the initial physical obstacles could be overcome. The advent of the prefabricated steamboat which could be carried in pieces from the coast to the upper river solved the problem. Henry Stanley transported the *En Avant* from the coast to Stanley Pool, from where the upper Congo was accessible. Savorgnan De Brazza similarly had the *Ballay* carried to the Congo and Samuel Baker had the *Khedive* transported to the upper Nile. Particularly spectacular was the transport and use of the prefabricated aluminium steamer, the *Leon Blot*, to the Lake Chad region in the 1890s, to aid the French conquest of the area.

After the pioneers, more regular services were introduced (Lederer, 1965). Stanley established Leopoldville in 1882 as a base for ships steaming on the upper Congo. The river provided the means of transport whereby the Congo Free State was explored and exploited. The railways linking Matadi and Leopoldville, Stanleyville and Ponthierville, and Kasongo and Kabalo, were constructed to link the various sections of the navigable Congo, bypassing the rapids. The system covered about 4,000 km of navigable rivers when fully utilised (Huybrechts, 1970). Leopoldville consequently became one of the larger ports of Africa, handling 1.6 million tons of cargo in 1959. Major port and transhipment facilities were constructed to handle the specialised fleets of sternwheelers and barges. A similar system was operated by the French between Brazzaville and Bangui.

Few other rivers and lakes were suitable for major transportation use. Systems were developed on the Senegal, and the upper Niger by the French. The upper Nile and Lake Victoria were used to more limited extents by the British. Owing to the greater aridity of the northern and southern parts of the continent, neither North or South Africa developed a river transport system, and the rivers were seen essentially as barriers to be crossed by road or rail. Similarly the East Africa Rift Valley lake system was exploited to a limited degree owing to the isolating nature of the topography. Only the lower Zambezi was used to any extent and this required the establishment of a base at Chinde for the transhipment of goods bound for Nyasaland (Baker, 1980).

Owing to disease only limited parts of the continent were suitable for animal hauled transport. Ox-wagons were used for bulk transport in the extreme north and south of the continent, until the advent of motor vehicles in the 1920s and 1930s, but they were slow. Speeds of approximately 20–30 km per day resulted in journeys measured in weeks rather than hours. The demand for a swifter means of movement was fostered in South Africa by the discovery of the diamond fields in the vicinity of Kimberley in 1870. Stage coaches were introduced and a network of regular services was built up serving the major towns south of the Zambezi River (Zeederberg, 1971). The coaches required substantially better roads and so contributed to the improvement in land transport through the construction and maintenance of a system of graded roads, linking Cape Town and Salisbury by the early 1890s. However, the coaches were superseded by the railway system in the course of the 1880s and 1890s.

Railways

Colonial and metropolitan governments were particularly enamoured with the construction of railways. Lines were viewed not only as a means of transport but also demonstrated the technological skills of the colonial power and appealed to the humanitarian movements in the metropoles. The problems of transportation, especially porterage, were emphasised. The system drained labour from the routes as some were forcibly recruited and others fled to avoid empressment, and it acted as corridors along which human and animal diseases were transmitted. The Brussels Conference of 1876 recommended 'the construction of railroads for the purpose of substituting economical and rapid means of transport for the present head porterage' (Headrick, 1981, pp. 192-3). Estimates were produced to show that one train could do the work of 13,333 porters. However, there were few parts of Africa in the late nineteenth century where there were sufficient goods for 13,333 porters to carry. Railway construction often had to be viewed in terms of prestige rather than profit. More recently the whole undertaking has been reinterpreted in terms of promoting regional inequalities and underdevelopment (Pirie, 1982).

Railway construction was expensive (Christopher, 1976a). In South Africa before the First World War, the average cost of building the standard (1.067 m) gauge lines was £4,665 per kilometre, and difficult sections had cost over six times as much. To justify this expenditure railways needed either a considerable traffic in passengers and manufactures, or raw materials from mines and farms. Except for the Alexandria-Suez route and a few local lines in North and South Africa, the former were not present until late in the colonial period when railway building had largely ceased. Thus the colonial railways were mainly geared to the transport of minerals and crops from their sources to the ports. Opportunities for profitable railway construction were therefore few, and the enterprise was often undertaken by the government. Railways were usually built as cheaply as possible, on narrower gauges than in Europe and avoiding tunnels and expensive bridges where rivers could be forded by ferries. Station platforms could be dispensed with as indeed could signalling on single track lines. Sir Frederick Lugard thus advocated maximum railway construction at minimum costs in order to obtain the benefits of cheap transportation for landlocked Northern Nigeria (Lugard, 1965). His advice was heeded elsewhere on the continent where light railways were frequently constructed as feeder services for the main lines.

The lines may be primarily regarded as links between the ports and the interior. Few were built to link one port to another and the regional integration of railway systems was rare. Only the two extremities of the continent where European settlement was of paramount importance created railway networks as opposed to isolated individual lines. The earliest railways on the continent were constructed largely for passenger conveyance. The first lines from Alexandria to Cairo and Cairo to Suez were built in the 1850s as a means of speeding passengers in their voyage between Europe and India, linking the steamer services which had superseded the Cape of Good Hope route. In the following decade short lines were built in the Cape Colony, Natal and Algeria to link the ports with areas of dense European settlement in the immediate hinterland. By 1875 under 1,000 km of railways had been constructed in Africa, excluding the Egyptian system. This lack of progress was not for lack of plans. The first proposals in Algeria were framed in 1844, but it was 18 years before the first line was opened (Brant, 1971). Similarly in southern Africa the railway mania of the 1840s produced no tangible result and only two short lines at Cape Town and Durban were opened in 1860. In Senegal the time lag between plan and completion was even longer. The St Louis–Dakar line (263 km) proposed in 1854 by General Faidherbe was only completed in 1885.

Advances in technology in the second half of the nineteenth century were such that by the time the main African lines were built, they were regarded as feasible engineering feats. The completion of both the transcontinental railway in the United States and the Suez Canal in 1869 illustrated the possibilities of transcontinental lines and the cutting of canal links to irrigate the deserts. The interior of the continent offered a greater potential than had been previously apparent as disease and indigenous powers could more readily be overcome and technology applied to the development of the continent's resources. Railways were to play an essential role in this development. Grand schemes were envisaged by both the British and the French. The French were attracted to the idea of a railway across the Sahara (Brunschwig, 1967). In 1879 the Commission for the Trans-Saharan Railway was established to investigate the feasibility of a link between Algeria and the Niger. Lines were projected from Algiers to Conakry in French Guinea and Ouidah in Dahomey in the early 1890s and were later extended across the Sudan to Obock and the Congo. Even Johannesburg was suggested as the terminus for the French line in 1895. As late as 1914 a railway for Greater France from Dunkerque to Brazzaville was suggested as a practical proposition. The British continental theme was the link between the Cape and Cairo (Strage, 1977). This was proposed by southern African interests and particularly espoused by Cecil Rhodes. Links between the Cape of Good Hope and territories to the north were progressively negotiated and constructed. The British South Africa Company and its affiliates pushed the line 3,705 km from Cape Town to reach Elisabethville in the Belgian Congo in 1910. However, gaps remained in areas to the north which were particularly unpromising economically and the scheme lapsed. Even in the 1940s a project to link the East African and Rhodesian railway systems was rejected on both economic and technical grounds (Great Britian, 1949).

In practice railway building was not undertaken on this scale. The major advances came with the expansion first of the North and South African economies and secondly the individual lines of exploitation in the tropical colonies to convey the main minerals and crops to the export terminals. In North Africa, the Algerian railway system was expanded in a piecemeal fashion to total 3,337 km in 1911 with a further 1,800 km in Tunisia. The lines did little more than serve the needs of the European farming and commercial community settled within 100 km of the Mediterranean Sea. In South Africa 11,225 km had been built by 1911 and a further 3,650 km constructed by Rhodesia Railways. Elsewhere on the continent the two largest systems were the French West African, which totalled 2,457 km and that of German South West Africa where 2,372 km had been laid. The former, however, was broken up into four separate colonial lines for Senegal with its link to Upper Senegal and Niger (half the total length), French Guinea, Ivory Coast and Dahomey.

The southern African system at the outbreak of the First World War represented over half the total length of railways in Africa. Its evolution from an initial series of disconnected lines linking the main ports to their immediate hinterland was the result of the economic booms associated with the mineral discoveries. Diamonds at Kimberley and gold on the Witwatersrand transformed the subcontinental space economy by attracting large numbers of Europeans to the undeveloped interior (Christopher, 1976a). Lines were built from the main ports of Cape Town, Port Elizabeth and East London in the Cape Colony, Durban in Natal and Lourenço Marques in Moçambique to tap the wealth generated by the new mining centres. The latter line was designed by the Transvaal republican administration to provide a link with the rest of the world, independent of British control. The manipulation of freight rates, and the granting of subsidies resulted in a highly complex pattern of competition for the trade of the southern Transvaal, which was only resolved in 1910 with the unification of the various lines into the state controlled South African Railways. The construction of the main lines in the 1890s was extended to the Rhodesias through Bechuanaland as the British controlled line from Cape Town bypassed the Transvaal. Salisbury was at first linked to Beira before the connection to the main system was made.

There followed a period of railway elaboration as branch lines were constructed effectively providing cheap transport facilities to the developing agricultural regions and outlying mining centres. Over much of the Orange Free State and southern Transvaal, the railways preceded and indeed stimulated commercial crop production. Furthermore, the exploitation of minerals acted as the first stage in industrialisation in which the railways played a vital role.

A similar series of political calculations revolved around the railways built to carry the copper of Katanga and Northern Rhodesia to the sea (Haefele and Steinberg, 1965; Katzenellenbogen, 1973). Rhodesia Railways reached Broken Hill in 1906 and Elisabethville four years later. Through its control of the only accessible coal supplies at Wankie in Southern Rhodesia it was able to guarantee that all Northern Rhodesian and a high proportion of Katangan copper was transported southwards over its system. The use of Beira and later also Lourenço Marques was relatively lengthy both in terms of distance travelled and in the extra 4,000 km involved in shipment around Africa to Europe, but politically Rhodesia Railways was in a dominant position. To counter this dominance two further lines were laid to shorten distances and provide a non-British route to the sea for Katangan copper. The first was promoted by the Belgian government which constructed a line from Katanga to Port Francqui on the Congo from whence goods were taken by boat to Leopoldville. Transhipments at Leopoldville and Matadi reduced the competitive advantages of the line. A sliding scale of freight rates was intended to promote the use of the 'national way' and overcome its obvious logistical disadvantages. The second line was constructed from Lobito in Angola to the Katangan copper belt. It was only completed in 1931 and its use was controlled by international agreement. Attempts in 1956 to equalise rates failed as Rhodesia Railways offered discounts to maintain the flow of copper to southern and eastern coast ports.

Railway construction in tropical and equatorial Africa was more problematic as the economic bases were limited. Light railways were laid for specific purposes such as the military line in the Gold Coast in 1873 or the Senegalese line linking St Louis and Dakar in the 1880s. However, significant projects only got under way after Joseph Chamberlain became Colonial Secretary in Great Britain in 1895 and Bernard Dernburg in Germany in 1906. Both brought a more urgent approach to the exploitation of colonial resources and a greater awareness of the possibilities of economic and social advancement within Africa. The result was a major extension of railway construction. The Uganda Railway from Mombasa to Kisumu on Lake Victoria completed in 1901 achieved significant results (Hill, 1950). The journey from the coast to Lake Victoria was cut from two months to two days and freight rates fell from £100–£300 per ton to £2.40. The initial demand for the railway had been political, linked to the consolidation of British control of the headwaters of the Nile and the suppression of the slave trade. It was condemned as a line which went nowhere and was dubbed 'the Lunatic Express' (Miller, 1971). However, it did facilitate the trans-formation of the economies of the two countries through which it passed, by fostering the expansion of African cotton production in Uganda and the commencement of European settlement in Kenya. These in turn prompted further railway extensions to serve the areas of crop production (Van Dongen, 1954).

Other lines were built to develop particular products in demand in Europe. The Nigerian system was designed to link the palm-oil region directly to Lagos, while the extension to Kano was expected to stimulate cotton production in Northern Nigeria. The German line from the port at Douala was built to penetrate the coastal forest zone and reach the apparently more profitable savannah lands of the interior. The Germans built railways rapidly and by 1914 their four colonies possessed some 4,500 km of track. The most extensive system was in South West Africa which linked the two ports of Swakopmund and Luderitz to the interior pastoral lands around the capital, Windhoek, and the copper mines in the north of the colony (Pool, 1982). Equally comprehensive was that in German East Africa where the Dar es Salaam to Lake Tanganyika railway was completed in 1914 and work on the branch line to Lake Victoria was under way. The railway systems in the former German colonies were virtually completed by the First World War, with little further development in the colonial period.

The railways were built on several different gauges according to the calculations of each colonial railway administration. Thus the initial Cape railway was built with a 1.435 m gauge, but when the major line to Kimberley was planned the cheaper 1.067 m gauge was adopted in view of the engineering problems encountered in mountainous terrain. Linking the various systems has thus been difficult. The entire South West African system was converted by the South Africans to their own gauge after the two were linked. The problems of differing gauges for the Rhodesian and East

African systems were encountered when the Tazara line was built. Even within one territory more than one gauge was used. Both Algeria and South Africa adopted a narrow gauge lightweight system of feeder lines to supplement the main system. Transhipment stations were thus required and the later railway administrations have been faced with the problem of differing gauges and system integration.

The colonial administrator, Sir Philip Mitchell, wrote in 1936 'it is not as caretakers that we shall be judged in the eyes of posterity, but as builders' (Ehrlich, 1973). In terms of building, the communications systems, more especially the ports and the railways, stand as some of the most spectacular physical monuments to the colonial era. The railway lines in particular were allocated a high proportion of the capital which was available for colonial development. Capital development costs on the South African Railways system had amounted to £85 million by 1914. The German government spent or guaranteed private loans to the value of 265 million marks (£13.3 million) between 1906 and 1914 for African railway construction. These costs were viewed as essential for the stimulation of the colonial economies, and could be recouped by later revenues once the railways had led to increased production and large freight loads. Nevertheless, injudicious railway construction could effectively bankrupt colonial economies, where administrators overreached themselves with optimistic concepts of progress. The saga of Nyasaland Railways was one of impoverishment of the colony which had to bear the high costs of the Trans-Zambezi Railway, as a first call upon its treasury, yet failed to promote agricultural development (Vail, 1975). The prestige of a railway project was often too great to be deflected by the lack of exploitable resources when powerful settler interests were involved and stood to gain most from the railways' operation.

The engineering feats were often remarkable, involving a high degree of organisation and experimentation in conditions unlike those of the metropolitan country. The railways required substantial labour forces for construction and operation. These were often not available locally. Thus the Matadi-Leopoldville line built between 1892 and 1898 to bypass the rapids on the lower Congo experienced severe problems (Goffin, 1907). Labourers from Macao, the West Indies and finally Senegal were imported to work on the line. The high death-rates on this line and the later French line from Pointe Noire to Brazzaville similarly consumed its workers at a devastating rate. The Germans imported poor White South Africans for work on the Swakopmund-Windhoek line, while the British imported Indians to work on the Uganda Railway. As in so many cases the 'development' of Africa was undertaken by European managers using imported labourers, many of whom stayed to establish permanent interests in the continent when the project had been completed. Substantial staffs were required to maintain and run the systems and again many railwaymen came from other continents or parts of Africa.

Railway construction involved engineering works of a high order. The lines tolerated gradients and curves which reduced their operating efficiency in European terms, but this was the price to be paid for their construction in a short period of time. Constant improvements and realignments have been necessary. The major bridges including the Victoria Falls Bridge, the Zambezi Bridge in Moçambique and the Niger Bridge at Jebba acted as major innovations in themselves, enabling vehicles and pedestrians to cross the rivers. The problems of rapid ascents were frequent on the edge of the African plateaux and in the East Africa Rift Valley system. Elaborate solutions were devised in the form of circular tunnels and reversing stations borrowed from American and Indian experience.

Despite the spectacular characteristics of water and rail transport, goods continued to be carried by people, animals and vehicles on tracks and roads. Roads for the passage of wagons and horses were built by the governments in North and South Africa from the inception of European settlement. Temporary tracks for porters were demarcated in central Africa. Later, road systems were graded in every colony for motor transport. The more prosperous progressed to surfaced roads, at least around the main towns, although the all weather road networks of most colonies were still rudimentary at the end of the colonial era.

The first major road construction schemes were undertaken by the authorities in the Cape of Good Hope and Algeria in the first half of the nineteenth century. In the Cape of Good Hope the major transport problems of a permanent link across the Cape Flats between Cape Town and Stellenbosch and graded roads across the mountains into the interior, were solved by the construction of new all weather roads. The first, early in the century, involved the compaction of the sand dunes, and at mid-century included the major construction works of the mountain passes. As in Algeria much of the road construction was for military purposes and was aided by the presence of a permanent garrison which built the trunk routes for the transportation of military supplies.

Except in problematic areas such as mountains or at river crossings, roads outside the settled agricultural regions were usually no more than tracks, until new phases began about the turn of the century. Roads were then built and graded on an increasing scale. In Togo the Germans built a system which was integrated with the railways to provide a comprehensive network for the entire colony. Such a plan was ahead of its time, although clearly designed for motor transport, it was extensively used by bicycles. The bicycle proved to be an essential element in tropical Africa for overcoming the lack of transport animals. Roadbuilding accelerated after the First World War as motor transport became more general and a boom in bus and lorry services led to increasing integration of colonial economies and societies. Again North and South Africa were far in advance of other parts of the continent with the development of regional tarred road networks by the early 1960s.

The Missionaries

Missionaries played an often vital role in the colonial penetration of Africa. European enterprise was viewed from a European perspective as a civilising force in which Christianity, trade and industry were inseparably bound (Rea, 1976). The degree of evangelical zeal varied with time and nation. The Portuguese initiatives in the Congo or on the Zambezi in the sixteenth century were not repeated on any scale until the nineteenth century, when the religious revival in Europe inspired individuals to seek the conversion of distant peoples to Christianity. A number of religious orders and societies were formed with this object in mind. However, there were major problems so far as Africa was concerned. The northern half of the continent had been converted in varying degrees to Islam. Christian missions could therefore be established only with difficulty in Moslem areas, and usually required the security offered by an established colonial power to do so. Hence missions in northern Africa were generally weak and post-dated the imposition of colonial administration. Early missionary activities were therefore largely directed towards the southern portion of Africa, more especially towards the major centres of sedentary indigenous population.

The original missions were established on the coast to serve the peripheral settlements, but the missionary 'fields' always seem to have lain elsewhere (Prickett, 1969). Hence the importance of exploration and the trade routes to the populous parts of the continent for the expansion of missionary activity (Johnson, 1967). Stations were frequently established not only in the densely populated areas but also at suitable points along the main routes. The Missionaries' Road in southern Africa is one example of a chain of stations linking the interior with the base at the coast. The attraction of the interior, whether in terms of the people it offered for pastoral care, or for the more hospitable climates, resulted in some remarkable attempts to create lines of missions whether in Gabon in the 1840s or Angola in the 1880s. The mission chains thus became a significant element in the landscape, as few were founded in complete isolation from their neighbours.

Missionaries, possibly more than members of other branches of the colonial establishment, aimed at the radical transformation of indigenous society. Few clerics recognised any intrinsic value in African beliefs and cultures and in consequence tried to impose European ideas and ways of life upon the indigenous population (Magubane, 1979). They therefore sought, whether consciously or unconsciously, the destruction of pre-colonial societies and their replacement by new Christian societies in the image of Europe. In general, therefore, missions only gained adherents on any scale after the undermining of African polities and the imposition of colonial control. Even then it was often the ancillary services of education and medicine which were in demand rather than the missionaries' religious message and this in part influenced the form which the stations took.

In establishing a Christian society the missionaries introduced concepts such as the moral benefits of work and industry both for their own sake and as a means of entering the money economy. Agriculture and industry were fostered and converts were encouraged to acquire imported goods and other trappings of a European-style Christian society. The dual aspects of breaking down pre-existing modes of behaviour and their replacement by new ones required a high degree of supervision and even at times partial isolation from the remainder of African society, or in the European settler states, isolation from the colonists.

The mission station was thus often viewed in far more all-embracing terms than the construction of a church and a parsonage

or presbytery in an existing settlement. Entire villages were envisaged. Some of the earliest were created for freed slaves either
after emancipation in South Africa or those freed in the course of
anti-slavery patrols in East and West Africa. Thus Napier and Elim
in the Cape Colony or Freretown near Mombasa were conceived as
self-contained settlements under missionary control. This approach
was also adopted where indigenous society had disintegrated or was
partially broken. Thus the first Cape Colonial missions were
intended for the Khoikhoi peoples whose traditional economy had
been undermined by the loss of their grazing grounds to European
settlers. In Natal individuals who had been displaced by the wars
preceding the imposition of colonial rule were encouraged to settle
with missionaries on lands specially set aside for the purpose by the
government.

Clearly such settlements reflected European concepts with the
layout of villages, agricultural lands and grazing commonages. The
earliest settlements in the Cape Colony were strictly regulated in
plan and construction, producing a remarkably uniform set of
villages, with whitewashed thatched cottages erected on a gridiron
pattern of streets, usually focusing on the main church buildings.
Additional structures for the parsonage, school, stores, offices and
other buildings were frequently located around a square to create a
distinctively European-style village green. Industrial buildings and
the agricultural stores were located adjacent to the village (Figure
3.1). Because the converts' previous social organisation had disintegrated it was possible to establish a high degree of ecclesiastical
and planning control over the settlements.

A different approach was necessary where the missionaries
sought the permission of the indigenous authorities to found a
station. Reaction varied from active encouragement and the establishment of a major adjunct to the existing settlements, to the
virtual imprisonment of the missionaries within the local capital.
Christian missionaries were viewed in some cases as allies in local
power struggles. Here they were encouraged to settle and transfer
their skills to the indigenous population in the concrete form of
schools, medical facilities, technical and commercial enterprises
and the more general aspects of dealing with an alien culture. In
these cases missions of great importance were established, and
included those in eastern Nigeria and Uganda. Proliferation of
activity resulted in the foundation of daughter stations and a general
infilling of missionary activity. The major missions were often large

Figure 3.1: Genadendal Mission Station

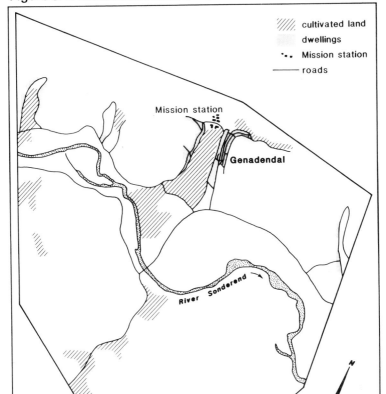

with schools, hospitals, training centres and workshops, as well as the church and halls. The Roman Catholic mission at Roma in Basutoland had developed into a small town by the end of the colonial period, with the addition of convents, seminaries and a university college – but this was exceptional. Most were appendages to the pre-colonial settlements, rather than the instigators of a new pattern. The planned village was missing. The degree to which the mission was able to influence the settlement pattern depended upon the extent to which the indigenous society had been disrupted and this in turn reflected the impact of European settlement.

Within the areas of European colonisation missionaries often acted as settlers themselves, purchasing or acquiring farms as a means of establishing missions or for speculative support for other church activities. In South Africa and Southern Rhodesia, the early church leaders acquired substantial properties, many of which became areas of African settlement in otherwise European owned farming areas. Such activity was inevitably unpopular with the settlers who demanded African labour and the removal of places of refuge. Thus some of the early mission stations were abandoned in southern Africa under settler pressure and the missionary protective role proved to be temporary. In other cases the mission was secularised and the village was left as an African settlement in the midst of European settlement. These proved to be particularly vulnerable to the post-1936 segregation policies in South Africa and the 1965-79 era in Southern Rhodesia.

The major concentrations of missions were to be found in the most densely populated areas of the southern half of the continent, with a marked concentration in Natal. This colony was viewed by several missionary societies as one of the most promising in Africa. The favourable circumstances of a dense population, ease of access, relatively healthy climate, and a highly romantic image of the Zulu population indicated to several societies that Natal offered a suitable field of endeavour. Furthermore knowledge of the area began to be circulated in the 1830s and 1840s as a result of the early involvement of the British government and the encouragement given to missionaries by the colonial administration. The colonial government introduced a special form of Mission Reserve for control by the societies, mainly the American Methodists. Some 74,000 ha were set aside for this purpose. The government was generous with land grants to churches. By 1860 the churches held some 12,000 ha in the rural areas, which was expanded to 54,000 ha by 1910 as a result of the judicious purchase of land for the foundation of mission stations. In addition mission churches and attendant facilities were built in the urban areas.

It is noticeable that Africa was not partitioned into separate missionary fields by the different denominations (Langlands and Namirembe, 1967). Mission stations often predated the establishment of colonial control, and although the missionaries frequently pressed for that control, many stations ultimately fell within the colonies of other nationalities. Religious toleration had been guaranteed under the General Act of the Berlin Conference of 1885 and although certain concentrations of Roman Catholic endeavour in French colonies and Protestant activity in British colonies is apparent, the two were not mutually exclusive. The most complex situation developed in the Belgian Congo, where ease of communication by river led to the assignment of spheres of influence between contending Protestant sects. Once colonial rule was firmly established this policy became easier, as governments usually had to approve the establishment of a station and competition was not encouraged.

The missionaries played a significant yet controversial role not only in the establishment of stations and the spiritual welfare of their converts. Indeed as a group it is difficult to disentangle many of their activities. It was necessary for them to explore and select new sites for stations and identify areas for their work. They sought to establish industry and redirect trade, and were thus often engaged in both running trading companies and establishing cottage industries. Missionaries sought to influence governments. They frequently acted as intermediaries in the early years of colonial rule between African and European, for they served as advisors to indigenous rulers. In this role their influence was usually biased towards colonial governments and the rapid cultural Europeanisation of the African population (Lamar and Thompson, 1981). Their imprint is therefore more widespread and possibly less specific than that of most groups identified in this volume. Furthermore, missionaries came from countries without direct colonial ambitions on the continent, so that the distinctive national architectural styles of Finland and Sweden may be seen on mission stations in Namibia and Natal respectively. However, it was the colonial powers themselves which impressed the ecclesiastical landscape of the continent most noticeably, whether German-style buildings in Namibia and Tanzania or French edifices in Senegal or Morocco. Exposure to European nationalisms expressed in stone, brick and even iron churches was a part of the acculturation process which the missionaries pursued throughout the colonial period. Churches, because of their physical size and embellishments are major features of many African landscapes, reflecting the diverse national styles of their founders.

4 HUNTERS, GATHERERS AND PLANTERS

Commercial exploitation of Africa had the elements of a robber economy. The vegetable and animal resources of the continent were available to those who could mount the enterprises to gather or hunt them. Pioneer hunters and gatherers were able to skim the surface of the continent taking profitable products and making no provision for later regeneration. Thus species of animals were hunted to extinction and the plant cover was ruthlessly cut down. Belated consequences of this exploitation were the conservation of the remaining wild animals and the orderly replanting of commercial crops either under government or commercial control. The initial environmental impact of the colonial era however was often devastating and was carried out by only a small group of men.

Hunters

Africa was the home of the elephant which as a source of ivory was one of the major living resources in demand, both in industrial Western Europe and, more traditionally, in Asia (Wilson and Ayerst, 1976). Ivory attracted traders and hunters to the continent in search of substantial profits. One of the results of the Portuguese explorations had been the opening of the ivory trade in Europe. Prior to this ivory had been traded through North African centres such as Cairo, which probably remained the principal ivory market on the continent until the mid-nineteenth century. In the sixteenth century small quantities were diverted to Europe. Some 15 tons per annum passed through Sofala at that time.

The unprecedented demand for ivory occasioned by the industrialisation of Europe and the United States led to a major expansion of hunting and ultimately to the destruction of the elephant herds in large parts of Africa. Ivory came into growing demand for ornaments, piano keys, billiard balls and a host of other items, thus maintaining high prices which promised profits to traders and professional hunters alike. The hunters, particularly in East Africa, became more effective as special elephant guns were perfected and the indigenous peoples sought a means of earning money for goods introduced by the traders. The Zanzibaris extended chains of trading posts across the East African mainland to the Congo Basin in the course of the nineteenth century and by 1891 Zanzibar accounted for three-quarters of the world's supply. In the second half of the nineteenth century the quantity passing through Zanzibar rarely fell below 200 tons per annum. The number of elephants killed must have amounted to an astounding 40,000–60,000 per annum, clearly a rate which could not be maintained indefinitely. The ivory trade had initially been linked to the East Coast slave trade and operated through the trading stations established by the Swahili traders.

Ivory constituted one of the major export commodities for many African colonies in the years immediately following their foundation, but it declined in importance as the elephants were destroyed and alternative products assumed importance. Thus ivory made up a third of the value of exports from Natal in 1853, but seven years later it had fallen to less than a tenth of the total. Later commercial enterprises such as the Congo Free State and the French Congo were even more dependent on ivory as a source of income. Between 1889 and 1895, ivory accounted for over half the value of the exports of the Congo Free State, reaching a maximum of 5.8 million frs. in 1895. The French Congo production maximum of 4.0 million frs. was attained later, in 1905. In both cases decline in the present century was rapid as the elephants were decimated.

Hunting continued for a long period to supply a living and a sport for those attracted to the pursuit. In the 1830s, W.C. Harris undertook an expedition through South Africa and concluded that hunting for ivory and trophies could be profitable. At the same time R.C.G. Cumming undertook a hunting expedition in South Africa and paid for it through trade and the sale of his book 'Five Years of a Hunter's Life in the Far Interior of South Africa', which was published in 1850 and continued to be reissued until 1911. Hunters' tales proved to be highly popular and the attraction of the continent was enhanced. A steady flow of hunters and tourists visited Africa and contributed to the mass destruction of the wild animals. Lions, elephants, rhinoceros and gorillas were all hunted and reduced to restricted areas. Some, including the quagga and the Cape lion, were exterminated. A late example of large-scale hunting was presented in the period of uncertainty in the Lado Enclave of the southern Anglo-Egyptian Sudan, while it was nominally under the control of Leopold II of the Congo Free State (Collins, 1971). The lack of an effective government between 1907 and 1909 attracted dozens of hunters for the last big elephant hunt on the continent, resulting in the extermination of the herds numbering several thousands in a matter of two years.

From the mass destruction came the beginnings of the conservation movement. Concern was first expressed in South Africa, where the advance of European settlement and the concentration of hunting had been most devastating (Pringle, 1982). The Transvaal established a game reserve in 1894 on the Pongola River and the Cape Colony followed in Bushmanland in 1896. Both proved to be ephemeral as the rate of destruction over-whelmed the conservation effort. In the latter case one lone police trooper was unequal to the immense task of deterring the poachers. However, in 1898 the Transvaal established the Sabi Game Reserve, the forerunner of the modern Kruger National Park, and other reserves in southern Africa were established soon afterwards.

Increased official intervention led to the signing of the Convention of London in 1900, which provided for the protection of wild animals in that part of the continent lying between 20°N and the Zambezi River (Great Britain, 1898, 1906). Thereafter the colonial powers became attached to the concept of game reserves which were proclaimed, particularly in British and German territories. Even the British Somaliland administration established a major reserve in the interior of the protectorate on land not yet under British control and whose suitability for a game reserve was questionable. Other waste lands such as the Etosha Pan in northern South West Africa and the Wankie region in Southern Rhodesia were proclaimed as game reserves, as there was no demand for such land either from the indigenous population or from European colonists.

The system of game reserves was elaborated and expanded throughout the colonial period. The Kenya government (1959, p. 2) expressed the desire 'to preserve game in Kenya to the greatest extent possible having regard to human interests and financial possibilities'. Clearly there were real conflicts of interest. Agricultural and pastoral production were incompatible with the concept of a game reserve. The Kruger National Park was only freed of domestic grazing animals in the late 1920s, when the government expropriated all private landowners and removed their stock from the Park. Later proclamations often faced greater problems as pressures of population built up. Thus the Tsavo Reserve in Kenya established in 1948 experienced large-scale poaching as the lands taken for the reserve were traditional African hunting grounds, which had been used without regulation prior to 1948. The legal distinction between hunting and poaching was a nicety. This was particularly evident in the various East African colonies where special hunters' licences were available by 1897 as a means of attracting wealthy tourists. Game viewing as opposed to game shooting was a comparatively late innovation, while facilities to do so, such as Treetops in Kenya, were only in a rudimentary stage at the end of the colonial period.

Game reserves were organised almost entirely by governments. The boundaries were drawn so as to interfere as little as possible with vested interests and their administration was viewed as being of low priority. However, in terms of extent the areas set aside were large, particularly in southern and eastern Africa. Several parks in excess of one million hectares were demarcated, the largest being the Kafue Park in Northern Rhodesia, covering 2.2 million hectares.

Gatherers

Trade and profit were the vital elements in the exploitation of most of the tropical empires acquired in the last quarter of the nineteenth century. The Congo basin became, in the 1880s and 1890s, a sphere of particular interest as its luxuriant vegetation suggested apparent riches. The problem of human diseases had been partially solved, certainly well enough for the risk of a prolonged stay in the tropics not to deter potential traders and their agents. However, the transportation problem remained as the rapids on the lower Congo effectively barred ocean-going vessels from the middle Congo. Furthermore, reliance upon human porterage in the absence of animal transport limited the range of products which could be exploited, as well as making the flow of such products uncertain.

The exploitation of the Congo basin therefore still involved a high risk factor, which deterred state investment, so that it was largely private capital which was invested in the Congo enterprises. The largest undertaking was that founded by King Leopold II of Belgium in 1876, under the title, 'The International Association for the Exploration and Civilization of Africa'. At the Congress of Berlin, the king gained international recognition for his Association and in 1885 the Congo Free State was founded, which was to remain his private domain until the Belgian annexation of 1908. Finance was gained from many sources, although increasingly it was Belgian capitalists who became involved in the loan structure of the Congo Free State. On the northern side of the river the French were able to establish their control by linking up with Gabon. Their problem was the same as Leopold II's: how to exploit the resources of the territory, and their solution was the same: the attraction of outside capital with the promise of substantial profits.

The king was able to raise capital through the offer of land concessions to exploit the natural resources of the Congo basin. The apparent fertility of the soil projected an image of great wealth awaiting the first men to reap it; but this was largely illusory. The two products the country possessed which were commercially exploitable in the early stages of European enterprise were basically non-renewable, namely ivory and rubber. In the period up to the development of the major rubber plantations in Malaya and the Dutch East Indies, the demand offered a large profit on rubber gathered from the natural rubber trees and vines of the Congo basin. It was a matter of organising the gathering of these riches as efficiently as possible.

The Congo Free State and French Congo administrations offered large land concessions with exclusive rights to utilise the natural resources at attractive rates, to encourage the exploitation of the territories. In the Congo Free State a few large concessions were offered in the 1890s (Harms, 1975). The Anglo-Belgian Indian Rubber Company (ABIR), founded in 1892, received a 30-year concession for approximately 8 million hectares in the Maringa-Lopori river valleys, and other companies received similar tracts. The territories were then occupied and administered by the companies on behalf of the Congo Free State government. A base station was established at Basakusu and further posts were set up along the rivers at intervals of 30-50 km. ABIR established 31 stations and only by 1900 was the area effectively occupied. Each post then established control over the indigenous villages by means of a local police force, members of which were stationed in each village to control production.

Once the territory had been occupied the administration proceeded to extract goods and services from the Congolese. The villages close to the transport routes were called upon to supply porters, canoe paddlers and food. Those further away were required to deliver rubber. In theory, taxation was limited to 40 hours per month in government service, but what this represented in kind depended upon the local administrator. Increases in production were achieved by varying taxes and prices and by forcing women and children to gather rubber. By 1906, ABIR had 47,000 rubber gatherers on its books, and the search for wild rubber spread. The rubber vines and the few rubber trees were quickly exploited and destroyed. Around the base at Basakusu a 10 km radius had been demolished within 18 months of occupation. Clearly a crisis was inevitable as the resources of the country and the people were exhausted. Armed resistance to coercion began, resulting in the construction of forts and the extraction of reprisals. In some parts of the concessions the inhabitants abandoned their villages and hid in the forest to avoid the ever increasing extortions. Those who remained were incorporated more effectively into the structure of villages and trading posts.

In 1903 ABIR exported 1,000 tons of rubber but thereafter production slumped and the concession reverted to the state in 1906. However, it was reformed in 1911 as the Compagnie du Congo Belge under new terms. The later concessions were directed towards a combination of direct gathering and the planting of rubber trees. Efforts were made as early as 1896 to force the concessionary companies to plant rubber trees so that there would be a continuing trade after the natural rubber had been destroyed. Government regulations stipulated that at first 150 rubber trees were to be planted per ton of rubber collected. In 1902 this was increased to 500 trees. By 1903 ABIR had planted over one million trees, a pointer to the future.

Several other colonies in tropical Africa including the Cameroons, Angola, Moçambique and the French Congo followed the example of the Congo Free State in the organisation of colonial exploitation through commercial enterprises (Coquery-Vidrovitch, 1972). A concessionary system was instituted in the French Congo, which lacked even the limited financial resources of its larger neighbour. In part this was the outcome of French policy which in 1900 was formally adopted as the principle, long approved, that colonies must be self-supporting and not be a monetary burden to metropolitan France. The success of the Congo Free State in raising revenue through the use of private capital encouraged the French to do the same. In the 1890s profits from Congo Free State concessions were such that ABIR which paid dividends of 2 frs. per share in 1894 was able to pay 2,100 frs. in 1900. Similarly the Société Anversoise with a capital of 1.7 million frs. made a profit of 3.4 million frs. in 1897, 4.0 million frs. a year later, and its shares, with a nominal value of 500 frs. in 1892 rose to about 12,000 frs. in 1898. Speculative capital was enticed to the French Congo with the prospect of achieving equally profitable ventures.

Generous land concessions were offered. The first in Gabon in 1893 was to the Société du Haute-Ogooué which covered some 11,000,000 ha of forest land. The main impulse took place in 1899 and 1900 when most of the southern French Congo was acquired by concessionary companies in blocks of land in excess of 10,000 ha. The largest, the Compagnie des Sultanats du Haut-Oubangui covered 14,000,000 ha, an area larger than Tunisia. A total of 40 companies acquired some 80,000,000 ha which was to be administered and exploited for 30 years. Conditions regarding improvements and freeholds complicated the agreements but were not regarded as important in the first stages of gathering the resources of the colony.

The regime which ensued was not a replica of the Congo Free State as the French Congo suffered from a gross misunderstanding of the country, a lack of capital, limited manpower, and inadequate official supervision; and consequently there was no system of exploitation as there had been under Leopold II. As a result stagnation followed, rather than development. Many companies were unable to pay any dividends as the concessionaires found their lands to be underpopulated, infertile, sandy or marshy, and without elephants or rubber plants. The country was thought in 1900 to be inhabited by a population in excess of 10,000,000, yet by 1914 estimates had been lowered to 2,500,000. No reconnaissance surveys of soils and resources had been undertaken, so that rubber and indeed any other commercial commodity were lacking on the lands of some companies. Communication problems were such that the savannah lands of Tchad took four months to reach from Gabon with access by porterage and consequently they were deemed unexploitable. On the rivers malaria and sleeping sickness took their toll on the lives of both the European traders and their African workers.

Despite these problems the concessionary companies did create a surge of economic activity in the first decade of the century as the resources of the colony were gathered. Again rubber and ivory were the main items sought. Ivory reached a peak export of 210 tons in 1905, declining to 97 tons in 1920. Rubber reached a peak of 1,950 tons in 1906 but production fell rapidly thereafter. A more successful enterprise was the export of timber. In 1913 some 150,000 tons of lumber were exported compared with 2,000 tons in 1898. In order to achieve even these modest results a ruthless regime was imposed enforcing what Coquery-Vidrovitch (1971, p. 341) aptly described as the 'economy of pillage'.

The situation in the lands controlled by the Compagnie des Sultanats du Haut-Oubangui illustrates the impact of this economy. In 1901 the Company signed a treaty with the sultan Bangassou confirming the commercial rights obtained from the colonial government. There followed a steady elaboration of the network of trading posts. In 1901 four posts had been established manned by eight European agents, while two years later there were seven posts and 20 European agents. By 1914 some 19 posts and 27 subsidiary establishments had been erected. Although the Company could boast of 144 buildings, only three had been constructed in brick. Nine of the posts were closed in 1914 on the outbreak of war. Rubber and ivory were bought by the traders at a tenth to a twentieth of prices on the French market. The result was a high financial return for the Company and its shareholders. In 1910 declared profits of 3.3 million frs. hid real profits of the order of 5 million frs. or a 100 per cent return on capital invested. Rubber production reached a peak in 1912 and declined thereafter except for the brief wartime boom of 1916-19. Ivory similarly reached a peak of 60 tons in 1905 and then fell to an average of 20–30 tons per annum.

Other companies such as the Compagnie Française du Haut-Congo also started by exploiting the ivory and rubber resources of the concession area, but as production fell so a search for alternative sources of income began. Palm-oil was collected but again anticipated production levels failed to come up to expectation. Installed refining capacity of 10,000 tons in the late 1920s contrasted with production averages of only 700 tons. The loss of the monopoly of exploitation when the original concession lapsed in 1930 was serious as it was needed to maintain even these levels of production. Smaller monopoly areas and plantation zones were negotiated as the companies changed over to an industrial economy based on private enterprise and reduced the level of coercion (Figure 4.1). By the end of the colonial period concessionaires held only 1 per cent of the area of the original concessions. This reflected the changed assessment of the value of the land and the use of only the most accessible and suitable. Thus small plantations, processing plants,

Figure 4.1: Middle Congo Concessionary Areas *c.* 1930

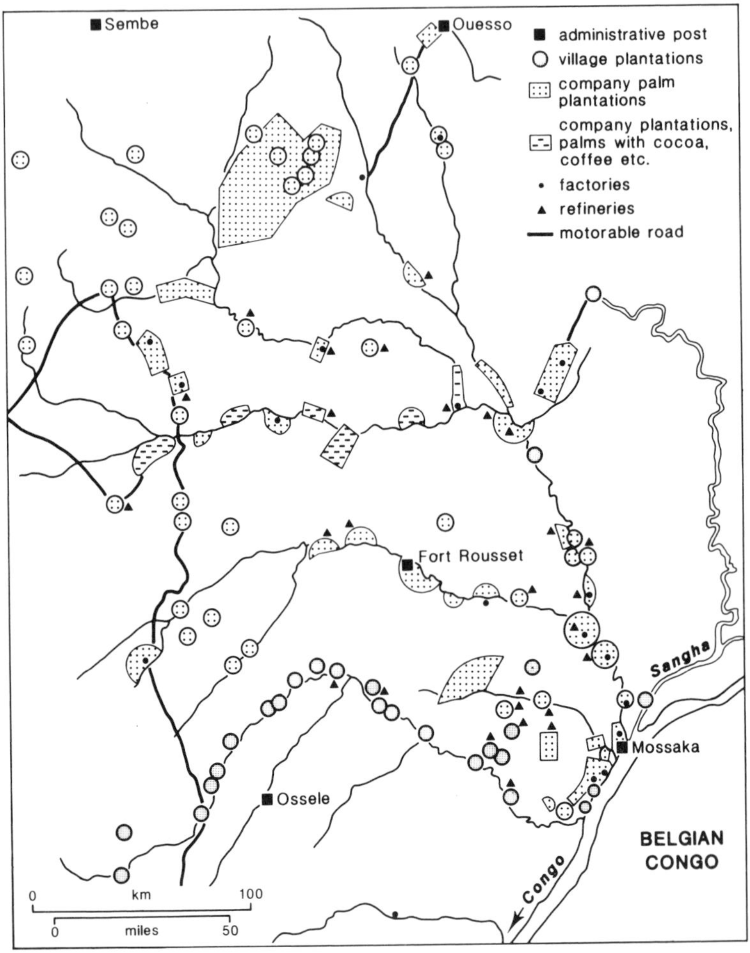

timber concessions and industrial processing plants were located along the main communication lines and the indigenous inhabitants retained the remainder. Transportation remained the most serious impediment to the exploitation of the French Congo, and the lack of funds to develop an infrastructure was in marked contrast to the Congo Free State. Nevertheless improvement did take place, canoes were supplemented by steam boats, and porters partially replaced by motor transport, but the colony lacked sustained investment. Even the Congo-Ocean railway was built several decades after the Belgian line and it was related to political demands rather than economic requirements.

The transition from gathering to commercial planting may be illustrated by the experience of the Unilever enterprise in the Belgian Congo (Fieldhouse, 1978). The unfavourable publicity attracted by the Congo Free State over its concessions policies resulted in the Belgian administration after 1908 assuming a cautious approach to the exploitation of the colony. Thus the Unilever subsidiary, Huileries du Congo Belge, (HCB) established in 1911 to tap the palm-oil resources of the colony, had to undertake substantial improvements before a permanent title could be obtained. In addition specific services such as housing, health and education were to be offered to the African workers and their families by the company. The Belgian government offered Sir William Lever monopoly gathering concessions over the areas of five circles of 60 km radii — a total of some 5,700,000 ha. In return £1 million was to be invested in the scheme with oil mills in each of the five circles capable of processing 6,000 tons per annum. In addition a road and river transport system had to be established and conditions on the use of Belgian machinery and supplies were written into the agreement. Once all the conditions had been fulfilled HCB would receive some 750,000 ha in freehold title, but no more than 200,000 ha could be incorporated in any one circle.

The Unilever enterprise began as a gathering concern and although it had received optimistic images of the circles' capabilities, costs far exceeded the estimates. By 1926, HCB employed some 335 European and 23,000 African workers. Over 1,000 km of road and 70 km of light railway had been built, while a fleet of 19 steamers and 72 barges plied the Congo and its tributaries. Labour was encouraged to work through government taxation measures and administrative pressures on chiefs. Rather than resort to widespread coercion it was found easier to establish depots in the villages so that workers did not have to leave their homes. Collection failed to show a marked profit, while the depression and its associated lowering of commodity prices forced the Company to reassess its position. Organised plantation production was considered as the solution. In 1930 the HCB had planted only 3,170 ha but by 1960 some 46,839 ha were planted to oil-palm and lesser extents to rubber, cacao and small plots to coffee and tea. The switch to a plantation based enterprise resulted in the acquisition in freehold of 350,000 ha, of which 60,000 ha were under plantations and the remainder acted as a cordon sanitaire devoid of indigenous agriculture. The plantations remained a poor investment compared with other Unilever enterprises mainly because of the continuing dependence upon gathering and the consequently large labour force employed, with attendant social service expenses.

Gathering enterprises were remarkably widespread in Africa. The timber cutting companies of Gabon were replicated elsewhere on the West Coast in the early twentieth century. At an earlier stage the Dutch and others had cut the forests of the coastal belt of South Africa for constructional timber for ships and buildings. The longevity of this enterprise virtually exhausted the available resources of the Cape Colony, resulting in conservation measures having to be introduced. Outside the equatorial forests Africa's timber resources were limited. Other products such as gum were widely collected. Senegal in the early nineteenth century became a major exporter, but as in the case of natural rubber, overproduction killed the trade late in the century.

Planters

Although plantations were established on the West African islands of Madeira, Grand Canarie, Fernando Poo and Sao Tomé as early as the fifteenth and sixteenth centuries, the expansion of plantation production took place elsewhere, mainly in the Americas. Mauritius and Reunion followed the experience of the West Indian sugar colonies through the eighteenth and twentieth centuries (Lefevre, 1976). Subsequent attempts in the eighteenth and early nineteenth centuries to engage in this form of production on the West African mainland failed on meeting opposition from West Indian planters and encountering the severity of the disease environment. As a capital intensive undertaking, investors required security and hence the layout of plantations followed the imposition of colonial rule and their distribution reflected the policies of the colonial powers towards large-scale enterprises. Definition is difficult as many settler estates, although run on plantation lines, might be better dealt with under settler agriculture. The sugar plantations of Natal and the olive plantations of Tunisia are interwoven into the mainstream of settler agricultural expansion. Estates in tropical Africa outside the areas of European settlement, such as Cameroon or Somalia, clearly fall into the category of plantation; although the symbiotic development of plantation and indigenous smallholding went side by side in both cases.

The most important requirement for plantation agriculture once a suitable region and crops had been identified was secure title to a portion of land large enough to justify long-term investment. Capital was required and was lured by the prospects of eventual profits. Labour was also required to plant, tend and harvest the crops, which usually involved the employment of a large, highly organised and skilled force. Few ventures in Africa were able to secure the necessary land, labour and capital for success, let alone a suitable crop to grow. African plantations did not develop along the lines of those in South East Asia. The major problem in the colonial period was the shortage of labour, except where the colonial governments had been able to undermine indigenous societies so as to force labour on to the market. In addition many colonial governments were unfavourably disposed towards plantations. The unsuccessful attempts by Sir William Lever to obtain land concessions for plantations in Nigeria are particularly well documented (Pedler, 1974). British administrations in West Africa were exceptionally zealous in their defence of African land rights. However, the Germans viewed plantations as a part of colonial development and they were actively encouraged in Cameroon and East Africa. Certain 'empty' lands such as the East African coast in Kenya and Somalia were developed by the British and Italians, following Zanzibari precedents, but in general land proved to be remarkably difficult to obtain for extensive plantation development.

It is scarcely surprising that some of the earliest plantation development took place in Natal, where the majority of African land rights had been extinguished in the late 1830s. The coastal belt, because of its apparent soil fertility and hot, rainy climate was assessed in official reports as ideal for the cultivation of tropical and subtropical crops (Christopher, 1971b). The British administration began selling plantations of 100–250 ha apiece in 1846. However, experiments in growing a wide variety of crops from indigo to cotton were largely unsuccessful in producing the return considered necessary to establish commercial plantation agriculture. Sugar, after a number of vicissitudes, proved to be the most successful crop. Strains of sugar cane, expertise, and machinery were imported from the established sugar producing island of Mauritius. Labour supply became an immediate problem. The African population was reluctant to work for white planters, so long as there was still the option of relative independence in the designated Reserves. Thus in common with other sugar plantation regions, labour was introduced from overseas. Following the success of the Mauritian industry, the Natal government recruited Indian indentured labourers in 1860 and importation continued until 1911 when the practice was stopped by the Government of India.

The Natal sugar industry was highly complex in its organisation and landscape, with a range of enterprise extending from the major milling and refining companies owning and planting thousands of hectares to smallholdings of a few hectares apiece (Osborn, 1964). The initial plantations were mainly in the range 100–250 ha as the colonial government sought to encourage the settlement of a large number of planters. However, substantial tracts of land in the coastal belt had already been alienated to the Cape-Dutch pastoral settlers, who had mostly sold their lands to speculators in the late 1840s and early 1850s. Land speculation was rife, with individuals, syndicates and local and metropolitan land and development companies attracted to Natal in the expectation of profitably exploiting the coastal lands. A large number of companies were floated, the most important being the Natal Land and Colonization Company in 1860 (Slater, 1975). It undertook experimental planting in an effort to boost the prospects for land sales, but owing to the general oversupply of land in the colony, less ambitious plans were pursued. A number of individuals and companies were able to prosper and develop plantations with their own mills and employing substantial labour forces. By the 1880s some 70 mills were in operation and 7,300 ha planted to sugar-cane. Sugar then accounted for a quarter of the value of colonial exports, second only to wool. Sugar planting was highly erratic as problems associated with pests, diseases, fluctuating prices and technical innovation confronted the industry. The area under sugar-cane grew to reach 66,000 ha by the First World War, in a zone extending from southern Natal to Zululand, although there was little evidence of a continuous sugar belt at this date.

By the 1890s the larger companies had begun a programme of rationalisation whereby the individual mills were abandoned and milling was centralised in a number of large, more efficient factories. Between 1878 and 1888 the number of mills fell from 74 to 38. In addition major companies such as Natal Estates, Huletts, and Tongaat Estates purchased land to extend their holdings, which by 1900 exceeded 15,000 ha. This process of consolidation led to the emergence of a small number of large highly capitalised plantations. In addition the smaller European estates continued in being and were actively encouraged by the colonial and later dominion governments in the opening of new areas such as Zululand, where the companies were barred from planting. Also the Indian population was able to purchase land, but because of the limited land resources only small blocks could be obtained. Few received the land promised in lieu of a return passage in terms of their indenture contract. Indian purchases were facilitated by the large speculative concerns such as the Natal Land and Colonization Company, which were willing to cut up their holdings into small blocks of land for people of limited means; a process which the individual European planter opposed. Thus the three distinctive settlement elements of the sugar industry rendered the Natal coastal belt one of the most complex areas of immigrant settlement on the African continent.

Although sugar was the most successful plantation crop in Natal, others were tried and experimentation was lengthy and expensive. Tea, coffee, and cotton companies were floated in the period before the First World War, more in response to the state of the overseas market, than promising experiments in Natal. Thus the areas planted or planned were large. Tea plantations in 1914 covered 1,500 ha but were abandoned in the following decade. Coffee was even less successful, while cotton plantations were revived periodically. In 1848 the Natal Cotton Company received the largest grant of land ever made in the colony (almost 10,000 ha), but was unable to establish a viable industry. In 1863 the Cotton Plantation Company sought to benefit from the shortage caused by the American civil war, and acquired 32,500 ha for the purpose. The company exhibited considerable enterprise, introducing for example the first steam plough to Natal, but it went bankrupt in 1870 in the wake of the slump in cotton prices.

Greater success was achieved by John van der Plank at Camperdown, midway between Durban and Pietermaritzburg with the wattle tree, introduced from Australia. The bark of the wattle could be processed and used as tannin in leather manufacture. The success of the enterprise led to a spate of plantings after 1886 when the processes had been refined and its profitability demonstrated. By 1904 some 32,000 ha had been planted and this increased to 108,000 ha only seven years later. Planting continued after the First World War reaching a peak of 300,000 ha in the 1960s. A distinctive timber belt had been created by that stage with over half the area of some

Natal Midlands districts planted to wattle. Again the industry was dominated by a number of major wattle companies, with relative smallholders planting only a few hundred hectares of wattle as a part of a farming enterprise. Private, as opposed to state, afforestation was possible as a result of the short growing period (approximately 14 years) compared with conifers which took twice the length of time to reach a marketable stage.

Natal, although it had many elements of plantation agriculture, was peculiar in the sense that it was linked to a substantial European settlement. This led to a high degree of permanence on the part of the planters and also increasingly to the use of local capital as well as the need to satisfy the local market rather than overseas exports.

Elsewhere in Africa the attraction of cheap land, the prospects of good growing conditions, and secure and sympathetic political control resulted in an inflow of capital for plantation enterprises, yet on a far smaller scale than the Asian and central American developments. In much of intertropical Africa suitable conditions for plantation economies were only established in the 1890s. Hence, unlike the Natal plantations, most African enterprises were largely the product of the present century. A number of crops, including cotton and groundnuts, were adopted by African smallholders and European plantings were limited. Production of others such as coffee, tea and sisal was expanded under European control. Occasionally competition between European and African farmers was eliminated by a ban on African production, such as that imposed in Kenya on African cultivation of coffee. Effective restrictions on African production were maintained through the limitations of agricultural extension services, the non-availability of credit facilities and a pervasive discrimination against African producers. Planters sought land unencumbered with indigenous ownership rights, which in theory meant a limited range unless the colonial government resorted to large-scale expropriation of the land resources. This was achieved by an often deliberate misinterpretation of African landownership and occupation practices, and the application of European laws of tenure which inevitably worked badly for the indigenous population. Thus there was rarely a major problem for the planters in areas which were deemed suitable for European use.

In 1898 the French government established the Commission on Colonial Concessions, which offered large tracts of land for gathering crops and undertaking plantation work. The experience of the

French Congo has been outlined, while concessions in French West Africa were limited to under 100,00 ha, but some 1,500,000 ha were granted in Madagascar (Koerner, 1969; Thompson and Adloff, 1958). The Portuguese government through its chartered companies, the Moçambique Company, Nyassa Company and Zambezia Company similarly offered favourable terms to concessionaires. Plantations, as previously mentioned, were laid out as a second stage of the initial gathering concession, when the natural resources were exhausted or depleted. The first major plantation enterprises were thus devoted to rubber production. The decline in natural rubber collection in the first few years of the century and the rising world demand for the product caused a steady increase in the London price, to reach a peak of £1.10 per kilogramme in 1910 (Munro, 1981). A major boom in speculative rubber plantations ensued. In British Africa between 1905 and 1914 some 55 companies were floated with a nominal capital of £5.9 million. The enterprises were linked to major consortia as for example the Vine and General Rubber Trust, which controlled interests in Madagascar, Natal and Moçambique. Despite the financial activity little actual planting took place. In West Africa only 2,700 ha were planted and the majority of companies were unsuccessful. In East Africa plantings were larger as estates were more plantation than collection orientated. However, interest in African rubber was dissipated as the estates in Malaya and the Dutch East Indies commenced production. Thus African production, which exceeded Asian until 1911, amounted to only a tenth of Asian production in 1914. East African rubber plantations continued with limited production after the First World War. The largest producers, however, were those in the Belgian Congo and Liberia, but their origins too were related to the gathering phases.

Large concessions for plantations were comparatively rare owing to the financial and political problems involved, as had been demonstrated in the French Congo. However, the example of the Societa Agricola Italo-Somala instituted in 1920 illustrates the scale at which it was possible to work (Scassellati-Sforzolini, 1926). The concession on the Webi Scebeli provided 25,000 ha for a sugar project. The infrastructure development involved the construction of a 109 km railway to the port at Mogadishu, some 30 km of primary canals and 670 km of secondary canals. The labour problem caused by the Somali reluctance to work on the scheme was solved by the importation of Black Africans. The town of Villabruzzi was laid out and 16 villages were established for the workers in a network across the concession. By 1940 approximately 10,000 ha was cultivated under irrigation. Parallel with the plantation, each of the 2,400 families employed received one hectare of irrigated land, half of which was used for subsistence and half for cash cropping, mostly cotton (Hess, 1966). Following the success of this scheme, other plantations were established in Somalia, which by 1940 covered some 65,000 ha, half of which was under cultivation.

Similar extensive plantations were established on the East and West African coasts in British, German and Portuguese colonies (Figure 4.2). Sisal was introduced to German East Africa in 1891 and proved to be highly successful. The German authorities increasingly viewed the colony in plantation terms rather than for European settlement. Thus by 1913 some 313,000 ha had been assigned mostly to plantations. In the Cameroons concessionary companies paralleled those in the French and Belgian Congos with single awards of up to 5,000,000 ha, but their demise concentrated attention upon plantations (Ardener, 1960). The first plantations had been established by the major trading firms such as Woermann, immediately after the declaration of the protectorate in 1885. In general grants of 2,000–5,000 ha were given to individuals while syndicates received larger areas. The total area involved was relatively small as by 1913 only 107,000 ha had been granted. In common with areas alienated for settlement, Native Reserves were established in the Cameroons plantation regions to provide living space for the intended labour force. Thus few parts of a plantation were more than 5 km from a Native Reserve. The active encouragement afforded colonial plantations by the Germans lapsed under the mandatory regimes which followed the First World War. Concessionaires cultivated only limited tracts of their estates, so that in the British Cameroons only half the plantation areas had been used in 1955.

Commercial ranching also attracted metropolitan capital, although on a smaller scale than for crop plantations. Large portions of Africa were suited to ranching, but little of it was devoid of indigenous population. Thus outside southern Africa few areas were available for European pastoralism. There was also a notable reluctance on the part of meat production companies to engage in African enterprises, largely because of the disease environment. It was only after American and Australian ranches had been developed that Africa was opened to commercial ranching in the early

Figure 4.2: Taita Sisal Estates, Kenya

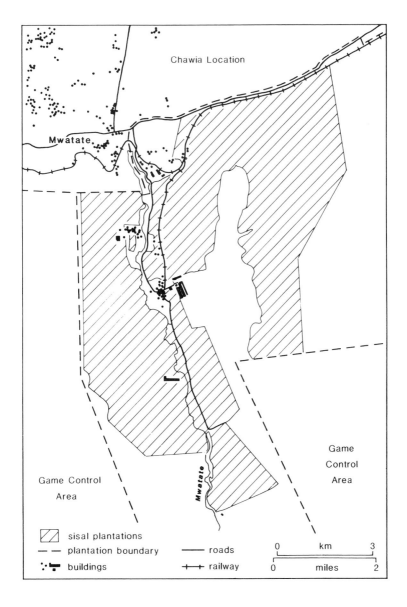

twentieth century.

The most suitable regions were in southern Africa where the local colonial governments encouraged the influx of capital to use lands which were marginal to settler interests. Thus extensive tracts of the Southern Rhodesian lowveld were offered to companies such as Sir John Willoughby's Mashonaland Investment Company (300,000 ha), with a view to establishing a meat export industry. Inevitably in the economic climate of the 1890s much of the activity was purely speculative and the commercial aspects were neglected. However, renewed interest after 1907 led the British South Africa Company to attract firms such as Leibig's Extract of Meat with a grant of 500,000 ha. In the following decade the Nuanetsi Ranch extending over 1,100,000 ha was organised for the British South Africa Company to develop its own cattle industry. These enterprises were however not the start of the major export trade which had been anticipated. The length of communications to Cape Town or Beira, together with the established position of Argentine beef in the British market, effectively prevented the emergence of large-scale ranching in southern Africa (Phimister, 1978). Leibigs' attempt to develop ranches in South West Africa in the 1920s failed and those which had been established continued to function as portions of the essentially settler economy.

Commercial ranching was undertaken to a limited degree elsewhere on the continent. Other settler colonies such as Kenya encouraged cattle raising in the northern drier fringes of the settler farming region. In other parts of the continent the ranchers met established African pastoral interests. Ranching in Nigeria was a case in point. The attempt by African Ranches Ltd to develop a cattle ranch in northern Nigeria between 1914 and 1923 failed as the British and Nigerian governments were unsympathetic towards ranching enterprises which might encroach upon the perceived rights of the Fulani pastoralists (Dunbar, 1970). The Company therefore was only able to obtain 10,500 ha, and not the 200,000 ha, which it considered to be essential for the maintenance of a viable cattle ranch. As a result it was forced to surrender its land as only 1,000 head of cattle could be kept. Other enterprises such as the Ranch de l'Ouadi Rimé in Tchad were more long lasting but equally problematical because of the conflicts of interest between European and African, and pastoralist and agriculturalist.

5 MINERS

Mining activity had taken place in Africa for millennia prior to the arrival of the Europeans. Control of the gold trade of the Sudan and Orphir, which reached the Mediterranean world via North Africa, was one of the immediate objectives of the Portuguese pioneers and their successors. However, physical control of the goldfields eluded the Europeans until the 1880s and 1890s when the political partition of the continent took place. Until then production and trade had remained in African hands. Indeed African miners in the Gold Coast and Southern Rhodesia had been able to extract a considerable portion of the accessible reserves by the time European prospectors reached them. The international investors' disappointment in the 1890s at the extent of the mining activity of the 'Ancients' in Southern Rhodesia undoubtedly depressed the territory's economy. Similarly copper had been mined and smelted in Katanga for a long period prior to the imposition of colonial rule, where it was used as an exchange currency in trade with the Arabs and Europeans. Iron had also been mined and smelted on an extensive scale. Pre-colonial mining was limited by the technology available so that many minerals such as zinc, aluminium and uranium were useless, and deep level deposits could not be tapped.

The colonial mining industry attracted large numbers of Europeans to the continent and even more significantly attracted substantial capital investment. In the second half of the nineteenth century imported British and American mining skills had advanced sufficiently to enable exploitation of deposits which the indigenous population had been unable to tackle. Furthermore the pace of technological innovation quickened as new mining and metallurgical problems were encountered and overcome. In the last 20 years of the nineteenth century mining increasingly became dependent upon the employment of salaried specialists. The individual prospectors and diggers could skim the surfaces of deposits but as soon as problems were encountered, geologists, engineers, surveyors, analysts and managers were required. This development demanded both organisation and finance. In order to attract manpower and the capital required, security of investment had to be guaranteed and there had to be the promise of a high financial return. Capital flow from Europe to Africa from the 1880s onwards was largely directed towards mining ventures and public works, especially the railways, designed to transport mining supplies to the mines and minerals to the export terminals (Frankel, 1938). The large-scale development of mining required incentives to be offered to attract both the European and other labour needed and in numbers demanded new organisational skills. Mining therefore introduced a new element into the colonial economy of Africa.

South Africa

Mining developments in South Africa, which was effectively under colonial rule earlier than the remainder of the continent, provided a model upon which much of the later activity was based. European mining began in the 1850s with the exploitation of the copper deposits of Namaqualand (Smalberger, 1975). The deposits had been discovered in the late seventeenth century, but their distance from Cape Town and the aridity of the local environment was such as to deter any large-scale mining enterprise. By the 1850s technical innovation had resulted in their being considered sufficiently attractive to investors, who had experience of the Australian and American booms, to hope for similarly rich returns in South Africa. Problems of transportation hindered the mining companies until the tramway and railway were built to the new export terminal at Port Nolloth. Labour recruitment, however, presented comparatively few problems as the numbers required were small. Thus even in 1875 only 3,400 persons lived in the four mining settlements. The largest at O'okiep comprised half the total. In terms of production the Namaqualand industry, prior to its cessation in the depression of the 1930s, only exceeded 40,000 tons once in 1888, but between 1872 and 1917 production did not fall below 10,000 tons. Violent fluctuations in export were reflected in equally spectacular fluctuations in output. The towns were laid out as villages with houses, churches, shops and huts built on a grid pattern. Apart from the mine itself the settlements were similar in appearance to that of their agricultural counterparts and thus did not constitute any radical break in colonial town planning.

Diamonds

The major revolution in European mining activity in southern

Africa came with the discovery of diamonds in the Cape Colony in 1867 (Roberts, 1976). The chance finding of a diamond in the Northern Cape led to a major rush to the banks of the Vaal River. The alluvial workings attracted several thousand European diggers lured by the vision of instant wealth. Claims were staked along the banks of the river and primitive digging and sorting techniques resulted in the emergence of a jumble of mining camps water furrows and spoil heaps. The area was effectively outside the administrative control of Great Britain and the Orange Free State and Transvaal republics, with the result that the diggers organised their own ephemeral republic. Metropolitan political and commercial activity nevertheless ensured that this state of affairs did not persist and British sovereignty was proclaimed.

Alluvial diamond workings were not the basis of a major industry and a search was instituted for the source of the stones. This was discovered in a series of intrusive kimberlite pipes to the south of the alluvial workings. The major pipe at Colesberg kopje (hill) attracted the diggers to New Rush in 1870. The site ultimately became the Big Hole and the settlement was renamed Kimberley in honour of the Secretary of State for the Colonies. The new diggings were again divided into claims of 10 m x 10 m which were excavated by the miners as best they could. The surface layers had been partially decomposed and were easy to excavate, but on reaching solid 'blue ground', new techniques were required. The first diggers had possessed little capital and indeed many were part-time farmers and traders who returned home when their profits declined. As the diggings went deeper so the problems of labour, drainage, shoring up unworked claims and the removal of the broken ground to the sorting areas, assumed greater significance. The mining landscape was one of the utmost complexity as each claim was worked at a different rate and each had its own surface haulage system, area for crushing and sorting the rock, and spoil heaps.

The problems associated with the uncontrolled digging of diamonds together with the search for greater profits led to moves to concentrate financial and managerial direction. Amalgamation of workings under a number of companies with access not only to Cape finance, which had sustained early development, but overseas capital, became essential. The period of amalgamation was ultimately concluded by Cecil Rhodes who in 1887 consolidated control over the De Beers mine and later the other mines. De Beers Consolidated Mines was then able to regulate the marketing of the gems to ensure a high and stable price. Supervision of marketing extended to companies operating in other African countries where diamonds were subsequently found, such as South West Africa, Angola, the Belgian Congo and Sierra Leone, as well as British Guiana. The profits gained from the mines were largely spent and reinvested in mining ventures in southern Africa.

Concentrated and ultimately unified control allowed the rationalisation of the operation of the mines and greater supervision of the workforce (Smalberger, 1974). One of the major problems confronting the industry had been the illicit diamond trade which in the early 1880s was calculated to account for 25–40 per cent of all diamond finds. The sorting process, which enabled the broken rock to decompose on the surface prior to washing and sifting, gave ample opportunity for the workers to hide the gems they found. The fencing of the surface working areas did little to reduce the illicit trade. Furthermore compulsory searching of the workers led to strikes and bloodshed. The solution to the problem was found in the introduction of the mining compound system, which involved the mining companies housing their Black workers in a series of segregated houses. The workers were not allowed to leave the mine or compound for the duration of their contract and so were effectively cut off from the outside world and hence from the illicit diamond buyer. The first compound was opened in 1885 and soon virtually all Black workers on the diamond fields were segregated. A similar, but limited attempt to segregate the White mine workers followed two years later with construction of the village of Kenilworth where De Beers hoped to establish a self-contained town. However, the rigorous conditions imposed upon the African workers could not be applied to the Europeans. An added advantage of amalgamation for the mining employers was elimination of competition for labour. Hence wage rates could be set by the companies. Such developments marked a departure in mining practice and were significant for the future of mining organisation in southern Africa.

The town of Kimberley which grew up adjacent to the main mines was the first European-style industrial town on the continent. It was laid out with little regard for future regulation, with a highly irregular street plan and little provision for services. The first buildings were largely constructed of prefabricated corrugated iron. In time, structures became more elaborate but the town retained much of the appearance of a mining camp until the early twentieth century. In terms of population there were 19,000 inhabitants by 1877 and this had increased to 39,000 by 1891 when it was the second largest town in southern Africa. At the later date 17,200 Europeans were resident in the town. However, growth ceased with the transfer of many functions such as the School of Mines and financial organisations to the Witwatersrand after the Anglo-Boer War of 1899–1902. The population of Kimberley enumerated in 1936 barely exceeded that of 1891.

Although the four Kimberley mines were of most importance, other diamond bearing kimberlite pipes were discovered in the Orange Free State at Jagersfontein and Koffiefontein in the 1870s and at Cullinan, near Pretoria, after the Anglo-Boer War in 1902. It was at the Premier Mine near Pretoria that the largest diamond, the Cullinan (3,025 carats) was discovered in 1905, and presented by the colonial government for incorporation into the British Crown Jewels. Although formal towns were laid out at Jagersfontein and Koffiefontein, neither approached Kimberley in size or in organisation, so that they were reduced during periods of depression and mine closure to small country towns dependent upon their links with the agricultural community.

Diamonds were also discovered at Kolmanskop in the Namib Desert of German South West Africa in 1908. At first this gave rise to small-scale workings and a temporary boom town. However, the gems were deposited upon a series of marine terraces, subsequently covered with sand, which made the cost of recovery such as to suggest the need for large-scale operations. The Sperregebiet (Prohibited Area) was proclaimed on the coast and strict control was exercised over mining personnel. The major mining companies were reorganised after the South African occupation of the territory and integrated into the De Beers conglomerate. The mines were worked by huge earth moving machines which scraped the sand overburden from the terraces and then sifted the diamonds. A similar operation was begun south of the Orange River in Namaqualand in the 1920s.

Gold

The discovery of gold on the Witwatersrand resulted in the most spectacular mining venture on the African continent. Gold strikes had occurred in the eastern Transvaal in the vicinity of Pilgrims Rest and Barberton in the preceding 13 years, but the output had been limited. The mining camps had been short lived and although some were substantial settlements at the height of the boom, in the following slump they were all but obliterated as the prefabricated houses, shops, offices, hotels and mining equipment were moved to other sites. The discovery of the Witwatersrand fields resulted in a major rush from the earlier workings, followed by an influx of diggers from elsewhere in the subcontinent and from overseas, which because of the magnitude of the operations led to sustained growth on a scale far exceeding that on the diamond fields.

The gold outcrops were located in a belt of conglomerates which formed a ridge in the southern Transvaal, and were later traced beneath later deposits over a much wider area (Scott, 1951). Owing to the mining techniques required to extract the gold from the ore, there had been no previous African mining and it was possible for the first diggers to work the surface layers. Thus a chain of small surface mines and shallow shafts were dug along the line of the outcrop. In order to cater for the influx of population a series of towns was laid out by the government from Krugersdorp to Germiston, of which Johannesburg was the most important. It was significant that the plots surveyed in these towns (230 m²) were substantially smaller than those in other government towns (670 m²) where it was assumed that gardens would be used for subsistence cropping. Prompt government action ensured that the towns developed in a more orderly fashion than had been the case with Kimberley and that the authority of the administration would be in evidence from the beginning . It is also likely that the government envisaged the new towns as being no more long lasting or significant than Pilgrims Rest and Barberton before them.

On the contrary the gold bearing reef proved to be remarkably substantial. The value of production increased from £169,000 in 1887 to £4.5 million five years later. By 1898 production had reached £16.2 million and after faltering during the Anglo-Boer War continued to rise to reach £37.4 million in 1913. In order to achieve these results a considerable input of labour and capital was required, which resulted in an industry which influenced the entire subcontinent. The same pattern of events was evident on the Witwatersrand as on the diamond fields. The individual diggers could achieve little once the first surface deposits had been removed. Substantial inputs of capital were required to open the deep level mines and to overcome the metallurgical problems of extracting the gold from the ores, and much of this had to be obtained from Europe (Kubicek, 1979). Owing to the fine nature of the gold particles and the presence of pyrites, new methods of extraction such as the cyanide process had to be developed in the early 1890s to improve the extraction ratios. Reduction works involved enormous capital outlay both for research and construction. In addition the rocks dipped steeply, necessitating the sinking of shafts of up to 1,000 m in depth by the mid-1890s. Parallel with this development was the fact that extensive mining concessions were required to increase the length of life of the mine. There was thus little place for the individual digger, who was soon reduced to the status of a salaried worker.

Although the initial diggers were European, the bulk of the heavy unskilled work was rapidly assigned to Africans. The numbers required were large, resulting in the rapid growth of the gold mining settlements. By 1896 Johannesburg had attained a population of 102,000 of whom half were Europeans. The African population totalling 42,500 was 96 per cent male indicating the temporary nature of the migration. The rising demand for labour was such that the number of recruits was soon inadequate. The Chamber of Mines was established in 1889 to oversee recruitment and to attempt to reduce competition between the mining companies for the available Black labour. Labour recruitment increased from 14,000 African workers in 1889 to 97,000 a decade later (Taylor, 1982; Wilson, 1972). Two organisations, the Witwatersrand Native Labour Association and the Native Recruiting Corporation centralised and streamlined the procurement of labour and were thus able to reduce costs and depress wage rates. Much of the labour came from Moçambique which was regulated by international convention after 1909. African numbers rose to reach over 300,000 in the 1930s as new mines were opened and the area of mining operations expanded. Increasingly the impoverishment of the rural African Reserves accelerated the flow to the mines, so that the mining companies' main labour concern was to administer and house the temporary migrant labourers. Notably little attempt was made to recruit permanent African labourers as they would need to be housed with their families, thereby increasing costs. The compound system devised in Kimberley was therefore applied on the Witwatersrand, but without the aspect of enclosure.

The gold mining industry changed its location as the original mines on the central Witwatersrand were worked out and new areas were opened further from Johannesburg. The East Rand developed in the 1910s, the Far West Rand in the 1940s, and the Klerksdorp and Orange Free State mines in the 1950s. By the 1940s the Witwatersrand goldfields extended for over 80 km east to west along the line of the outcrop, with the Klerksdorp and Orange Free State fields as detached outliers some 100 and 150 km respectively to the south-west. Progressively as each new area come into production the mines were larger, often deeper, and designed to achieve a more efficient working of the ores. In landscape terms this resulted in larger mining settlements which were more widely spaced. Thus the continuous jumble of land uses which developed on the early mining areas of the central Witwatersrand goldfields gave place to a more orderly and planned segregation of land uses.

The more recently exploited Orange Free State goldfields illustrate the changes in organisation and planning which occurred within half a century. These particularly profitable fields were opened up after the Second World War by a small number of mining companies who sank comparatively few shafts to extract the ores over wide areas. The competition and overcrowding of mines and settlements evident in the central Witwatersrand were replaced by orderly planned development and co-operation between companies. The whole exercise benefited from the devaluation of the Pound in 1949 and the associated rise in the gold price. The change in mining landscapes may be illustrated by the town of Welkom, founded in 1947. It was designed according to the then prevailing town planning principles whereby the White residential areas of the town were divided into separate neighbourhood units arranged around a large civic centre. Road patterns were geometrical in design to reduce the volume of traffic in the residential areas and remove the particularly dangerous intersections of a grid plan city designed in the pre-motor transport era. Extensive areas of open land for schools, paths and playing fields represented a major break with past town planning practice. Yet the segregation of land uses also applied to the population. The adjacent Black township of Thabong was laid out in a grid pattern with little of the generous open space provision and few of the commercial facilities offered in the White sector of the town. In addition the mines retained the compound barracks system for the migratory workers which physically remained separate entities. Growth was rapid and not dissimilar in scale to that of Johannesburg 60 years earlier, as by 1960 the population stood at 96,000.

Gold mining provided a major stimulus to the South African economy through its demand for men, supplies and capital. Geographically it was able to reverse the traditional colonial space economy of coastal dominance (Browett and Fair, 1974). The Witwatersrand, more especially Johannesburg, became the core of the subcontinental economy and the coastal cities lost their dominant role. It was moreover the goldmining industry which provided the impetus for independent industrial development and the initiation of a significant heavy industrial base in the quest for import substitution.

The development of the Witwatersrand gold fields and their attendant services demanded considerable inputs of machinery and power. The former was supplied initially by massive importations. Mining gear from Great Britain, Germany and America was imported at great expense, as were the smaller and often minor items which were demanded by the mining and financial communities. Power, however, was supplied locally. Coal was discovered at Boksburg only 20 km from Johannesburg. Later discoveries in the eastern and southern Transvaal and Natal resulted in the availability of cheap local coal adequate for the needs of the expanding mining and secondary industries. The colliery towns remained isolated entities, attracting little processing industry as the coal was transported elsewhere. Mines increased in number, but particularly in size, as production increased. By 1910 some 7.2 million tons were produced in South Africa, over half of it in the Transvaal. In 1960 this figure had increased to 41.5 million tons.

Iron was the other basic element required for industrialisation. Iron ore was discovered in several parts of the subcontinent, but large scale mining was only initiated after the First World War. The state run South African Iron and Steel Corporation was founded in 1928 to commence local production. In 1934 the first iron ore mines were connected by rail to the newly opened iron and steel works in Pretoria. The mines were open cast and worked with a small labour force. Only 5,600 persons lived at the mining settlement in 1960. As in the case of the coalfields, the iron ore fields were not the location for the iron and steel plants which were erected in Pretoria and in 1942 at Vanderbijlpark, close to the main markets, and so contributing to the high degree of industrial concentration evident in South Africa.

Central Africa

The Witwatersrand goldfields presented political problems in that they were situated within the South African Republic (Transvaal) at the time of their discovery. They thus lay beyond the area of British rule and indeed the prosperity and prestige which the gold revenues afforded the republican government were viewed as detrimental to British imperial interests. In compensation, the idea that there was a 'Second Rand' to be found north of the Limpopo River was promoted, leading to the launching of another venture. In 1889 the British South Africa Company received a charter to exploit the goldfields of the region. The Company was able to raise sufficient capital and manpower to occupy Mashonaland in 1890, and, failing a large gold strike there, to occupy Matabeleland in 1893. The pioneers were attracted by tales of the 'Land of Ophir' and other accounts of mining by the 'Ancients'. More particularly they were offered the incentive of twelve mining claims apiece, in addition to land concessions.

Some 44,000 mining claims had been registered by mid-1894, and it was noted that in the following year, of the 2,050 European men in rural areas of Matabeleland, some 1,800 were engaged in prospecting. However, it was evident that in contrast to the Witwatersrand, previous workings had exhausted much of the value of the gold seams. Even after recovery from the fluctuations caused by war and disease, production in 1910 amounted to only £2.6 million, as opposed to £32.0 million in the Transvaal. Although production value continued to rise to £7.1 million by 1960, no major strikes were found, and the mining industry remained a small-scale enterprise with large numbers of producers located in the rural areas, by contrast with the major urban enterprises of the South African gold mining industry. In 1935 there were over 1,600 European producers. The number had shrunk by 1960 to 300 producers, but two-thirds still produced less than 14 kg per annum.

Intensive prospecting led to the discovery of other minerals, more especially asbestos and chrome, which provided major boosts for the Southern Rhodesian economy (Kay, 1970). For the advancement of the economy of central Africa in general, the discovery of high grade coal deposits at Wankie proved to be invaluable. Coal production in Southern Rhodesia reached 349,000 tons by 1914 and continued to increase to reach 1.2 million tons in 1928. The depression was a major set-back but recovery was such that by the late 1950s, 3.5 million tons were being raised annually. After the Second World War, Southern Rhodesia followed the South African example and embarked upon an industrial development programme and a major mining expansion. The exercise was repeated in the post-1965 era under the impact of international economic sanctions after the Unilateral Declaration of Independence (Stephenson, 1975). The state established the Rhodesia Iron and Steel Commission and constructed an iron and steel works at Redcliff based on local iron and coal deposits. Increased World demand for chrome and asbestos resulted in the growth of two major mining centres at Selukwe and Shabani respectively. Otherwise mining resulted in few urban foundations of any significance in Southern Rhodesia.

The 'Second Rand' failed to materialise in Southern Rhodesia, but on the Northern Rhodesia-Congo Free State boundary there was a major mineral zone; the future Copper Belt. The deposits had been known to the Belgian authorities from the time Katanga had been occupied, but they were thought to be too poor and inaccessible for commercial exploitation, located as they were in south-central Africa. The British South Africa Company, however, considered them to be a payable proposition when the Rhodesia Railways system was extended to the region. Through the agency of Tanganyika Concessions, the Union Minière du Haut Katanga was established in 1906 to exploit the deposits on the Congo side of the border. The main mining settlement was laid out at Elisabethville, which was built as a traditional Southern African grid pattern town in 1910 (Gann and Duignan, 1979b). The design was based apparently upon Bulawayo. The markedly segregated pattern with the mining camp, the administrative capital of Katanga, and the army headquarters in the European town was paralleled by similar divisions within the African settlements.

Copper production increased rapidly to reach 11,000 tons in 1914 and 139,000 tons in 1930. Elisabethville grew steadily and by 1929 housed some 33,400 inhabitants of whom 3,500 were Europeans (Fetter, 1976). The distribution of the population within the town at that date indicated the degree to which the initial mining camp had been modified as it assumed increasing administrative and commercial functions. Some 11,300 Africans lived in the mining and other compounds, but a similar number lived in a special *cité indigène*, modelled according to the pattern of South African urban locations. The remainder lived in the European town. Only a quarter of the European population worked for the mining companies but a high proportion was dependent upon the services provided for them. The depression of the early 1930s had a disastrous effect upon the town. Copper production was reduced to 45,000 tons in 1932, and by 1934 the population of the city had fallen by a quarter and nearly half the Europeans had left. Recovery was nevertheless fairly rapid as copper production increased to reach 150,000 tons in 1937 and was maintained at over 200,000 tons per annum between 1952 and 1960. By the latter date Elisabethville housed 219,000 inhabitants, the second largest town in the Belgian Congo.

Exploitation of the copper lodes on the Northern Rhodesian side of the border was slower. The ores were of a lower grade and new processes were required to make extraction profitable. Financial organisation was also required, which was only brought about after 1923 when the British South Africa Company initiated the development of its Northern Rhodesian mineral rights. It was only after intensive geological exploration, that the extent of the lodes became apparent, and so attracted the attention of two large mining combines, Anglo-American Corporation and Rhodesia Selection Trust. The opening of the copper mines however coincided with the onset of the depression, but was pursued despite the low World prices. Thus in 1931 only 9,000 tons were produced, but in the following year production exceeded that of Katanga. In 1940 some 253,000 tons were produced and this, subject to fluctuation, reached over 300,000 tons in 1951, a level which was maintained for the remainder of the colonial period.

A line of mining towns based on Kitwe, extending from Luanshya in the east to Bancroft in the west was constructed around the major mines (Northern Rhodesia, 1960). These towns were laid out as South Africa mining settlements with gridiron plans and separate residential areas for European and African miners, and compounds for the migratory workers. By 1961 the population of the Copper Belt towns had reached nearly 325,000 including 42,000 Europeans. The mining industry employed some 7,600 European and 39,000 African workers. Production was concentrated upon a number of large producing mines which were linked to local smelters and refineries. The substantial demand for coal and power was supplied in the colonial period almost entirely by the Wankie coal mines in Southern Rhodesia. Initial power supplies were partially satisfied, as in the case of the early railways, by the use of the woodlands. Some 100,000 ha of forest was cut in the 1950s alone, and timber plantations were established around the mining areas to replenish the supply for pit props. Additional electric power was available in 1960 with the completion of the Kariba Dam scheme on the

Zambezi River.

The problem of food supplies for the mines was largely overcome by increased African production but European settlement was officially viewed as a desirable complement to mining activity. Similar moves had taken place in the vicinity of Elisabethville in the 1910s, but had been unsuccessful (Cornet, 1965). In Northern Rhodesia by the 1950s over 1,000 smallholdings and 160 small farms had been laid out on the Copper Belt, but only half were occupied. A survey in 1959 found only 1,600 ha cultivated on European farms and a further 280 ha by the mines. In terms of attracting European population it was the booms associated with the opening of the copper mines in the late 1920s and the sustained post-1945 boom which resulted in massive immigration. The European population of the colony tripled between 1921 and 1931 and again between 1946 and 1956. It was the revenues from the copper mines which financed many of the projects of the short-lived Federation of Rhodesia and Nyasaland (1953-63).

The Remainder of the Continent

Compared with the Southern African experience, mining activity elsewhere in Africa during the colonial period was on a comparatively small scale. The most famous mining region on the West Coast was no exception (Silver, 1981). The goldfields of the Gold Coast were opened to European miners in the late 1870s, but at first production remained in African hands as mechanisation proved to be less successful than had been anticipated. Attempts to float companies in Europe and obtain government concessions on the goldfields were highly speculative. A number of companies were launched to exploit the alluvial fields near Tarkwa and the adjacent gold bearing reefs. By 1882 there were only six companies actually engaged in mining. An interesting commentary upon the state of the transportation system was the fact that all machinery had to be carried to the site and hence its size was limited. Production levels remained low until the early part of the present century, when the virtual cessation of South African production spurred Gold Coast exploitation. In the period 1900-1 some 3,500 mining concessions were issued, but no more than 40 were developed into successful mines or dredging operations. As a result output increased from 3 tons in 1901 to almost 200 tons by 1914. Despite fluctuations a peak of 300 tons was produced in 1938. Although the indigenous inhabitants had considerable experience of mining, the impact of expanded production meant once again the need to recruit labour from outside the immediate vicinity. Even in 1904 when only 17,000 African labourers were employed, a third came from outside the Gold Coast. This dependence upon imported labour continued throughout the colonial period and resulted in the emergence of migratory labour settlements akin to those developed in South Africa.

Other minerals such as diamonds in the Belgian Congo, Gold Coast and Sierra Leone attracted mining capital, but the results were questionable, as the workings were run parallel with indigenous small digging operations. This was particularly noticeable in Sierra Leone where in 1932 the Sierra Leone Selection Trust was granted a monopoly of diamond working throughout the colony. The main alluvial fields were remarkably rich and large stones were found, including a 770 carat gem in 1945. Output reached 0.75 million carats by 1936-8. However, in 1952 African diggers were legalised, although within prescribed areas. Small surface digging commenced and the result was a distortion of the local market, as such mining took place in the zones still within the exclusive concession of the mining company. By the late 1950s the struggle for control of the diamond fields had become intense as the indigenous diggers' sales exceeded that of the monopoly company.

Most African countries possessed some minerals which were exploited in the colonial era. It was, however, only after 1945 that prospecting was intensified. New deposits were located and the more accessible and valuable were extracted. The bauxite on Kassa Island in French Guinea first exported in 1952 and iron ore at Ngwenya in Swaziland in 1964 are but two examples of the accelerated pace of mining. The most spectacular discoveries were those related to petroleum. Exploration began in North Africa in 1946 and the first strikes occurred in 1949, but the major discoveries were made in 1956 in the Algerian Sahara at Hassi Messaoud and Edjeleh. The development of the Saharan oilfields required vast capital investment and this in turn necessitated the introduction of non-French oil companies. Production was soon under way, with export facilitated by a series of pipe lines constructed to terminals on the Mediterranean Sea. In 1961, the year before Algerian independence, production had reached 16 million tons. Exploration in other parts of the continent met with varying success. The search in

Nigeria, instituted in 1937, was only rewarded 20 years later, and production had barely begun at independence. Similarly the discoveries in Gabon and Angola in the late 1950s were only in the process of being brought into production at the time of independence. Thus for much of the continent mining has been a feature of the post-colonial era, bound up with the multinational companies which controlled most of the mining, marketing and processing of the minerals.

Mining is by its very nature an economy of plunder. The main feature of mining exploitation in Africa in the colonial period was the extraction of minerals for the benefit of the metropolitan economy. Thus the majority of minerals produced left the continent for processing elsewhere. The railway and other transport lines were built to ease this movement with the result that many railway lines were of dubious economic value to the colony. The nature of the mining economy is perhaps best illustrated by Africa's last mainland colony, South West Africa, which although predominantly semi-arid, possessed a valuable assemblage of minerals (Lanning and Mueller, 1979). The Germans opened the copper mines at Tsumeb in the north of the territory and constructed the railway to the coast in 1908. Since 1945 the mines have been controlled by the American Tsumeb Corporation. Diamonds were also discovered in 1908 and are worked by the South African Consolidated Diamond Mines. More recently in 1976, Rio Tinto Zinc has opened a large open cast uranium mine at Rossing. Owing to the difficulty of obtaining accurate statistics the value of mining production is subject to dispute. However, there has been a major boom with exports rising from R53 million in 1961 to an estimated R250 million in 1977. Undoubtedly the generous terms offered by the colonial power encouraged this vast mining enterprise, little of whose profits have remained in the territory.

6 SETTLERS

Without doubt the greatest imprint upon the colonial landscape was wrought by settlers who came to Africa to establish a permanent home. In this they differed from the majority of other groups who came to the continent to make their living, preferably their fortune, and then return to the metropoles to retire or to enjoy their new-found affluence. Settlement reflected an ambivalent attitude which sought to establish a new and improved Europe or Asia, but on the African continent. The new home was nevertheless not a straight-forward reproduction of the old home country, although great emphasis was placed on the immigrants' cultural heritage within colonial society, often to stress the differences between coloniser and colonised.

The presence of numerically superior indigenous populations forced modifications of a drastic nature as, despite the ethos of colonisation, Algeria, Kenya, or South Africa did not develop on mid-latitude colonial lines. Settlers always remained a minority, often a small minority, who were as much subject to the pressures of the metropolitan government as were the politicians and traders. This was paralleled by the class-selective nature of much of the emigration to Africa. As the unskilled work was usually performed by the indigenous population or Asian immigrants there was little place for European manual workers in colonial society (Christopher, 1976a). At the other end of the social scale, aristo-crats with a firm place in metropolitan society exhibited little tendency to emigrate permanently, although they might initiate schemes for others. The majority of European colonial societies were therefore restricted in terms of class and also in the concepts by which they functioned when comparison is made with metro-politan society. Clearly numbers were of vital importance to the imprint and nature of colonial society, as were the origins and the length of time settlement was in progress. An additional factor was the degree to which the settler community was able to influence and even gain control of colonial policy, sometimes to the detriment of the metropolitan power. Natal earned Winston Churchill's con-demnation as 'the hooligan of the British Empire' for its govern-ment's independent handling of the indigenous population (Hyam,

1968, p. 251).

It will at once be clear that no two colonies were exactly alike and that a great range of colonial settler experiences was evident on the continent. It is proposed to examine some of the broader themes of colonies of settlement before examining in more detail the specific aspects of the imprints of three groups, namely the pastoralists, agriculturalists and townsmen.

Origins and Numbers

Permanent European settlement in Africa was largely a nineteenth- and twentieth-century phenomenon. There were probably only 25,000 European settlers in Africa at the beginning of the nine-teenth century, after more than 300 years of colonial contact between the two continents. However, substantial migration from Europe to Africa, allied to high birth-rates and the checking of mortality rates resulted in a rapid increase in numbers thereafter. By 1860 there were 320,000 Europeans living in Africa and this number had grown to 2.2 million by 1911. Thereafter the rate of growth slackened, but in absolute terms the increase in the later colonial period was remarkable. The European population of Africa attained a peak of approximately six million in 1960, with a further one million Asian immigrants living on the continent (Figure 6.1).

The experiences of the two main areas of settlement, French North Africa and British South Africa, were not coincident in demographic progress. The highest rates of net migration to Algeria occurred between 1841 and 1891 when numbers in excess of 10,000 per annum were recorded. By contrast South Africa only ex-perienced such migratory growth in the period after 1890, with a peak of 40,000 per annum in the first five years of the twentieth century. The net outmigrations experienced by Algeria during both World Wars were not made good by subsequent inflows. In con-trast, with few exceptions South Africa continued to register net gains in the same period. The third major area of European settle-ment, Portuguese Africa, experienced its peak inward migration at the end of the colonial period with a rise of over 400,000 people in the 13 years, 1960–73. The demographic origins and histories of the European settlers in Africa are diverse and often complex, not least in the distinctive and durable character of the South African component.

Figure 6.1: Distribution of Europeans in Africa, *c.* 1956-60

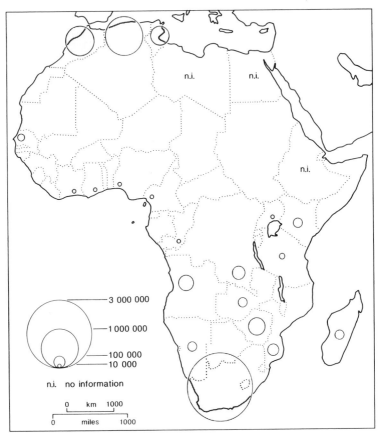

The Dutch and the British

The largest and most long-lasting group of colonists was that in southern Africa. The Cape of Good Hope settlement was established in 1652 as a refreshment station for ships of the Dutch East India Company plying between the Netherlands and the Dutch East Indies. The station was expected to fulfil its function through the cultivation of a Company fruit and vegetable garden and by barter with the indigenous population for livestock. However, the Company was unable to grow sufficient cereals and found the local inhabitants unwilling to barter large numbers of animals. In 1657 the Company therefore took the momentous step of freeing a group of its servants to become free burghers, and granting them small portions of land within the vicinity of the settlement to cultivate crops, and later keep cattle. The numbers freed in this manner were small. Twenty-five years later (1682) the free population still amounted to only 318 persons. It was supplemented by an influx of French Huguenot refugees after the Revocation of the Edict of Nantes in 1688, together with Dutch and German settlers, such that by 1700 the free White population totalled 1,265 persons. Significantly the French were not located as a group but were rapidly integrated into the existing Dutch and German settlers to form a distinct Cape-Dutch population (Elphick and Giliomee, 1979). By 1716 the free White population had risen to 1,828 persons, but the available arable land was considered to be exhausted and official free immigration ceased.

There followed a long period of limited immigration and high rates of natural increase. In contrast to tropical and northern Africa, the southern extremity of the continent proved to be remarkably healthy although it experienced a series of smallpox epidemics, which however proved to be more inimical to the indigenous population. As a result the free White population rose throughout the eighteenth century and numbered 25,000 by 1806. The natural rate of increase of 2.6 per cent per annum has been ascribed to the removal of the restraints placed on population growth in Europe, through the presence of an open land frontier and a plentiful food supply (Lamar and Thompson, 1981). Further, the lowering of the age of marriage encouraged large families which could be supported through the exploitation of frontier resources.

The degree of isolation was significant for the community to evolve distinctive traits such as language and a feeling of emotional separation from Europe. This development was enhanced by limited government supervision outside Cape Town. The Dutch East India Company was concerned with its East Indian ventures and the Cape settlement was highly peripheral to those undertakings. There was thus little coherent policy towards it in the eighteenth century as it offered little prospect of substantial profits. Isolation was further enhanced by the events at the end of the eighteenth century. In the course of the French Revolutionary and Napoleonic Wars, the Cape was captured by Great Britain in 1795, retroceded to the Batavian Republic in 1803 and recaptured by Great Britain in 1806. The Netherlands finally relinquished its interest in the settlement at the end of the Wars in 1814. During this period the fate of the colony was undetermined and little effort was made to interfere with the local population, giving rise to an uncontrolled frontier (Duly, 1968).

The British administration after the Napoleonic Wars instituted a large number of reforms with the aim of bringing the colony into line with nineteenth-century ideas and Imperial practices (Fredrickson, 1981). Inevitably friction arose as the colonists found their high degree of freedom circumscribed by new rules and regulations, administered by a much larger and more efficient civil service. New laws concerning matters such as land tenure, the treatment of free Blacks and finally the emancipation of slaves interfered with accepted ways and, added to the language barrier, reinforced in many Cape-Dutch speakers the feeling of separation from the government. The ruler-ruled cleavage in White society therefore acquired political overtones, but they were by no means clear cut. The frontier districts were most noticeably affected through the official restrictions on frontier expansion which sought to establish a permanent line between the Colony and the African indigenous population. This proved to be as unacceptable to the White frontiersman of South Africa as had been an earlier (1763) proclamation to restrict those of North America.

Political pressures allied to the perceived need for more land for an expanding population resulted in the Great Trek of the late 1830s. Frontier farmers had been on the move throughout the eighteenth and early nineteenth centuries, taking their flocks and herds to better pastures, even when these lay beyond the colonial boundary. But they had remained politically and economically tied to the Cape Colony. Those who embarked upon the Great Trek sought to leave the Colony permanently and establish a new state in the interior of Africa as far from British colonial rule as possible. The trekkers entered areas which had been laid waste by the wars occasioned by the rise of the Zulu military monarchy early in the nineteenth century, and were erroneously assumed to be uninhabited. Thus the areas of the present Orange Free State, Transvaal and Natal were deemed suitable for the establishment of this free state where the traditional eighteenth-century political economy could be practised without Imperial interference. A series of republics was formed by the various emigrant groups, the most important of which was Natal (1838) which gained independent access to the sea. However, the British government, fearful of the impact of the Great Trek upon the indigenous population and its implications for the Cape Colony, annexed Natal in 1843. The republics were thus after a period of conflict and confusion confined to the Transvaal (South African Republic) and Orange Free State.

Immigration recommenced in 1820 with the arrival of several thousand British settlers in the eastern part of the Cape Colony and later (1849) in Natal. These settlements established two zones of British rural population, and significantly provided a substantial base for the development of the towns, as many of the immigrants and even those originally placed upon the land were, before emigrating, urban dwellers with industrial and commercial skills. The numbers involved however were small (4,000 to the Cape in 1820, 5,000 to Natal in 1849-51). Despite the influx of 800,000 Europeans between 1815 and 1914, many subsequently left, so that British settlers were always outnumbered by the Cape-Dutch speaking White population in southern Africa as a whole, although in Natal after 1850 there was an English speaking majority. A small German military settlement was established in British Kaffraria in the late 1850s and a small number of free German settlers followed.

Thus by 1860 there were approximately 150,000 Europeans in southern Africa. The majority were concentrated in the Cape Colony, with only 30,000 spread across the Orange Free State, Transvaal and Natal (Christopher, 1976a). The settlement of the northern Transvaal was so weakly based that it was temporarily abandoned in the 1860s. The growth of the European population was such that by 1880 it had reached approximately 400,000 of which 100,000 lived outside the Cape Colony. There followed a period of rapid expansion related to the advance of mining, particularly the development of the Witwatersrand goldfields after their discovery in 1886. The White population of the Transvaal increased from 43,000 to 119,000 in the course of the 1880s in response to the opportunities offered by the changed space economy of the sub-continent. The economic development associated with mining was such as to attract substantial immigration which reached a peak immediately after the Anglo-Boer War of 1899-1902.

Just as in the 1830s there was a remarkable expansion in the geographical extent of European settlement so in the 1880s and 1890s new territories were occupied, if only to a limited degree (Christopher, 1982a). In many respects this paralleled the political expansion of European control associated with the Age of Imperialism. Ephemeral republics were formed in the early 1880s on the eastern and western margins of the Transvaal, where land was seized from the indigenous population. British interests retaliated with the annexation and occupation of Bechuanaland (1885) and Northern and Southern Rhodesia (1890). European settlement in these extensive territories was minimal for many years. In 1895 only 5,000 Europeans had penetrated north of the Limpopo River despite the expectations from mining and other enterprises and few were agriculturalists. Small groups of South African Afrikaners, as the Cape-Dutch could now be described, migrated to other countries in the same period (Olivier, 1943; Strydom, 1976). Angola, South West Africa, even British and German East Africa received groups who were dissatisfied with conditions in South Africa.

Apart from the South African acquisition of South West Africa during the First World War, there were no further opportunities for the expansion of the White South African settlement area by 1914. Expanding numbers had therefore to be accommodated within the existing area. Population growth continued through limited immigration and natural increase, although the former was erratic and lower than that prior to 1914, while the latter has shown a steady decline throughout the present century. Thus the White population of southern Africa which stood at 1.2 million in 1911 expanded to 2.1 million in 1936, but slackened its rate of increase to reach 3.4 million by 1960 and 4.8 million in 1980 (Christopher, 1982b). These totals mask substantial shifts as rural-urban and inter-provincial and inter-colonial migration took place. Whereas only 53 per cent of the White population lived in towns in 1911, by 1960 some 83 per cent was classified as urban. Within South Africa, work opportunities in the Transvaal attracted Europeans from the Cape and Orange Free State, so that by 1936 it had become the largest province in terms of White population. In addition the two frontier territories of South West Africa and Southern Rhodesia attracted lesser inflows of population. In 1911 only 38,000 Europeans lived in the two territories, but by 1960 this figure had increased to some 295,000. However, Southern Rhodesia then experienced a markedly unstable situation until the end of the colonial period in 1980 when the European population was little changed from that of 20 years before. In South West Africa a similar exodus began in the 1970s.

Southern Africa is the largest and most durable European settlement area on the continent. Owing to its isolation from Europe, a distinctively separate nation with Dutch roots evolved. The Afrikaner nation developed its own language, Afrikaans, as part of the symbolic break with Europe; whereas the English speakers retained direct links with Great Britain. However, the English-

Afrikaans dualism led to conflict which culminated in the Anglo-Boer War of 1899–1902. The subsequent reconstruction government led by Lord Milner attempted to change the balance in the composition of the European population through a massive British immigration drive (Streak, 1970). This failed as the mining industry was unable to produce the revenues and jobs necessary to sustain the growth needed in the economy and because there was no place in society for poor immigrants (Denoon, 1973). Throughout recent South African history the more menial tasks have been done by other racial groups whether Asian slaves or indentured labourers, or by African workers (Christopher, 1976a). Thus even in 1900 when the total European population stood at only one million, it was impossible to attract immigrants on a sufficient scale to outnumber the Afrikaners and create a British dominion. Lord Milner's administration gave way to the recognition that Afrikaner political dominance was inevitable and ensuing administrations never challenged that assumption. Thus the proclamation of a republic in 1961 marked the political conclusion of the colonial period so far as South African politicians were concerned.

Within White South African society a number of well marked principles evolved which had markedly geographical implications, of which the policies associated with segregation were the most significant (Davenport, 1977). The indigenous population was segregated from the White population in the rural areas during the course of the nineteenth century and in the urban areas during the twentieth century. Asian immigrants were also subjected to increasing pressure to return whence they came, or failing that to segregation. A remarkable consensus existed among colonists, whether Afrikaans or English, over relations with other peoples. No one who was not European 'to the tenth degree' could hold land or possess political rights under the Transvaal constitution. The practice was emulated in the Orange Free State. In Natal limited political rights were theoretically available for Asians and Africans but every effort was made to ensure that few people acquired them. Mahatma Ghandi's early expeiences in Natal illustrate the divergence between theory and practice (Huttenback, 1971). In the Cape Colony a theoretically colour-blind approach was limited politically by property qualifications which barred the majority of the non-European population from voting, and socially by attitudes akin to those of most colonial societies. After 1910 the Cape was steadily brought into line with the remainder of South Africa (Tatz,

1962). Southern Rhodesia followed Cape practice and Cecil Rhodes' dictum of 'equal rights for all civilised men'. Definition of civilisation remained a European prerogative throughout the colonial era and proved to be remarkably colour conscious. The result was a fragmented society reflected in a fragmented landscape.

The French

The French settlement of North Africa was of much shorter duration and supported fewer immigrants than its southern counterpart. An attempt was made to recreate France overseas, as there was a constant reference to the extension of France on to the southern shore of the Mediterranean Sea. Settlement was thus tightly controlled and for its entire history the colonisation of Algeria, and to a lesser extent that of Morocco and Tunisia, were directed from Paris. Because of the territories' proximity to France and the lack of any rival French colonies of settlement, the Algerian enterprise received much greater governmental supervision and the population was subject to a greater degree of regulation, unthinkable in a contemporary British colony. Settlement was designed as an integral part of French society, rather than as a new and better society on the model of British colonies.

The conquest of Algiers in 1830 began a long French involvement in North Africa terminating in 1962 with the granting of independence to Algeria (Ageron, 1979). For much of this time France was embroiled in military operations and maintained a substantial army in the country throughout the colonial era. The wars presented a number of advantages for French colonisation. First and foremost military campaigns led to large-scale confiscation of land such as that of the late 1830s and early 1870s, which was then made available for colonists. Secondly the army built and maintained the basic infrastructure of roads, ports and canals, and at the same time undertook the construction of villages, farms and agricultural improvement schemes. Indeed it might be claimed that the disastrous start to colonisation in the 1830s, when high death-rates resulted in a considerable excess of deaths over births, was only overcome through the military colonisation plans of Marshall Bugeaud. In the period of his administration (1841–7) the European population increased from 37,000 to 109,000 (Breil, 1957). Although death-rates continued to exceed birth-rates until the late 1860s, no thought of abandonment was possible after this period. Migration was maintained at fairly uniform rates until the end of the century. Although the peak of the early 1840s was never again attained, the 1870s as a whole added 116,000 immigrants to the European population. Marshall Bugeaud's settlement resulted in Algeria overtaking the European population of southern Africa. It was only in the course of the 1880s that rising rates of immigration to South Africa resulted in Algerian numbers being overtaken. French satisfaction could still be expressed in the 1890s that French North Africa as opposed to British South Africa (which excluded the Transvaal) possessed a larger European population.

However, despite continuing high rates of natural increase from the 1870s onwards, immigration declined in the 1890s. To some extent settlement was diverted to Tunisia and, after 1912, to Morocco. In 1911 some 900,000 Europeans lived in Algeria and Tunisia. While limited immigration continued after the First World War, it was Morocco which was the main recipient, recording nearly 600,000 Europeans by 1954 (Morocco, 1956). Thus in the mid-1950s, French North Africa had 1.9 million European inhabitants. This was not as rapid a rate of expansion as in South Africa, or indeed tropical Africa in the 1914–60 era, and reflected in part the weak demographic position of metropolitan France. Further the issue was complicated by the presence of large numbers of Spanish and Italian settlers. The latter in particular were the subject of considerable concern owing to the Italian government's pro-German alliances prior to both World Wars. French demographic weakness had been recognised as early as 1871 when the indigenous Jewish population had been reclassified as European to boost settler numbers (Ageron, 1979). In 1891 the Oran Department enumerated 102,453 Spanish settlers as opposed to only 78,880 French settlers. In Tunisia in 1911 the 46,044 French colonists were outnumbered by 88,182 Italians (Tunisia, 1914a). Almost two-thirds of the European population of the city of Tunis was Italian. It is an interesting reflection upon the times that the threat to French security was seen in European continental political terms, not in relation to the 1.7 million Moslem inhabitants of Tunisia. As a result of ingenious reclassification and the inclusion of all Europeans born in North Africa in the French population, the balance was soon changed (Bernard, 1937b).

As with most frontier societies, the French in North Africa adopted attitudes and outlooks at variance with those in the metropole. By the 1890s French observers were noting this divergence and hinted at the eventual loss of Algeria as Great Britain had lost the North American colonies in the previous century (Ageron, 1979). The degree of government supervision was however far greater, and the officials who administered the country were integrated into metropolitan society with little opportunity to develop peculiarly Algerian traits and attitudes. The fiction of protectorate status in Morocco and Tunisia reinforced the restraints on any such development. Algeria, however, became increasingly dependent upon the French connection after the First World War as the French market was available for Algerian basic products and protected from external competition. Further the French stake in Algeria was strengthened as a result of the Second World War, as it had been the possession of an overseas French Empire which had retained a place for France among the major powers. There was thus a general consensus on the position of Algeria in the French polity. The War of Independence after 1954 only increased the dependence of European settlers in Algeria upon the French government. This dependence was maintained to the end of the colonial period and it was General de Gaulle's breaking through traditional patterns of thought which enabled France to hand the country over to the people it had been fighting for eight years. The colonists returned to France and were reintegrated into metropolitan society.

The Portuguese and the Italians

Other attempts at European colonisation in Africa were on a smaller scale and chronologically later. The Portuguese interest in their African possessions was revived in the twentieth century, particularly after the establishment of the *Estado Nova* in 1928. The European presence in Portuguese Africa in 1911 was little more than 20,000 persons, concentrated mainly in Angola. In the mid-1930s it still amounted to little more than 50,000. However, after the Second World War immigration increased rapidly, reflecting a concerted effort on the part of the government to redirect a portion of the continuing Portuguese emigration away from Brazil to their African possessions. Thus in 1950 there were 126,000 Europeans in Angola and Moçambique and by 1970 the numbers had increased to approximately 495,000. The peak figure attained in 1973–4 was probably close to 600,000 (Bender, 1978; Middlemas, 1979). Mass migration to Portuguese Africa was late in the colonial period, indeed over half took place after most of the continent had been decolonised. Furthermore in the African context a great deal was accomplished in a short period of time as a result of close government supervision. Although much attention was directed towards the agricultural settlements, it was the main towns which received most of the immigrants. Associated with the European settlement of Angola and Moçambique was a secondary movement of Cape Verdians to the mainland colonies. Once more the attainment of independence after the *coup d'état* in Lisbon in 1974 resulted in the mass exodus of colonists.

The Italians also initiated a major colonisation programme in the 1920s and 1930s (Istituto Agricolo Coloniale Italiano, 1945). This was largely directed towards Libya, the northern districts of which were regarded as integral parts of Italy by the end of the colonial era. By 1930 only 300 families had been settled in Libya, however the rate accelerated as colonial land settlement policies achieved a higher priority in Italian official circles. The impetus came from the idea of redirecting part of the massive Italian emigration towards the colonies as a means of expanding national power (Fowler, 1972). In the rural areas by 1937 some 27,000 families had been settled and in the next three years the total climbed to 59,000 families. Attention was focused upon agricultural settlement but as in the case of the Portuguese experience, most settlers migrated to the towns. In 1941 there were some 110,000 Europeans in Libya, of whom 70,000 lived in Tripolitania. After the Second World War, Libya gained independence in 1951 and the majority of the Italian settlers emigrated.

The Tropical Highlands

The other major area of European colonisation was that associated with the belt of highlands which ran through East Africa between South Africa and Ethiopia. Within this zone European agricultural settlement was officially considered both possible and desirable owing to the altitudinal amelioration of the tropical climate. Bowman described a line of 'tolerable temperatures' which increased in elevation towards the Equator, but above which it was possible for Europeans to work normally (Bowman, 1931). Thus large tracts of Southern and Northern Rhodesia, parts of Kenya and Tanganyika and small detached portions of the Belgian Congo were suitable for settlement. Within these zones plantations were the largest utilisers of land granted to Europeans, but colonists were able to acquire land and develop a settler economy augmented by a substantial permanent urban population.

Within the highland belt, Nyasaland and Uganda were declared to be areas of African paramountcy of interest and European settlement was discouraged. Tanganyika, after its conquest by the British was similarly regarded as being an area of African dominance. Only Kenya and Northern Rhodesia developed a traditional settler economy, but owing to the restraining influence of the British Colonial Office neither was able to obtain responsible government and complete control of internal affairs. The numbers of settlers were therefore limited. In 1960 only 75,000 Europeans lived in Northern Rhodesia and 61,000 in Kenya. In both cases this represented considerable percentage increases over the previous 15 years, but not sufficient to dispense with metropolitan officials and control. The end of the colonial period also resulted in a substantial decline in European numbers, although the imprint of the colonial period was less abruptly terminated than in Algeria, Angola or Libya.

The Asians

Europe was not the only source of colonists. Asians migrated to Africa in considerable numbers, first as traders and settlers in East Africa, where they exerted a significant influence on the Swahili town system of the pre-Portuguese period. This influence continued, as it was Oman which displaced the Portuguese from the coast north of Moçambique at the end of the seventeenth century. The number of Asian settlers was small and was absorbed by the indigenous Islamic population. In the course of the colonial period large numbers of Asians migrated to Africa, but most were not assimilated by the African population and thus became a further element of diversity in the continent's population.

The first colonial migration was associated with the Portuguese who used Indian slaves and freemen from Goa to supplement their own limited manpower on the East Coast. The numbers involved were small and the distinguishable Goan element in the population of Moçambique amounted to only a few thousand. On a larger scale was the Dutch use of Asian slaves at the Cape of Good Hope. In 1657 the Dutch East Indian Company decided to use slave labour from the East Indies, rather than indentured or free White labour. This reflected the position of the colony as a dependency of the government in Batavia, which was resistant to the concept of a White colony of settlement. The decision on labour policy was questioned as late as 1715, but the demand for slaves rather than White colonists was overwhelming and a steady flow of Asian and African slaves entered the colony. The slaves, including the Cape Malays, were partly Moslem and originated from the Dutch possessions in India and the East Indies as well as other parts of Africa. At the time of emancipation (1832) there were some 35,000 slaves in the colony. Economically and socially they merged with other peoples described as 'Coloured' and were enumerated as such in subsequent censuses. This grouping included Mulattos, and remnants of the indigenous population of the Western Cape, numbering 525,000 by 1911.

The major migration of Indians to the African continent only began in the second half of the nineteenth century. The first migrants responded to the European demand for labourers on the sugar plantations. On the island of Mauritius, in common with other sugar growing colonies, after the abolition of slavery, plantation owners resorted to the employment of indentured Indians. When Natal began to develop its sugar industry in the 1850s, it adopted many Mauritian approaches ranging from the cane varieties and machinery to its organisation and recruitment of Indian indentured labourers. The first labourers arrived in Natal in 1860, and numbers increased rapidly as the plantations were developed. Labourers were indentured for five years with an option of a further five-year indenture in return for a passage to India or a grant of land equivalent in value to the passage money. The majority chose to stay, although few were able to obtain a land grant from the colonial government. In addition free Indians migrated to Natal to establish shops and professional services and to farm on their own account. Thus in 1891 there were 11,000 indentured labourers and 30,000 free Indians in the colony. Numbers increased rapidly to a total of 152,000 by 1911, but conflicts between the governments of India and South Africa over the conditions under which the Indians laboured were such that in 1914 immigration was halted. Despite restrictions on the Indian population of the country, and enactments encouraging them to return to India, a steady growth took place to number 220,000 in 1936, 477,000 in 1960 and 780,000 in 1980.

Indians were later attracted to other parts of Africa, particularly to East Africa. The Uganda Railway was constructed by Indian labourers, and many subsequently stayed when the line was completed. Some 12,000 Indians were enumerated in British East

Africa in 1911. Business and professional services afforded further opportunities throughout East and Central Africa and a steady migration and growth took place. Thus by 1936 some 44,000 Indians were living in Kenya, and this had increased to 177,000 by the end of the colonial period. Rapid growth of the Indian population was also evident in Uganda and Tanganyika after the First World War, while small numbers settled in Northern and Southern Rhodesia and Nyasaland. The communities were predominantly urban with a trade and service orientation, as opportunities for agriculture were limited owing to the extent of prejudice against them in the European settler community. Their position remained insecure in the post-independence period, as the fate of the Ugandan Asians testifies. In West Africa it was the Syrians and Lebanese who fulfilled the same commercial and professional functions in the French colonial possessions, while in the Portuguese colonies small numbers of Indians and Chinese settled in the main towns. In neither case were the numbers large. It is noticeable that Chinese migration to Africa was limited. Chinese miners were introduced to the Witwatersrand after the Anglo-Boer War but were later repatriated. Thus in 1960 there were probably under one million Asians living in Africa.

The Eurafricans

Linked to the immigrant groups were the people of mixed racial parentage such as the Coloureds of Southern Africa, the Mestiços of Portuguese Africa and the Creoles of West Africa and the Indian Ocean islands. Owing to their mixed ancestry they bridged the gap between European and African society and were often an influential group within the urban based commercial and administrative network (Bender, 1978). Indeed, in the colonial period they acted as a middle caste within society. However, by their very origin numbers are difficult to ascertain as definition was often impossible; as the South African legislators found in 1950 when formulating the Population Registration Act which sought to classify everyone according to racial origin. Miscegenation between European men and African women took place in all pioneer societies, but tended to become less significant with the arrival of European women in Africa.

The Portuguese through their concept of luso-tropicalism contemplated integration through racial mixing of the Portuguese immigrants and indigenous Africans to produce a new people on

Brazilian lines, although theory and practice did not match in reality. The most successful example of luso-tropicalism was the Cape Verde Islands, where by 1950 some 69.6 per cent of the population was Mestiço. However, this was a reflection of the peculiar nature of the islands and the small size of their population (148,000). When the islands were discovered in the fifteenth century they were uninhabited. Colonisation took the form of the settlement of African slaves and the outcasts of Portuguese society such as convicts and Jews, expelled by the Inquisition, in addition to a small governing and planter class. Few Europeans settled permanently on the islands after the end of the slave trade, so that this isolated and socially limited society was not materially disturbed until the end of the colonial period. The Cape Verdians, because of their particular origin and degree of assimilation to Portuguese culture, provided a small additional source of manpower for the colonisation of the mainland colonies. The number of Mestiços in Angola (53,000) and Moçambique (31,000) in 1960 was small and tends to suggest that the extent of miscegenation in the mainland colonies was not remarkable, particularly when it is remembered that many of those enumerated came from the Cape Verde Islands.

Paradoxically the main region of racial mixing proved to be South Africa, where the amalgam of slaves, indigenous peoples and Europeans resulted in a highly complex pattern of society (Elphick and Giliomee, 1979). In 1865 the first census in the Cape of Good Hope recorded 133,000 Coloureds (mixed race) and 82,000 Hottentots (indigenous) who thereafter were generally merged both for statistical purposes and in reality through intermarriage. These totals compared with 182,000 Europeans enumerated in the Colony at the same time. By 1911 there were some 525,000 Coloureds in South Africa, and the numbers increased rapidly through natural increase and racial admixture to reach 1.5 million in 1960 and 2.6 million in 1980. At that date they were still settled predominantly (85.9 per cent) in the Cape of Good Hope, suggesting a low degree of racial mixing in areas of nineteenth-century settlement. Laws and rules against racial mixing were enacted in several colonies and the degree of miscegenation was usually limited by the time the main thrust of colonial expansion took place late in the nineteenth century. The majority of children of mixed parentage then tended to be absorbed into established African societies and so did not emerge as a separate grouping as they had in the earlier stages of the colonial era when European colour consciousness was not pronounced.

The Pastoralists

The most extensive group of settlers in terms of land usage were the pastoralists. It would probably be true to say that few European settlers migrated to Africa with the intention of establishing pastoral farms, but a large number found it to be the main, often the only way of making a living in arid and semi-arid lands. Thus although the tending of livestock was an essential part of most colonial settlements and farms, particularly in the period before the mechanisation of transport and farming practices, it was only after the reassessment of initial colonisation objectives that pastoralism became a dominant form of economic activity. European pastoral farming was largely limited in extent to the southern parts of the continent with outliers in the highlands of Central and East Africa. Elsewhere on the continent animal husbandry was left to the indigenous population and little attempt was made to establish European ranching enterprises.

The Cape of Good Hope

The key area was southern Africa, where by the late 1650s the authorities at the Dutch station at the Cape of Good Hope found that the supply of livestock from the indigenous population was insufficient to meet the demands of the passing ships. Thus the Dutch East India Company undertook its own herding and allowed the free burghers to keep animals. Livestock raising was meant to be only a subsidiary activity to the main occupation of raising crops. However, the livestock element grew in importance and the range of grazing grounds was extended beyond the settled colony. At first animals were driven to summer pastures in and over the mountains of the south-western Cape, but later they were permanently pastured beyond the settled area until needed for market. In the early eighteenth century livestock farming had become a means whereby poorer Europeans could obtain the funds to acquire an arable farm. By the mid-eighteenth century it had become an end in itself, and in the nineteenth and early twentieth century a pervasive way of life (Guelke, 1976; Harris and Guelke, 1977).

There were a number of distinctive features to this development of pastoralism which distinguished it from the later commercial expansion of cattle and sheep farming on other mid-latitude frontiers in the nineteenth century. Foremost were its longevity and low degree of commercialisation. Related to these were the emergence of a semi-subsistence economy and society with tenuous links with the metropolis, and the development of a free frontier mentality and isolation from Europe. In tangible form the emergent society evolved a distinctive manner in appropriating and organising the land. The result was an increasingly rapid migration of pastoral farmers across the environmentally suitable regions of southern Africa, until the final closing of the free land frontier in the present century. There are thus many parallels with the experience of the United States and Australia, and other mid-latitude lands of colonisation, but modified by the peculiar circumstances of a location on the African continent.

Owing to the limited areas suitable for crop farming in the vicinity of the western Cape, and problems and cost of transportation to the market in Cape Town, commercial agriculture was severely restricted in extent in the first 200 years of the Cape settlement. Expansion was only possible through the development of grazing which accorded with the potential of the poor, often semi-arid environment of the Cape Colony and the costs of long distance transportation (Van der Merwe, 1938, 1945). Temporary and later permanent settlement took place in the eighteenth century through the movement of farmers across the mountains and otherwise beyond the limits of the colony. In the first decade of the eighteenth century the Dutch East India Company sought to control this movement by licensing grazing activities. At first general licences were issued, but owing to the unsatisfactory nature of intermingling flocks and herds, exclusive grazing rights to limited areas were soon made available. The prospective pastoralist was able to select his grazing area by marking its midpoint (ordonnantie) and then walking or riding on horseback at walking pace in several directions for half an hour to demarcate its boundaries. The circular tract so described measured approximately 2,500 ha. Clearly such farms had to be situated at least one hours' walk apart and in practice they were often further distant from one another, leaving extensive tracts of nominally unoccupied government land between the legal grazing areas.

The pastoralist registered his claim and received a licence for a limited time for his tract, officially described as a loan place. Initially only grazing for a period of six months was allowed but by the 1730s the licence validity had been set at 15 years and both grazing and cultivation were permitted. Few licencees were disturbed for far longer periods if they chose to remain permanently on their farms, nor indeed were many dispossessed for failure to pay the licence fee, as lengthly testing periods were allowed before the licence was even applied for. Land was freely available and appeared to be unlimited until the 1780s when the leading colonists had ventured 1,000 km from Cape Town and had been checked by the Xhosa. Official attempts to limit the spread of settlement and extend a measure of control over the frontiersmen were ineffectual as the government machinery under the Dutch East India Company was small scale and stretched over a wide area. As late as the 1780s there were only two magistrates stationed outside Cape Town to administer an area measuring almost 1,000 km by 500 km. In such circumstances it is hardly surprising that the frontier farmers were able to develop their own approaches to land and land ownership with little regard for the wishes of the government, and that these approaches through practice by successive generations took on the air of permanency.

The commercial aspects of the pastoral economy inevitably weakened the further the colonists migrated from Cape Town. The controversy over their degree of participation in the colonial and world economies has suggested that even in the eighteenth century trading links with the metropolis were maintained by all the stock farmers. Neumark stressed the importance of trade in providing the frontiersmen with the essential supplies such as guns and gunpowder, and wagons, upon which the enterprise depended and by which military supremacy over the indigenous population was maintained (Neumark, 1957). The frontier farmers had comparatively little to trade in return. Owing to the great distances involved, the metropolitan market for sheep and cattle was supplied by the regions of the south-western Cape. Only a small fraction of the total colonial herd and flock was marketed. Income was derived on most farms from hides and skins, tallow and the products of hunting expeditions such as ivory, and these were sufficient to maintain the farmers above the subsistence level. Furthermore, links with Cape Town were maintained in order to baptise children or seek government assistance, and these visits generally had strong commercial overtones as stocks were obtained for considerable periods in advance. Thus the pastoral economy was largely subsistence with food and basic materials supplied by the frontierman. Game animals were hunted and shot for food, clothing and implements. The farmers' own herds and flocks were maintained as much for food and clothing as for commerce, but they also fulfilled the vital means whereby capital could be accumulated. In addition to the pastoral activity most frontier farmers cultivated small areas for fruit and vegetables, and where conditions were suitable, for grain. However, without irrigation, grain cultivation was often not successful in the erratic climatic regime of the Cape Colony. Hence springs and watercourses were eagerly sought by the farmers and in a semi-arid land, farm names reflect prized water sources, not the desolation. The situation outlined was clearly not static. The colonial economy increased in prosperity in the eighteenth and early nineteenth centuries and in response frontier farmers increased their demand for greater luxuries including exotic items such as coffee and printed cloths. The interaction between the frontiersmen and the markets depended upon the state of the colonial economy, distances, and the itinerant pedlars. Only in the nineteenth century with the development of the wool trade and the growth of towns did the frontier farmer begin to produce primarily for export and the commercial system become elaborated.

The numbers involved in the first century of the expansion of the pastoral frontier were small. By the time of the final British occupation of the Cape Colony in 1806 there were only 1,736 loan places in the entire colony (Duly, 1968). There were many more farms for which no title had been requested as squatting had become prevalent on the eastern frontier of the Colony. Furthermore, because of the extensive tracts of land left between the loan places, farmers used far more land than they were entitled to. The change of government was reflected in a changed attitude towards the freedom which the frontier farmers enjoyed. The British administration considered that the defects in the system they inherited were such that radical reforms were necessary. The major objection was seen in the impermanence of the tenure and hence the discouragement of any investment in permanent improvements. The same problem had concerned the Dutch administration, which in 1732 had offered freehold tenure to 50 ha of a grazing farm, where permanent improvements could be undertaken. However, few farmers had gone to the expense of availing themselves of the opportunity. In 1813 the governor, Sir John Cradock, promulgated new regulations which provided for the survey of farms and the granting of perpetual leasehold tenure in lieu of loan place status. In this manner the extent of farms could be determined and security of tenure offered to the proprietor. It also offered the government the means of ascertaining the extent of its own holdings with a view to their more profitable use.

The reforms instituted by the Cape government in 1813 were such that the areas of farms were limited to 2,500 ha. Patterns of square, rectangular and even circular farms were laid out in the various districts as the work of surveying proceeded. It was not until the 1830s that recognition was given to the arid nature of the interior of the Colony and that larger units were permitted upon payment of additional fees. The outward expansion of settlement was encouraged as frontier farmers grazed their animals further from established farming areas, when the increasing numbers in each generation sought lands of their own. Animals were grazed beyond established boundaries in periods of drought and small groups lived beyond such boundaries on a permanent basis. The government usually only followed settlement and practice by extending the area of the colony and recognising settler actions; it did not initiate settlement on any scale until the middle of the nineteenth century or even later. The land reforms were slow in operation and the British government in the 1830s and 1840s embarked upon the idea of systematic colonisation on Wakefieldian principles. This clearly was impractical as the balance between land, labour and capital required for its success clearly did not obtain in the Cape of Good Hope. The result was a break with the free land frontier and permanent European emigration beyond colonial control.

Expansion of the Settlement Area

In the late 1830s and early 1840s some 15,000 colonists emigrated from the Cape Colony on the Great Trek and settled in Natal and the areas beyond the Orange and Vaal Rivers, which became the Orange Free State and Transvaal respectively. Their economy and mode of approach to land tenure was based on that developed in the previous 120 years in the Cape Colony. Thus 2,500 ha farms were offered to all the citizens of the new states. Two farms were granted to those who had pioneered particular parts of the country or rendered special services to the government. The operation of the land laws became remarkably flexible as the colonists lacked qualified surveyors and farms had to be laid out as best they could. The circular farms of the Cape Colony were recognised to be wasteful and square farms with sides of one hour's ride at walking pace were instituted. The area was thus increased to 3,200 ha per farm. However, horses could be ridden at greater speeds than that prescribed, resulting in farms which proved to be two, three, even four times their nominal size when regular instrumental survey was undertaken either later in the nineteenth century of early in the twentieth century. Substantial new areas were opened up but malaria and trypanosomiasis defeated attempts to enter and colonise the lands north of the Limpopo River or the lowlands of the eastern Transvaal (Van der Merwe, 1962). In the northern Transvaal the indigenous inhabitants forced a temporary withdrawal in the 1860s, but the general movement was one of encroachment upon African lands. The consolidation of these gains took half a century, as even by 1880 there were only 100,000 Europeans in the Orange Free State and Transvaal occupying approximately 20,000,000 ha (Van Zyl, 1967).

The continuing expansion of the European population and the extensive nature of frontier farming resulted in further attempts to obtain land through the exploitation of internal weaknesses in indigenous societies and the occupation of their lands. In the 1880s a series of new states was established on the borders of the Transvaal including Stellaland and Goshen on the west, which offered standard sized farms to all who took part in their conquests. In the case of the New Republic in Zululand there was insufficient land for all the claimants and grants had to be scaled down to 1,500 ha. Within the Transvaal a disastrous attempt was made to colonise the north of the country under greater government control.

The 1890s witnessed a major advance with the colonisation of lands north of the Limpopo River and in the Kalahari Desert. In Mashonaland the British South Africa Company offered half farms (1,250 ha) and mining claims to pioneers whose main interest was mineral exploitation and full farms to those whose interest was farming. After the conquest of Matabeleland in 1893 the Company offered full farms to all. In the Kalahari region, the Kalahari Desert State offered its citizens increased size (12,500 ha) farms because of the poverty of the environment, while the British South Africa Company offered 5,000 ha farms at Ghanzi on the South West African border. Both settlements represented a limit of settlement and few permanent colonists were forthcoming until the large-scale sinking of boreholes in the present century.

The system of free distribution of land which had evolved in the eighteenth century had continued until the early part of the twentieth century. The adjunct to this element in the land disposal system was the concept of standardisation of size of holdings. The 2,500 ha unit was part of the cultural baggage of the Afrikaner population who constituted the majority of the rural European population, and was adhered to as far as possible until the First World War as a unit for pastoral farming (Christopher, 1976b). The British South Africa Company finally jettisoned the idea of standardisation in 1915 in favour of a more flexible approach (Southern Rhodesia, 1915). However, there were variations on the standard unit theme. Half farms (1,250 ha) were offered where the land was considered particularly fertile as in the case of the eastern Orange Free State conquered from the Basutos in the 1860s or in Mashonaland in the 1890s. As already noted increased standard areas were also offered in the drier and more inaccessible parts of the subcontinent.

Standardisation was abandoned in the Cape Colony in the 1830s as the government recognised that the aridity and variability of the climate necessitated larger farms for economic enterprises (Cape of Good Hope, 1876). Farms of up to 50,000 ha were surveyed as settlers penetrated the arid Karoo. Surveyors and government inspectors took an increasingly important part in determining farm areas through the evaluation of the grazing potential and the water resources. Thus economic units were designed, taking into account the varying capabilities of the grazing grounds so that farms would be neither too small to be unprofitable, nor so large that the purchasers could not use all the land. The process of survey and evaluation was slow but largely accomplished by 1900. In advance of the surveyors and the bureaucracy, squatters continued to use large tracts of land as their forefathers had done. Attempts were made to control them through temporary leasing agreements, but these were rarely the prelude to conversion to a permanent grant. Increasingly the diminishing land resources of the Colony were viewed as the preserve of the sons of established farmers. Capital sums and usually cash were required to purchase Crown Lands. Farm prices in the Cape Colony increased from £400 to £1,000 in the period 1850–1915. Clearly semi-subsistence farmers could not raise such sums and the squatters were increasingly dispossessed rather than given titles to the lands they had illegally occupied. In many respects this reflected the political control which the farming community had obtained under representative government in 1853, when the qualified franchise was tied to property.

The change to commercial concepts of government land disposal and colonisation was followed by the other states in southern Africa. Free land grants were finally abandoned in Natal in 1858, after which land could only be purchased at increasingly high prices and in areas limited to a maximum of 800 ha. The change was most marked in Southern Rhodesia where the 'Age of the Fortune Hunters' under Dr Leander Jameson (1891–6) gave way to the more parsimonious policy of Sir William Milton (1897–1914) (Palmer, 1976). The colonial and republican land settlement experiences were studied by the Germans in South West Africa where a system of inspection and valuation was introduced akin to that in operation in the Cape Colony, but with safeguards as to occupation and improvement which had often been conspicuously absent in colonial legislation. The policy of land sales after the evaluation of its farming potential and after the selection of suitable purchasers, became general after the First World War when colonisation was placed on a more scientific basis than had been the case in the previous 100 years. However, by that time there was little land available for European colonisation.

The speed with which the land resources of the subcontinent were acquired by individual European settlers, largely for pastoral purposes, was remarkable in the African context and paralleled the rise in population (Christopher, 1983). Between 1806 and 1860 approximately 36,000,000 ha were transferred to private European ownership, while in the following half century a further 76,000,000 ha were appropriated (Figure 6.2). There remained comparatively little land suitable for European settlement except in Southern Rhodesia and South West Africa, so that only 31,000,000 ha were alienated between 1911 and 1960. At the latter date nearly half the area of British Africa south of the Zambezi had been acquired by European farmers. The remainder was either held in African reserves (27.2 per cent) or was regarded as too arid or disease ridden (24.3 per cent) for permanent settlement.

The Pastoral Economy

The rise of commercial pastoralism in the nineteenth century was related to the export of a number of basic products in demand in the industrialising states of Europe and North America. The most important were wool, mohair, ostrich feathers and hides and skins. The latter had been a basic export throughout the eighteenth century and increased in volume in the nineteenth and twentieth centuries. Hides accounted for two-thirds of all Cape pastoral exports in the 1820s, but declined in relative importance thereafter as commercial wool production commenced. Wool exports which in the pre-1830 period had been negligible, expanded rapidly from

Figure 6.2: Area Occupied by European Farms in Southern Africa, 1806-1960

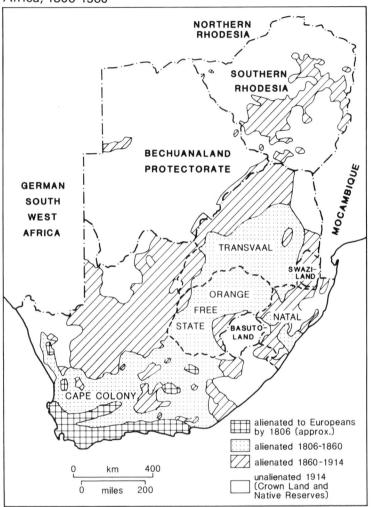

NORTHERN RHODESIA

SOUTHERN RHODESIA

BECHUANALAND PROTECTORATE

GERMAN SOUTH WEST AFRICA

MOCAMBIQUE

TRANSVAAL

SWAZI-LAND

ORANGE FREE STATE

NATAL

BASUTO-LAND

CAPE COLONY

alienated to Europeans by 1806 (approx.)

alienated 1806-1860

alienated 1860-1914

unalienated 1914 (Crown Land and Native Reserves)

0   km   400

0   miles   200

0.45 million kilogrammes in 1840 to 11.4 million kilogrammes 20 years later. Thereafter growth was less rapid in percentage terms but 80.3 million kilogrammes were exported in 1913. Despite fluctuations caused by wars and economic depression exports continued to rise in volume thereafter but at a much slower rate.

This was achieved by a dramatic transformation of the rural economy. Merino sheep were introduced in the 1790s but serious breeding only began in the 1820s. Thereafter the number of woolled sheep increased rapidly displacing the local, non-woolled, variety from the eastern part of the Cape Colony. Woolled sheep numbers increased from 2.3 million in 1849 to 8.4 million in 1865 as the wool export trade was organised and assumed a dominant position in the colonial export regime. In the interior, flocks in the Orange Free State increased from 1.0 million in 1856 to 5.1 million in 1880, but the pastoralists pushed woolled sheep into areas which were too drought prone and susceptible to disease. Overstocking ensued. In 1891 the Cape Colony enumerated 13.6 million woolled sheep, a peak not attained again for many years. Drought, rinderpest, locusts and finally the Anglo-Boer War wreaked havoc with the economy, but it was able to recover, in large measure as a result of the improved financial position of the colonies and the availability of agricultural credit. After 1912 funds from the Land Banks were available to provide low interest loans to effect improvements, but they were insufficient to halt the trend towards a steady European depopulation of the pastoral farming districts (Smit, 1973; South Africa, 1960).

Improvements took the form of fencing and the provision of water. In the early stages of settlement, farm improvements had been limited in the pastoral areas to stone pounds and shallow wells, prior to the introduction of cheap barbed wire and the drill and light metal windmill in the late nineteenth century. The result was the enclosure of grazing grounds, which was virtually completed by the 1920s, and the increase in the range of grazing as water from boreholes was provided in otherwise unusable backlands. The transformation allowed improved stock breeding, so that much of the twentieth-century increase in production was achieved through greater yields per animal rather than increased numbers. Enclosure also brought profound social changes as the squatters and nomadic graziers were displaced and constrained. Squatters who had been tolerated on the extensive farms, as they played a part as shepherds while maintaining their own flocks, had no place in the improved husbandry associated with pedigree breeding and rotational grazing. They were therefore displaced, adding to the rural-urban migration flow of the pre-Second World War period. Rising prosperity in the grazing areas was reflected in new farm houses replacing the basic structures such as the corbelled stone houses of the Karoo, or wattle and daub houses of the wetter regions, by more fashionable edifices such as the Malay-style Karoo house or the late Victorian and Edwardian decorated mansion. Particularly noticeable were the trees, usually Australian eucalyptus, which were introduced to the treeless regions and planted around the farm houses.

Other pastoral products were developed in the second half of the nineteenth century. The fashion demand in Europe for feathers resulted in the virtual extinction of the wild ostrich. However, the birds proved to be capable of domestication, with the result that the numbers on European farms grew rapidly from the 1860s onwards as fashion became more flamboyant. Breeders discovered that first grade feathers were produced by birds which were fed on lucerne rather than on the natural succulent bushes. Thus a marked concentration took place on developed irrigated pastures in the vicinity of Oudtshoom. Ostrich numbers increased to over 750,000 in 1913 when exports amounted to nearly 500 tons. However, overproduction, changing fashions, and the outbreak of the First World War resulted in the collapse of the industry, with only limited production continuing after the War. The irrigated pastures were converted to dairy and sheep fattening concerns after the collapse. Nevertheless, the considerable profits and the high short-term returns were such that Oudtshoorn developed a particularly ornate and grand Edwardian style of housing known as 'ostrich palaces' (Picton-Seymour, 1977).

Angora goats were introduced to South Africa in the 1850s in an attempt to provide a supply of fine mohair independent of Turkish control. Careful breeding and acclimatisation resulted in their prospering in the eastern part of the Cape Colony where 3 million were enumerated in 1891. The numbers rose slowly thereafter owing to the restricted range of suitable conditions and so only 4.4 million were counted by 1912. Drought, international competition and serious environmental degradation caused a rapid decline in numbers, which fell to stabilise at only a fifth of the previous level.

Immediately prior to the First World War the Germans introduced karakul sheep into South West Africa and they were similarly imported into the drier areas of the Cape of Good Hope. Karakul sheep were able to flourish in far more arid conditions than merino sheep or angora goats and so provided a commercial basis for farming in those areas, although stocking densities were extremely low, averaging only one animal per 5–8 ha in the south of South West Africa, when the flocks were fully established. Karakul pelt exports under the brandname, Swakara, became the most important aspect of pastoral production in South West Africa. By the early 1970s there were some 3.5 million karakul sheep in South West Africa and a further 1.9 million in the north-western Cape.

The developments in specialised small stock farming should not obscure the fact that non-woolled mutton sheep and farm goats remained in substantial numbers amongst the exotic breeds, but cattle made up a considerable proportion of the livestock population, particularly in the wetter eastern and northern parts of the subcontinent. Cattle and horses were an essential part of the rural economy until the 1940s when mechanical transport and farm machinery displaced draught oxen and transport animals. A commercial cattle industry came into being in the earliest days of the Cape settlement and the movement of cattle on a subcontinental scale was evident by the 1880s, when demands for meat in the mining camps were such as to attract stock from as far away as Barotseland, north of the Zambezi. This movement expanded as cattle ranching developed into a commercial enterprise in the twentieth century. Little of the trade was intercontinental, but the demands of the major urban and mining settlements were met by increasing African production and the commercialisation of European cattle farming.

Pastoral farming was pursued over a wider area by groups of Afrikaners who trekked beyond the colonial boundaries to reach Northern Rhodesia in the early years of the twentieth century where they were effectivel: blocked by the British South Africa Company (Fox, 1913). Other small groups moved further afield into Angola in the 1880s and established their traditional economy in the highland zone (Clarence-Smith, 1976). The Angolan group however remained comparatively isolated, as the religious motivation of their migration required. They depended to a high degree upon transport riding and hunting to earn a living. By the 1920s this way of life was undermined by the extermination of the game animals and the construction of the railway line, and they were repatriated to South West Africa in 1928. After the Anglo-Boer War, groups of Afrikaner families from the Transvaal left South Africa to escape British rule. They settled in various parts of the world including German and surprisingly British East Africa. In both cases they were initially encouraged and granted large pastoral farms (1,000–2,000 ha) (Iliffe, 1969). Most remained until the late 1950s developing economies parallel with those in South Africa, whence they returned upon decolonisation.

Commercial pastoral farming was undertaken to a limited extent by other groups of colonists and metropolitan based companies. Ranches were developed in such colonies as Kenya in the post-1920 period, but no purely pastoral settlements on the scale of those in southern Africa were established. European rural settlement in most other parts of the continent was geared to mixed or crop farming, from the beginning of colonisation. Southern Africa was unique in the evolution of European organised pastoralism and in the strength and permanence of its imprint upon the landscape. The later extension of crop growing was forced to take place within the framework created for and by the pastoralists.

The Agriculturalists

Agricultural settlers, as opposed to plantation managers, were characterised by a high degree of permanence upon the continent. Many enterprises were organised on a plantation basis using either locally recruited or imported labour, but the management was provided by a permanent European settler rather than a temporary paid employee. There were few farms on the continent which employed all White labour in the manner of mid-latitude settlements such as Australia, Canada or the northern and western United States. The presence of a substantial indigenous population was often stated to be an advantage for agricultural settlement as it could, through various coercive measures, be converted into an inexpensive labour force. The distinction between a plantation and a commercial farm is thus a fine and often arbitrary one, which must be defined largely according to the organisation and colony.

The main areas of agricultural settlement were the temperate northern and southern extremities of the continent, with outliers in the highlands of East Africa. Thus the two principal areas evolved in isolation from one another and along very different lines. The southern African region, colonised by the Dutch, and later the British, possessed limited agricultural potential before the advent of improved communications and techniques in the present century, although it was first established in the seventeenth century as an agricultural supply base. The North African region was initially developed in the nineteenth century by the French as an extension of the Mediterranean farming region of France. Colonisation was contemporary with the construction of the transport system, allowing exports to be effected and hence providing the commercial basis of the settlement virtually from its inception. Agricultural colonies established in the twentieth century clearly had fewer problems with crop development, as government agencies offered technical advice and financial assistance, while the communication system was built as a part of the scheme. Thus the Italian agricultural development of Libya, or the Portuguese colonisation of Angola and Moçambique, although all of short durations, were subject to close government supervision.

Agricultural development was limited in many aspects as colonists were conditioned by the established farming systems in operation in Europe. The majority of agricultural settlers, until the twentieth century, were therefore attracted to Africa by prospects of continuing a known system, rather than embarking upon a new one. Thus in the Cape of Good Hope, the European staple, wheat, was grown in often precarious circumstances and the mistakes made on one settlement were repeated in successive experiments as each group of settlers contended with an unknown environment. Only through a process of trial and error were problems overcome and new, but more suitable, crops planted. The interaction between the immigrants and the indigenous population was often beneficial to the farmer in transferring knowledge of suitable techniques and crops, while the produce of the indigenous population often tided the immigrants over the difficult initial period. Few agricultural settlements were established in areas devoid of a settled indigenous rural population, so that the dispossession of the African owners became an essential element of European agricultural development. The degree of seizure varied. In southern Africa approximately two-thirds of the potential crop land was confiscated, while in French North Africa approximately one-third was acquired by European settlers, although this was largely the best land (Isnard, 1939). The expropriation or purchase of land undermined the indigenous economy and so created a labouring class which had little option but to work for the settlers. It also induced African land hunger in all the colonies where substantial European rural settlement took place, a demand which was only partially satisfied in the course of decolonisation.

South Africa

European agriculture in southern Africa was initiated with the foundation of the Dutch station at the Cape of Good Hope. The first commander, Jan van Riebeeck, was given the task of provisioning the fleets of the Dutch East India Company on their voyages between Europe and the East Indies. A garden was laid out and maintained by the Company, but the cultivation of wheat proved to be problematical, thus the authorities decided upon a programme of farm settlement to make up the deficits (Elphick and Giliomee, 1979). In 1657 the first free settlers were given land in the vicinity of Cape Town in order to cultivate wheat. The farms were small, averaging only 10–15 ha in extent, as they were viewed in terms of contemporary crop farms in Europe, and the prospects of substantial numbers of rural settlers were entertained. However, conditions were unlike those in the Netherlands, as land was plentiful but labour and capital were not. Crop growing thus became extensive rather than intensive in character and the keeping of livestock soon complicated the picture. In contrast to the mixed farming economy in Europe, there was little integration of the two in the practice of, for example, manuring the crop land. The livestock were given considerable range, and crop land constituted only a small portion of the land in use.

Instead of settling hundreds of colonists near Cape Town, the land resources of the Cape Peninsula appeared exhausted by 1679 when only 40 farmers had been settled on 2,000 ha of farm land (Guelke, 1976). The remaining 125,000 ha in the Peninsula were not deemed capable of cultivation and were used for extensive grazing. Thus in 1679 the Stellenbosch area, separated from the Cape Peninsula by the sandy Cape Flats, was thrown open for settlement (Smuts, 1979). Larger blocks of land were offered on the basis of a freehold grant for all the land which could be cultivated within five years, so that the resultant farms ranged widely in size between 20 and 100 ha. The better watered lands along the rivers were selected and the interfluve lands were neglected except for grazing purposes. Again the settlement was soon filled and new areas were opened later in the century and early in the eighteenth century. By the time the Land of Waveren (Tulbagh) was made accessible to settlers, the distances to the Cape Town market were such that agriculture was becoming economically marginal. The later settlements, however, were more systematically organised with 50 ha-long lots pre-surveyed with short river or road frontages.

The extension of agricultural settlement virtually ceased in 1717 when immigration was halted. By that time some 19,000 ha had been granted within an area of 400,000 ha. The remaining government land acted as common grazing grounds for the settlers.

Approximately 400 grants had been made and some 1,400 Europeans lived in the rural areas outside Cape Town. The agricultural settlement was not significantly extended for 100 years and it evolved its own style of farming with its own architectural style (Fransen and Cook, 1980). Wheat proved to be relatively successful as an extensive crop in the winter rainfall environment, and steady progress was achieved until the early eighteenth century, after which the area sown remained fairly stable until the boom associated with the French Revolutionary and Napoleonic Wars. The commercial wheat area was then extended on to the extensive pastoral farms north of the settled area. Owing to the variability of the rainfall, yields fluctuated most markedly from year to year and decreased in the sandy lands where extensive and rotational cropping began. However, the farmers of the south-western Cape achieved most success with vine cultivation. The first experimental vineyards were established soon after the start of colonisation, but only in the 1680s did commercial production begin (Van Rensburg, 1954). Poor quality wines satisfied the passing ship trade but in the course of the eighteenth and early nineteenth centuries Constantia wines enjoyed a high reputation in Europe. Indeed until the rise in wool exports in the 1840s wine was the most important export from the Cape of Good Hope. The area of the vineyards was small and probably stood at no more than 3,000 ha in 1806, and this had doubled by the 1860s. Problems assailed the industry thereafter with the loss of preferential access to the British market in 1861 and the ravages of phylloxera in the 1880s. Expansion, however, continued with 14,000 ha under vineyards in 1911 and 73,000 ha 50 years later.

In the nineteenth century the British authorities undertook a number of agricultural settlement schemes in the Cape of Good Hope and Natal. The earliest and possibly most important was organised in 1820 in the Albany district of the eastern Cape. The British government was directly involved in the emigration of some 4,000 settlers to the frontier region of the Colony, where they were intended to act as a buffer between the Xhosa peoples to the east and the established colonial population on the west. The circumstances were therefore not auspicious and the terms offered, although apparently generous in the context of early-nineteenth-century England, were to prove inadequate in the face of the physical and economic environment of southern Africa (Nash, 1982). The colonists were organised into parties by proprietors who dealt directly with the government, and were granted 40 ha per family who accompanied them. The actual distribution of the land was a matter for each individual party. Some acted as co-operative groups and either distributed the land in 40 ha farms or selected small arable plots (4–10 ha) and retained the remainder as common grazing lands. However, a number of parties came under the firm control of their proprietors who retained most of the land for themselves in an attempt to recreate the medieval manor. The resultant settlement pattern was a mixture of villages and dispersed farmsteads, but as in the case of the Dutch settlement, the officials had been too ambitious and too optimistic in their assessment of the agricultural potential of the land at their disposal. The soil was poor, rust attacked the wheat, there was virtually no market for their products and the majority of the settlers had little or no experience of farming, being refugees from urban industrial depression. Such criticisms seem to have been almost universal for settlement schemes in southern Africa and were to be repeated at intervals for 100 years. Consequently there ensued the abandonment of holdings and a drift to the towns or to other parts of the world. Those who remained with the resulting larger farms turned to mixed farming with a major livestock emphasis, or indeed joined the ranks of the neighbouring pastoral farmers.

As a result of the setback in the Albany district, new agricultural settlement was abandoned for nearly 30 years until the late 1840s, when a series of schemes in Natal and British Kaffraria exploited the apparently more fertile soils of those colonies. Natal in particular, with its subtropical climate and coastal forest lands, appeared in emigration literature in glowing terms. A colonisation promotor, Joseph Byrne, sponsored a major scheme, acquiring large tracts of land on which he proposed to settle families on plots of 8 ha per person. As children counted as 'halves', a family of a man, his wife and a child would be entitled to 20 ha. Some 5,000 settlers migrated to Natal under the Byrne scheme and other smaller enterprises. In general they were based on village settlements surrounded by the farm plots and with small common grazing areas. Some 40,000 ha was acquired for the Byrne scheme and half of this area was divided into some 1,000 rural plots. However, nearly half the plots were either rejected by settlers or abandoned. In the more remote settlements abandonment was particularly serious with rejection rates as high as 90 per cent. As a result the villages failed to develop as the remaining settlers moved from their village plot on to their farm.

Thus villages such as New Glasgow, York and Byrne remained as open sites or with only the centralised functions such as churches, schools and post offices and attendant housing, paralleling the experience of the Albany settlement.

Possibly the most successful European agricultural settlement in South Africa was established in British Kaffraria in 1856 by the British-German Legion, which had been raised to serve in the Crimean War. After the war it was decided to locate the soldiers on the eastern Cape frontier as a defence force. They were settled in villages, many of which were named after German towns such as Berlin, Hanover and Frankfort. Arable plots of 0.4 ha were offered to the settlers and a further 1.6 ha were added when the original area proved to be inadequate. Extensive commonages were also laid out, recognising the importance of livestock in the colonial society. German officers and free settlers were located on larger blocks (10–12 ha) adjacent to the villages. The settlers were poor and owing to their low expectations, proved to be more stable than the British colonists.

Only restricted attempts to settle immigrants were undertaken thereafter with small-scale British and Scandinavian immigration into Natal in the 1880s and the sporadic settlement of Germans and British in the eastern Cape. These programmes, however, were linked to the concept of closer-settlement as a whole and reflected changing local attitudes to agricultural colonies as the free land pastoral frontier showed signs of exhaustion. In the twentieth century European farming immigrants were attracted by specific opportunities offered for such projects as sugar farming in Zululand or tobacco farming in Southern Rhodesia. Much of the experimental work had already been undertaken in these territories by government agencies such as the British South Africa Company's Central Farms, the agricultural colleges and experimental stations, in order to breed suitable strains of seeds and provide the basic infrastructure for the farmer. In this manner rapid increase in arable production took place as settler cash crops assumed greater importance throughout British South and Central Africa.

After the mid-1870s a number of southern African governments undertook agricultural closer-settlement projects. They were related to a growing awareness of the scarcity of land on the traditional pastoral frontier and hence attempted to settle colonists at increased densities in selected areas. The official projects took two basic forms, irrigation and dryland farms. Although a number of schemes were established on Crown Land on the edge of the contemporary frontier, the majority of the irrigation projects were located on lands acquired specifically for the purpose by the government. Occasionally provision was made for immigrants but in general the schemes were open to Europeans already in South Africa, which indeed supplied most of the colonists.

The irrigation settlements were initiated with the completion of the Van Wyks Vlei scheme in the central Karoo of the Cape Colony in 1880 (Cape of Good Hope, 1892). A number of pastoral farms were acquired by the government and a dam constructed to supply water for the irrigation of an extensive tract of flat land. A village was laid out with settlers receiving a town and garden plot and an 8 ha irrigation plot as well as access to an extensive commonage. Although over 300 irrigation plots were laid out, fewer than 100 settlers were located on the scheme. By the early 1890s the commonage had become so extensive (170,000 ha) that the agriculturalists neglected their irrigation lands to pursue livestock raising. Government control was therefore of the utmost necessity and the Bailiff pursued a frustrating campaign to keep the scheme and its settlers in order. Crops, such as wheat and lucerne, were grown on the irrigation plots and were in demand by the neighbouring pastoral farmers, who increasingly acquired the plots and ran them as adjuncts to their own farms. Other government projects were scarcely more successful and 'closer settlement' through irrigation was largely left to private initiative in the Cape Colony, except for church welfare projects designed to ease rising rural poverty among the settlers (Els, 1968).

In Natal less emphasis was placed on irrigation as it was assumed that settlement could be itensified by a more judicial use of the available water resources (Christopher, 1970). Thus the dryland approach was general, where the government purchased large pastoral farms and divided them into smaller units. The early schemes in the 1880s assumed a high degree of subdivision so that as many as 40 smaller farms were carved out of one 2,500 ha pastoral farm. The first scheme at Willow Fountains offered farms of an average of 34 ha with access to a commonage, for the anticipated 40 families. However, the usual problems of unsuitable land divided into small uneconomic sizes, lack of farming experience, poor planning and inadequate capital, arose. Furthermore, the government suffered a substantial financial loss on the entire transaction owing to the high cost of the land and the expense of laying out the scheme. It therefore pursued a policy of developing projects on Crown Lands whenever possible until the end of the century, in an effort to reduce these losses. Only the two major irrigation schemes at Weenen and Winterton deviated from this model, involving as they did capital expenditures not only on land acquisition and survey, but also dam and canal construction similar to those in the Cape Colony. However, the authorities provided greater assistance through agricultural extension and most important, the construction of railway spurs to serve the two irrigation schemes, in order to ensure their success.

Between 1908 and the amalgamation of the various South African Lands Departments in 1912, Natal embarked upon a major programme to encourage closer settlement (South Africa, 1913). Nine schemes covering 50,000 ha were divided into some 173 dryland farms. Closer settlement on the various projects was expressed in farms of average sizes ranging from 145 to 600 ha and they were clearly of a different nature from those envisaged in the previous century. Improved techniques of stock management, cultivation, and marketing had rendered the 2,500 ha pastoral farm obsolete in the better watered areas of the subcontinent capable of extensive cultivation. The intensive cropping regimes of Europe which had been introduced in the course of the nineteenth century had failed, but new styles based on extensive use of the land succeeded to make the closer-settlement movement viable. The villages and commonages which had been essential elements of most earlier schemes were abandoned and all the land was parcelled out to the incoming settlers, who were almost entirely of South African origin. This trend was continued in the various schemes undertaken in the twentieth century in the Orange Free State, Transvaal, and Southern Rhodesia.

The demise of the village and the commonage was of as vital a concern to the settler as to landscape development. The village as the basic unit of rural settlement had been a constant feature of closer-settlement schemes until the end of the nineteenth century. It had been inherited with European traditions which were often a source of inspiration in mid-latitude colonisation as an attempt was made to recreate the better features of rural Europe. Village settlement had an advantage over dispersion in respect of defence, although this was less of a factor in its longevity in South Africa than in Algeria. The non-farming community housed in the village provided the basic social and commercial services, but as a result of the often high degree of self-sufficiency on many pioneer farms and the often low population densities, little specialisation was possible. Thus villages often lacked service functions to any degree until the nineteenth century. Further the plots provided on settlement schemes were large and usually consolidated into one parcel. Thus the farmer found it more convenient to live on his farm and abandon his plot in the village. Only those villages which were advantageously situated and could develop their service functions, more especially the governmental functions, survived.

The commonage was usually associated with village settlement, although the two did not necessarily go hand in hand. The idea behind the commonage was the provision of grazing lands on a scale which would allow the villagers to keep sufficient livestock for their agricultural and domestic needs. The amount of land needed for a family was thus calculated as sufficient arable land for cultivation (the rural farm) and access to extensive grazing lands (the commonage). Medium-sized farms had the problem of being too extensive to be cultivated, yet inadequate for pasturage. The relative advantages of commonages over larger farms was subject to debate, but by the end of the nineteenth century, the commonage had largely been displaced as an element in settlement planning. However, those already in existence remained and subdivision amongst the remaining rights-holders took place, sometimes as late as the 1960s.

The final stage of government intervention in closer agricultural settlement in South Africa was the programme of major irrigation schemes undertaken in the period 1918–50. In that time some 150,000 ha were irrigated on a series of projects situated mainly in the Transvaal and northern Cape. The largest was the Vaal-Hartz scheme inaugurated in 1934, which brought some 40,000 ha under irrigation. These were large capital works which the government undertook in part to alleviate the problem of the poor White population which had been displaced from the land, particularly during the depression of the 1930s. Smaller poor White schemes had been commenced by the Dutch Reformed Church in the 1890s, but only the state had the resources necessary to pursue a policy on the scale required (Rossouw, 1951). Industrialisation in the course of the Second World War essentially removed the problem of poor unemployed Whites and hence few rural schemes were promoted after 1945. In layout the schemes followed on from colonial thinking, but because of their size and often remote situation, villages and towns were planned for service functions, although the colonists themselves lived on their farms from the start. Farms were designed to be placed entirely under irrigation without livestock. The sizes planned in the early schemes averaged only 10 ha but rose to over 20 ha by the 1950s. The two largest schemes, the Hartebeespoort and Vaal-Hartz, were planned for over 1,000 settler families apiece and constituted major changes in the landscape and economy in regions previously devoted to extensive stock raising.

The main process of agricultural development in the European areas of South Africa came through the gradual conversion in the twentieth century of some of the pastoral farms to crop cultivation. The transformation was lengthy as inevitably there was strong resistance to change from some of the more traditionally minded White farmers. Little government intervention was apparent, although the introduction of a wide range of technical advice and the establishment of Land Banks and agricultural colleges eased the difficult transition from herder to cultivator. The arable area of the European owned farms of South Africa increased from 2.4 million hectares in 1911 to 9.6 million hectares in 1960. Extensive areas were ploughed in the southern Transvaal and northern Orange Free State to create the Maize Triangle. Wheat zones in the western Cape and the sugar belt of Natal were smaller but equally distinctive developments. Even in the most intensively cultivated districts little more than half the farm areas were placed under crops by 1960 as livestock were not entirely displaced.

Farm subdivision reflecting the tradition of divided inheritance among the Cape-Dutch population was general and the large pastoral farms were divided and redivided once the free land frontier was exhausted (South Africa, 1960; Transvaal, 1908). Subdivision took the form of either physical division producing small and often uneconomic farms, or the expansion of the family dwellings to link several branches of the family living on the original grant. Inevitably this involved the intensification of land use to accommodate the increased population density, and gave a spur to commercial crop farming when the opportunities arose. Farm subdivision assumed serious proportions as in the Transvaal by 1900 over 10 per cent of privately-owned farms were held by six or more persons, and undivided fractions worth under 1 ha were inherited (Transvaal, 1900). In terms of physical division, the demand for access to scarce water resources resulted in farms of under 100 ha in area but with lengths of 10 km or more. The twin spurs of commercial opportunity and farm subdivision resulted in adaptation to new methods as each generation inherited smaller units. Irrigation potential was utilised with the construction of water furrows and extensive dryland cultivation was adopted on other portions of farms. This may be illustrated by the farm Middenspruit in the Orange Free State which at the time of its physical subdivision in 1930 had changed little in land use since the survey of 1862 (Figure 6.3). However, in the following 24 years a major transformation took place as the dryland potential was exploited and increased settlement occurred. It may be noted that extensive areas remained under pasture and that monocultural areas did not emerge. The increased degree of com-mercialisation was particularly evident after 1945, as dryland cultivation of maize was extended in areas such as the western Transvaal which were basically unsuited to sustained crop production.

North Africa

The European agricultural settlement of North Africa was of a very different nature from that in the South. The French conquest of Algeria was accommpanied by a programme of officially planned rural settlement, mostly within 100 km of the Mediterranean coast-line, which in turn was only 800 km from the port of Marseilles. The concept of North Africa as a 'New France', an extension of the French state across the Mediterranean, dominated official thinking (Isnard, 1954; Roberts, 1929). However, there were a number of major problems which beset colonial development in Algeria. One of the most serious and persistent was the shortage of agricultural land upon which to settle the colonists. The French government inherited little suitable land from the previous administration of the Bey, and what it did obtain was legally difficult to possess and even to identify from the extant deeds. Thus direct sequestration from particular groups and seizure of religious lands (habous) were vir-tually the only means initially available for acquiring sufficient lands for European settlement. In addition good arable land was limited. Only 5.9–6.8 million hectares were regarded as suitable for cultiva-tion and of this only 600,000 ha were considered first-class arable lands. Colonial estimates optimistically included extensive drylands and reached a total of 10 million hectares, but these lands were not exploited (Smith, 1978). The other major and finally most serious problem, as in southern Africa, was the presence of a disaffected indigenous population which was hostile to French rule and settle-ment, and which always greatly outnumbered the French colonists.

Colonisation until the early twentieth century was dominated by

Figure 6.3: The Farm Middenspruit, Orange Free State, 1862-1954

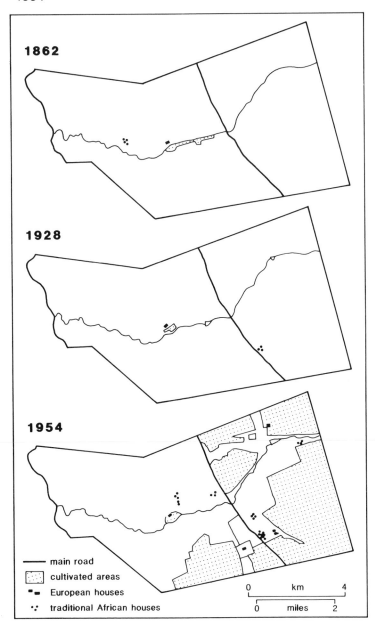

1862

1928

1954

—— main road

cultivated areas

■■ European houses

•:• traditional African houses

0   km   4

0   miles   2

three basic ideas (De Peyerimhoff, 1906). The first was that land should be granted to settlers, rather than sold, and that the Government could therefore largely control the course of settlement. Secondly official villages were to form the basis of colonisation rather than individual efforts on dispersed farmsteads. Thirdly small-scale farming enterprise was needed, not capitalistic estate farming. Although such guidelines might suggest the re-creation of French society on the African continent, it must be remembered that, as in southern Africa, most of the rural working population was indigenous and that even the small-scale European farming operation usually relied for its labour upon the pool of Moslem workers. They in turn, having been dispossessed of their lands and subjected to the imposition of taxation had little option but to become labourers for the European settlers, tending their previous family lands as employees.

The imprint of the French official hand in Algeria was remarkable when the majority of European settlement frontiers is considered. De Peyerimhoff (1906) suggested that the French colonist, although very enduring and perservering had little spontaneity or innovative ability, thus relying upon the state for constant direction. Furthermore the colonial enterprise was starved of settlers as the level of French emigration was far lower than in other European countries. Thus whereas in the 1870s emigration ran at 4–5 per cent per annum in most European nations, the French figure was only 0.2 per cent. In addition even when emigrants had been induced to come to Algeria, many of the rural settlers did not stay on their farms. In common with most nineteenth-century European overseas settlements, a large number of non-agricultural people were placed on the land and soon migrated to the towns. A survey of the 1183 families from Alsace-Lorraine settled in Algeria after the Franco-Prussian War, undertaken in 1899, found that only 387 were still residing on their plots, 519 were living elsewhere in Algeria, and 277 had left the territory altogether (De Peyerimhoff, 1906). The cost of their settlement had been some 4.8 million francs. The boosts to colonisation came from government actions in making settlement in Algeria either more or less attractive, largely through expenditure on basic infrastructure and subsidies. The initial phase of experimentation in the 1830s was superseded by policies of military settlement in the 1840s and peasant colonisation in the 1850s. Only in the 1860s did Napoleon III briefly embark upon a free capitalist system akin to the British systematic colonisation programme. Its collapse in 1870 resulted in a return to small-scale state settlement which persisted throughout the remainder of the French period.

The village was the basic element of the organisation of French settlement after the experiments of the 1830s. The task of colonisation was described by Marshal Bugeaud in military terms:

'The climate, the nature of the soil, the scarcity of water, the warlike and plundering character of the natives are enormous obstacles. In order to colonise, it must be stated, a warrior population accustomed to work in the fields, organised almost as the Arabs, to cultivate and defend the land is needed'. (Franc, 1928, p. 237).

The military settlements of the 1840s were generally small with village lands covering only 400–1,000 ha. Each settler received a plot for a house and garden in the village and a cultivation lot of not more than 12 ha. The nucleated villages were viewed as essential owing to the continuing hostility of the indigenous population, indeed the early villages were walled and the gates were closed at night. The European population of the village of Boufarik, already established in 1837, had suffered severely between 1837 and 1841 with 36 colonists killed, 37 carried off by the Arabs and 227 succumbing to fever and dysentry. Between 1841 and 1845 Boufarik was reorganised according to military principles. Water furrows for the village were dug, some 300 houses built and a school, church and other public buildings erected. Furthermore 150,000 trees were planted changing the appearance of the village and removing the bare frontier appearance of the site. On the rural lands, the main swamp areas were drained to the benefit not only of agriculture but public health and by 1845 some 600 ha of the 1,500 ha of the village lands were exploited (Figure 6.4). A measure of success may be taken from the rise in the European population in the same period from 430 to 1,928 persons. The same rapid transformation took place in other villages re-established or founded during the period of Marshal Bugeaud's command, and these in turn served as models for the foundation and organisation of subsequent villages.

The first major period of village foundation between 1840 and 1860 resulted in an increase in the rural European population from 30,000 to 100,000. As a result of neglect and conflicting policies this total had fallen to 90,000 by 1871. There followed a number of

Figure 6.4: Boufarik, Algeria, 1844-1930

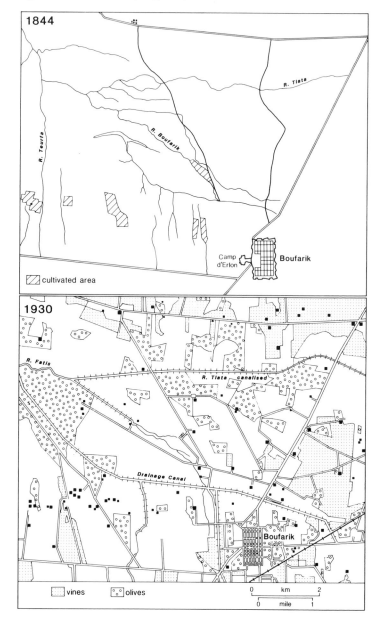

experiments, culminating in the official colonisation programme of the period 1878–1904 which was modelled upon the American Homestead Act of 1862. The government offered a free grant to a portion of land after a five-year preliminary testing period during which certain basic improvements had to be undertaken as a means of testing the determination of the settler to stay on his land. Nevertheless, in marked contrast to the American prototype, the village was retained as the basic element of organisation and settlement. In 1881 the ambitious Project of Fifty Millions was launched to spend 50 million frs. (£2 million) on 150 new villages. However, the pace of colonisation had slowed. Whereas some 264 villages had been established or enlarged in the 1870s only 107 were initiated in the 1880s while the number fell to a mere 46 in the following decade. The government villages founded in this period covered an area of 700,000 ha, which in addition to the townlands were divided into some 14,000 rural lots. The average area of the village was approximately 2,000 ha and the average farm size was approximately 50 ha, both substantially larger than those laid out during the military colonisation of the 1840s, and reflecting a major reappraisal of both land quality and the methods of crop production. Thus by 1900 there were 700 colonisation villages housing some 189,000 Europeans on 2,000,000 ha of land, mainly situated on the plains of northern Algeria. By the beginning of the twentieth century the government lacked further land for European settlement and expansion took place through the private purchase of Moslem lands.

The rural economy was based at first largely on commercial cereal growing. The substantial local markets of the towns and the army stimulated production, but few opportunities for export were available. Protectionism in France after 1885 did little to encourage large-scale export production in competition with the metropolis. The cereal area, mainly under wheat, totalled 900,000 ha by 1914 and it remained the most significant element in the land use of European farms throughout the colonial period. However, the major commercial development was the introduction of vines, which were to provide the majority of Algerian colonists with a livelihood (Isnard, 1949; Pechoux, 1975). The early vineyards had been small (e.g. 11,000 ha in 1874) and geared to production for local consumption. However, the spread of phylloxera in France resulted in a decline in wine production in the metropolis and provided the opportunity for Algerian farmers. Credit was freely available as banks, such as the Banque d'Algérie, founded in 1879, were able to provide agricultural funds for improvements, planting and mechanisation. Thus the vineyards had increased to 122,000 ha by 1895 when phylloxera reached Algeria. The setback was temporary for between 1901 and 1913 the amount of credit invested in the industry increased fivefold as mechanisation, modernisation and replanting with Californian phylloxera-free vines took place. The area cultivated continued to expand, covering 180,000 ha in 1928 and 400,000 ha in 1939. Overproduction occurred in the mid-1930s with the result that attempts were made to reduce the area in the 1940s.

The post-1920 period was one of consolidation and contraction. The peak of 239,000 rural European population was enumerated in 1926 and this fell to 196,000 by 1954. Consolidation of properties was such that in 1930 some 26,000 farms covered 2,300,000 ha, but by 1950 the number had shrunk to 22,000 on an enlarged area of 2,700,000 ha. Government programmes to reverse this trend had comparatively little success as there were few estates in Algeria large enough for a closer-settlement scheme to prosper (Bernard, 1932). In the confusion of the 1954–62 period the number of farms and European farmers shrank rapidly, although the larger enterprises were able to overcome most difficulties through utilisation of abandoned farms and the employment of cheap displaced labour (Ageron, 1979).

European colonisation in Tunisia commenced before the French occupation in 1881 and proceeded along markedly different lines from those in Algeria (Poncet, 1962). Organisation was based on large-scale capitalistic plantation enterprises, rather than the small-scale state-controlled settlement schemes. The first French colonisers were not agriculturalists but speculators, investors and planters who formed an aristocracy of usually absentee proprietors of large concessions. At the same time poor European agriculturalists migrated from Italy and Malta, and by 1881 constituted the majority of the European population. Thus in 1892 some 94 per cent of European owned land was held in estates exceeding 4,000 ha. The largest estates such as that at Enfida (96,000 ha) were organised with labour forces of 1,000–12,000, mostly Moslem. European colonists preferred to buy established agricultural land rather than create new farms from wasteland. Thus state control of land distribution was circumvented, particularly after the introduction of laws allowing for the individualisation of Moslem property in 1885. As a result costs were high. In addition to the price of land, usually

50-500 frs. (£2-£20) per hectare, the cost of establishing a vineyard of 100 ha was approximately 300,000 frs. (£12,000), and a modern cereal farm of 2,000 ha some 120,000 frs. (£4,800). Such investment required credit, a good market and sustained protection. All three were available within the orbit of the French Empire (Tunisia, 1914b).

Owing to the style of exploitation, the European rural population grew relatively slowly with only 38,575 enumerated in 1911, and only a small increment thereafter. However, the European owned area increased steadily to reach 0.9 million hectares in 1914. This area was divided amongst 5,000 properties, a noticeable difference from the situation 22 years beforehand. The change had been brought about through the subdivision of many of the large estates as speculators sought their profits (Société des Fermes Françaises de Tunisie, 1925). The Société Franco-Africaine, for example, was able to sell its rural land holdings at a threefold increase in value. In the vicinity of Tunis subdivided lands were often even more profitable to the early investors. The estates were predominantly broken up into farms of 100-500 ha apiece. The opportunities for the private purchase of land from Tunisians were soon exhausted and the government commenced an official colonisation scheme on lines akin to those in Algeria, but little came of it. The perceived problem of Italian immigration was such that a major effort was made to attract French agricultural settlers, but the administration lacked the means to actively intervene in the land market. European labour was provided by Italians who early in the century constituted three-quarters of the European population, but as tenants and employees, and only rarely as owners. Distinctions became blurred as a result of vigorous French programmes aimed at integration.

The European rural economy was supported largely by the export of olive oil. Extensive olive groves were planted by the colonists. Some 4 million trees were growing in Tunisia in 1881 but by 1955 over 26 million had been planted. The main olive estate areas were in the south at Sfax and Sousse. Yields were noticeably higher than those in the traditional production areas in Europe, reflecting the commercial and capital intensive basis of the plantations. Olive oil was the most valuable of Tunisian exports throughout the colonial period. Wine constituted the second export commodity, until the decline in prices in the 1930s. Vineyards though covered only 41,000 ha at their peak in 1933-4, having covered a

mere 15,000 ha in 1911. However, the subsequent decline in production was reflected in a reduction in vineyard areas to 27,000 ha
by 1948. The third crop, wheat, only assumed major importance on
European farms in the late 1920s. The area of the crop cultivated
increased dramatically from 49,000 ha in 1914 to 269,000 ha in the
early 1950s. However, in terms of acreage, if not production, the
Moslem sector of the agricultural economy remained more extensive, cultivating five to six times the area of European farms; and
because of the dual nature of the Protectorate administration, was
not subjected to the same degree of impoverishment as in Algeria.

The third French possession in North Africa, Morocco, was in a
different position as the French inherited the country and the
Protectorate was less integrated into the colonial machinery than
Tunisia. Land for European settlement therefore had to be
obtained by purchase from Moroccans. In 1916 the Comité de
Colonisation was established and proceeded to embark upon a
systematic programme of colonisation (Scham, 1970). A quarter of
the land was offered to recent immigrants, a quarter to soldiers, and
the remainder to those who had lived in Morocco for at least two
years, and were therefore conversant with farming conditions. No
free grants were available and land was sold at valuation except in
the case of large lots, over 400 ha, which were auctioned. Medium
sized plots of 200–400 ha proved to be most popular with prospective colonists. Although farms were grouped into rural settlements,
the village approach of Algerian colonisation was not enforced, as
the farms were substantially larger and colonists preferred to live on
their own lands. The first Resident-General, Marshal Lyautey
(1912–22) was also able to avoid the Tunisian example of large
estates through the direct rejection of large-scale concessions. Thus
by 1935 the 271,000 ha distributed by the government had been
divided into 1,735 farms. However, a further 569,000 ha had been
privately purchased and was generally held in smaller units. Thus in
1953 the average size of a European farm in the Protectorate was
only 50 ha. European settlement was dispersed throughout the
northern and central plains of Morocco, and few areas were exclusively in European hands. The French rural settlement of the
country was remarkable for the speed with which it was accomplished in the 20 years between the two World Wars; it is also a rare
example of colonial initiative in a period of neglected Empires.

The Italians viewed Libya as an extension of Italy on the African
continent (Segrè, 1974). Paradoxically as the French authorities

worried about the number of Italians migrating to Tunisia and Algeria, so the Italian government viewed the loss to their home country with concern. Italian perceptions of Tripolitania 'depended more upon analogies with southern Italy (including Sicily), Tunisia and the military colonization of Roman Libya than upon objective assessments of the land in northern Tripolitania' (Fowler, 1972, p. 628). The first official enquiry in 1913 reported that there was ample space for Italian colonisation as well as for the expansion of indigenous agriculture in the steppe lands. Little land belonged to the state (14,000 ha) and with an assessment that settlement was linked to economic holdings of 200–300 ha apiece, little progress appeared possible. However, pressure was exerted on Moslem holdings which were considered excessive in size and which would have to be reduced in order to provide land for Italian settlers. The First World War intervened and it was only in 1922 with the conquest of northern Tripolitania that the first tentative colonisation measures were introduced. A public domain was established and within ten years 200,000 ha had been nationalised in Tripolitania and a further 140,000 ha throughout Libya by 1940. This was achieved through the nationalisation of land which had not been in 'rational' cultivation for at least three years, and through confiscation of land belonging to those who resisted the Italian occupation. The former process was aided by the shifting nature of cultivation in the dry areas, making the recognition of titles contentious. The zones remaining in Libyan lands were thus restricted and in places limited to areas of shifting cereal cultivation.

European colonisation began first in Tripolitania and was only launched in Cyrenaica in the 1930s, once the military situation had been stabilised. The area of land concessions amounted to only 10,000 ha in 1922 but by 1931 had reached 120,000 ha. By 1940 at the outbreak of the Second World War some 375,000 ha had been obtained by Italian colonists and 3,900 families had been settled on the land (Istituto Agricolo Coloniale Italiano, 1945). Colonisation in the 1920s had been based on private estates but these gave way to colonisation companies intent upon peasant settlement, in line with Benito Mussolini's agrarian philosophy. As a result the smaller peasant farms were situated further from Tripoli and Benghazi than the earlier estates and greater reliance was placed upon irrigation from boreholes (Istituto Agricolo Coloniale Italiano, 1940) (Figure 6.5). The restricted areas available for settlement necessitated strict control and official agencies planned and effected many basic

Figure 6.5: Italian Settlement Schemes in Tripolitania

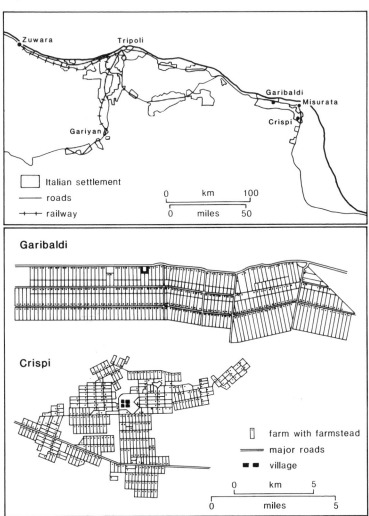

improvements before the colonists arrived on their land. As in southern Tunisia, olives became the most important crop on European farms in Tripolitania, with half the cultivated area under olive trees by 1940. Vines and cereals occupied most of the remainder. In large measure Italian settlement in Libya was still in its infancy when it was halted at the outbreak of the Second World War (Istituto Agricolo Coloniale Italiano, 1947). Wartime plans for its expansion were negated by Italy's defeat and loss of the colony.

Central and East Africa

Agricultural settlement in inter-tropical Africa was even more problematical than at the two extremities. The disease barrier deterred any concept of tropical colonisation until the 1880s. Even then few areas were deemed suitable for European settlement both for health and political reasons. Attention was directed towards the belts of highlands running from Ethiopia through East Africa to the Transvaal. At lower altitudes only the Portuguese, at the close of the colonial period, attempted anything more than plantation agriculture.

The first significant colonisation attempt was undertaken in Eritrea at the northern limit of the chain of highlands (Pankhurst, 1964). In 1885 Massawa was occupied by Italy following its abandonment by Egypt. By 1889 the Italians had conquered parts of the interior plateau around Asmara, which appeared to be suitable for European habitation. In addition to the temperate environment the plateau also seemed to present the advantage that it was virtually unoccupied and therefore offered large tracts for European settlement. These assessments were erroneous as although protracted military campaigns and human and stock diseases had afflicted the area before the Italian conquest, abandonment was only temporary, so that little land was available for state colonisation. Settlement began in 1893 with the official offer of 20–25 ha per family, but many immigrants were unsuitable and there was a lack of markets and of basic agricultural and technical assistance. Although some 5.8 million Italians emigrated between 1890 and 1905 only 3,949 lived in Eritrea at the latter date. By 1913 only 61 colonists remained on their land, cultivating a mere 1,146 ha. It was only in the 1930s that renewed attempts were made to introduce limited numbers of agricultural settlers. Schemes to introduce several thousand Italian settler families to Ethiopia were drawn up between 1936 and 1940, but lack of Crown Land, finance and the outbreak of the Second World War prevented their implementation (Sbacchi, 1977).

The major highland agricultural colonisation zones were those of East Africa and the Rhodesias. The most significant, Southern Rhodesia, was at first an extension of the South African settlement area. The initial settlers were largely pastoral, but following an official investigation by the British South Africa Company directors into the state of the territory's economy, agricultural settlement was vigorously pursued after 1907. The Company established a series of Central Farms where immigrants could receive agricultural training and practical farming experience, and where experimentation in crop and animal breeding could be conducted (Weinmann, 1972). In 1912 the Land Bank was established to provide subsidised credit and in 1920 the Settlers Board was formed to encourage rural settlement (Hodder-Williams, 1981). Various control boards and marketing schemes were introduced in the inter-war period to aid European farmers and eliminate African competition. The soldier settler scheme after the First World War was limited as only 46 farms covering 50,000 ha were granted. Despite setbacks such as this, progress was made, although the numbers engaged in agriculture and the crop land areas were small. Only 772 farmers had been enumerated in 1907 but this had risen to 2,355 by 1921 when 100,000 ha were cultivated. Agricultural progress continued steadily until the Second World War when 3,699 farms were recorded in 1944, and of the 8.6 million hectares of European farmland enumerated, 220,000 ha were cultivated. In the same year the Land Settlement Act was passed in an attempt to create a co-ordinated settlement procedure to place ex-servicemen, and later, civilians upon the land. By 1950 over 700 had joined the soldier settlement scheme, although only 400 eventually took up farming on a permanent basis. More success was achieved with civilian schemes and through the encouragement of the subdivision of extensive estates (Dunlop, 1971). The Land Settlement Board considered that 150 ha of arable land was required for an economic unit in the better watered parts of the country. Owing to the varied nature of the terrain, farm sizes of 600–1,000 ha were required to include sufficient arable land. As government land became scarcer, so the area suggested as necessary for economic viability was reduced. Partially as a result of the active settlement programme, by 1961 there were 6,437 farms in the country covering 13.4 million hectares, of which 400,000 ha were cultivated.

Arable agriculture in Southern Rhodesia was concentrated in the eastern half of the country, but over half the farms were directed primarily towards crop growing, which by 1960 accounted for four-fifths of production value. Cultivation had developed slowly as the initial European settlers had been able to purchase from neighbouring African farmers and their own tenants and workers. Thus in 1900 only 1,720 ha was recorded under maize on European farms.

However, maize, the main food staple, developed as a European commercial crop. By 1914 some 6,500 ha had been planted on European farms and this area continued to be expanded reaching 95,000 ha in 1945 and 165,000 ha in 1961. Production experienced considerable fluctuation according to the drought cycles, although through selective seed breeding yields, increased in better years. Thus average yields of 0.5 tons per hectare recorded in the 1910s had been doubled by the 1960s.

It was, however, in specialised crop growing that agricultural enterprise in Southern Rhodesia, and to a limited extent Northern Rhodesia and Nyasaland, was able to support European immigrants. Tobacco proved to be the mainstay of the European farming community which derived half its income from this single source in the 20 years between the Second World War and the Unilaterial Declaration of Independence. Experimentation began at the turn of the century. Both Virginia and Turkish tobaccos were planted, to the extent of 2,000 ha by 1914. After the setback caused by the First World War a steady increase occurred until the Second World War. Some 25,000 ha was planted in 1945. There followed the rapid expansion in cultivation and production for the area under tobacco to total 80,000 ha by 1960. During the same period the number of European growers increased from 800 to 2,700. In view of its importance in the colonial economy it is remarkable that tobacco was essentially a 'small growers'' crop, with comparatively small areas devoted to it. The impetus to the tobacco industry came from the increased British demand for the Rhodesian product. Before the Second World War, the United States accounted for 70 per cent of British manufacturing demand. However, as a result of the dollar shortage after 1945, tobacco cultivation within the British Empire was expanded. Thus in 1947 an agreement was reached on preferential access to the British market. The dependence upon one market was illustrated by the strains and cutback in the tobacco area following the imposition of economic sanctions in 1966. The diversification of European agricultural enterprises in the late 1960s and early 1970s followed. New crops such as cotton, sunflowers and groundnuts replaced tobacco and resulted in the expansion of the cultivated area until the process was checked by the turmoil of the war of independence in the late 1970s.

The 'White Highlands' of Kenya were developed on a similar basis to Southern Rhodesia. In 1902 the British East Africa government embarked upon a land settlement programme (Sorrenson,

1968). In part this was a response to pressure from South African interests and others such as Lord Delamere who considered the highlands to possess excellent agricultural potential. In addition the colonial administration was faced with the prospect of mounting losses on the Uganda Railway, which passed through undeveloped and therefore non-traffic generating lands. Official and settler interests coincided in promoting European agricultural settlement in lands which were apparently underpopulated as a result of war and disease (Wolff, 1974). Alienation of land was remarkably rapid and unsystematic with 2.0 million hectares granted to Europeans by 1914. The lands were viewed in terms of arable farming and various experiments with crops such as coffee, tea, sugar and pyrethrum were undertaken, as well as with the staples, wheat and maize (Huxley, 1935). Coffee proved to be the most successful with 41,000 ha planted by 1936. However, in response to international market-ing problems this had declined to 30,000 ha by 1961, out of a total cropped area of 486,000 ha. Nevertheless at the later date coffee contributed over one-fifth of all European farm income. The high profitability of coffee enabled many small European cultivators to make a living. In 1961 one-third of all European holdings were under 200 ha. Significantly the area occupied by European farmers in the latter date amounted to only 3,100,000 ha as a result of restrictions placed upon the alienation of African owned land in the 1920s and 1930s (Great Britain, 1934; Morgan, 1963). In common with other tropical colonies Kenya developed plantations, mainly in the coastal zone, and adjacent to Lake Victoria. In organisational terms they would be difficult to assign to farm or plantation, as often the planter was also a settler. However, tea and sisal tended to be large scale plantation crops. The European agricultural settlement of German East Africa was still in its infancy in 1914 and the British mandatory power did little to foster it after the First World War.

The Belgians encouraged settlers to emigrate to the Congo to grow foodstuffs to supply the Katangan copper mines in 1910, while the eastern highlands were also considered suitable for European settlement after the First World War. However, European farms did not form a consolidated block as in Kenya, as they were interspersed with African and vacant lands. The numbers involved (almost 2,000 by 1959) were small but through concentration upon high value, low bulk crops, particularly coffee, but also tea, pyrethrum, medicine and perfume plants, and tobacco, they were able to contribute substantially to the colonial economy from comparatively small units. In layout and concept Belgian colonisation was more akin to that of Kenya, than southern Africa, requiring as it did substantial inputs of capital and organisation for the production of an export crop (Jewsiewichi, 1979).

The last major programme of European agricultural settlement in Africa was promoted by the Portuguese during the period when colonial rule on the remainder of the continent was ending. Prior to the 1950s Portuguese settlement in Africa had been on a small scale (Henderson, 1976). Early attempts at colonisation had suffered from a lack of suitable settlers, as Portuguese emigrants held a negative image of Angola and Moçambique and few ventured to Africa. Those who did were generally not farmers and so were unable to make a living in agriculture, thereby contributing to the unfavourable picture of the colonies. Thus in 1950 under 3,000 Whites were engaged in agriculture despite the encouragement offered under the Estado Novo.

In the 1950s renewed government interest and intervention in Africa led to the decision to establish a series of major state-controlled colonisation schemes (*colonatos*). In addition to a number of small schemes, two large colonatos were designed in Angola at Cela and Matala and one in Moçambique on the Limpopo River. The plan of the Cela colonato made provision for the settlement of 8,400 Portuguese families totalling 58,900 persons in the period up to 1980. At Cela each colonist received approximately 20 ha of land together with an equipment and installation subsidy. At Matala the majority were offered only 5–6 ha although in both cases larger areas were available to suitable colonists with proven agricultural ability. The colonatos were based on village settlement with areas of communal grazing averaging 30–40 ha per family. The total areas of the schemes were large: Cela (300,000 ha) and Matala (420,000 ha). Despite considerable planning and investment only 300 families were resident on each of the two schemes by the end of 1960. The outbreak of fighting in Angola in 1961 led to a reappraisal of colonisation policies. In Angola a Provincial Settlement Board proceeded to speed up the process of settlement and was empowered to spend considerable sums on the projects as a means of maintaining Portuguese rule (Bender, 1978). Furthermore the scope of the schemes was widened to include Cape Verdians and Africans displaced by the War. The majority of schemes were segregated but a third of settlers were located on mixed schemes. By 1968 some 35 colonatos had been initiated in the two colonies. The turnover of European settlers was high with nearly two-thirds of settlers leaving within 18 months. The Cape Verdians and Africans proved to be far more stable. Furthermore the Cela settlement was by far the most successful in retaining its colonists, largely because they were able to achieve, mainly through dairying, an income ten times higher than the average of the other colonatos.

In Moçambique the Limpopo colonato was based on irrigation from the Limpopo Barrage (Morais, 1964). The irrigated area of 31,000 ha was shared amongst 3,000 families on 7.5 ha lots together with a number of other special uses. The costs of settling each family were estimated in the mid-1960s at some 350 Contos (£4,375), an indication of the vast investment involved. Intensive cultivation of horticultural products for the local and Southern Rhodesian markets provided the economic basis of the scheme. Preliminary plans were being drawn up in 1974 to establish an even larger colonato in the Zambezi valley using water from the Cabora Basa Dam project, but this was abandoned with the termination of Portuguese rule.

Townsmen

In common with most European overseas settlements, the urban areas played a major role from inception. Indeed it might be true to say that Europe brought an essentially urbanised view of society to Africa. Towns were the bases from which colonial expansion took place and they were in turn promoted by rural development, trade and government. The towns were an essential element in the linkage between Colonial Africa and the industrial, urban economy of Europe upon which it became dependent. However, the continent already possessed towns and European colonisation was restricted to adopting and adapting structures already in existence. In particular the Europeans were brought into contact with the Islamic towns of northern and western Africa and the east coast Swahili city-states. Within these zones European additions were made to the pre-colonial city producing the dual form of city noticeable in the contemporary Asian colonies (Giese, 1979; King, 1976). In contrast the southern and central parts of the continent were largely devoid of major pre-colonial settlements and it was the colonial impress which was dominant. Colonial cities were therefore of two basic forms, the new settler city attached to a pre-existing entity, and the planned city where it was the indigenous settlement which represented the structural appendage. The French towns of North Africa and the Anglo-Dutch towns of South Africa respectively illustrate the main contrasts and similarities between the two forms, representing as they do the two main areas of European settler urban colonisation.

North Africa

The North African settler town was generally built as an addition to an existing Islamic city, in the form of a new planned spacious layout. The majority of such towns were erected by the French and so reflect French town planning style and the urban characteristics of French civilisation, uninhibited by the physical heritage of a long history. British and Italian colonial governments encountered the same established Islamic structures but failed to evolve the cohesive policies and hence the imprint which the French attained. The striking feature of the dual town was the virtually self-contained nature of the two sectors, as the Islamic cities (*medinas*) with their walled enclosures continued to function in certain respects as they had before the conquest. The new European city (*nouvelle ville*) was established as an independent unit to serve the settler community and the colonial state. Those in North Africa were essentially towns designed and built by Frenchmen to house Frenchmen, and hence reflect the tastes and concepts of the metropole translated into a more spacious African environment. A high degree of segregation was instituted and maintained and occasionally enforced, as for example Marshal Lyautey's decree in 1917 that Europeans were forbidden to live in the Moroccan medinas (Stewart, 1964).

The new city was generally planned as a complete entity in North Africa with the designs of French cities, especially Baron Hausmann's Paris, much in evidence. Broad straight boulevards separated city blocks, which were in turn divided by more irregular street and plot systems. The object was to concentrate high density multi-storey buildings in terraces within the centre on the pattern of Paris or the French provinces. At first the concentration of housing and other facilities was essential in Algeria as the towns were fortified, with walls constructed around them. Algiers was enclosed by walls and elaborate fortifications as late as the 1850s, as indeed were the majority of smaller towns and villages (Figure 6.6). How-

Figure 6.6: Algiers, *c.* 1850

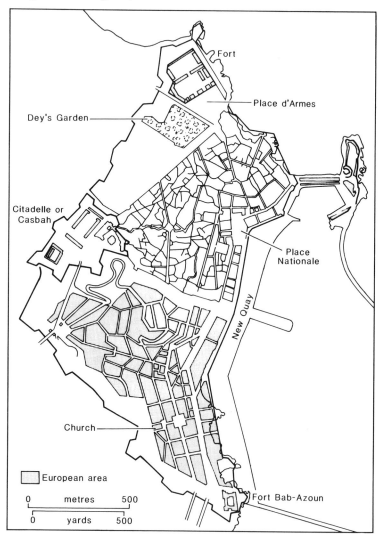

ever, although united by a common wall, the two halves of Algiers
differed with regard to plan and population (Taieb, 1971). The
isolation of the two halves was nevertheless not as complete as it was
to become in Morocco in the twentieth century. A steady encroachment by the European town upon the Moslem town was evident as
the boulevards were driven through the lower parts of Algiers'

medina in order to gain access to the port, and strategically placed blocks on the edge of the medina were incorporated into the European city (Eichler, 1977). It was however within the European city that most government attention was lavished with new structures for government offices, town halls, churches, and opera houses, built in contemporary French style, leaving a distinctively metropolitan imprint upon the landscape. Spacious parks, gardens and monuments were designed to give a similar image, but usually on a more extensive scale than in France, as land was more freely available and each sector of settler society expected to live and work in somewhat grander surroundings than had been possible in Europe.

The European settlement of North Africa was largely urban in character. In 1886 the European population of Algeria was 63.6 per cent urban and this rose to 78.3 per cent by 1954. The Moslem population remained essentially rural although increasing its urban percentage from 6.9 to 18.3 in the same period, as rural-urban migration began to gather momentum in the late colonial era. Algiers in 1866 enumerated 52,000 Europeans and only 13,000 Moslems. Even in 1926 with 193,000 Europeans living in the city only 73,000 Moslems were enumerated. Nevertheless, there followed an accelerating rate of Moslem rural-urban migration, which allied to a weak French demographic structure resulted in the recording of a Moslem majority at the time of the 1954 census, when 277,000 Europeans and 293,000 Moslems were enumerated in the city. The disparity had widened by 1960 when the figures stood at 307,000 and 543,000 respectively. Algiers was from soon after its conquest until the early 1930s, the largest European city on the continent in terms of its European population, and retained the number two position until the exodus following independence in 1962. Other major cities in Algeria similarly became predominantly European, both in population and character of the new towns. Oran for example retained a European majority until decolonisation.

Tunisia, however, owing to the different political character of the settlement retained a more Moslem character to the towns. It might be added that by 1956 Tunis alone housed over two – thirds of the 255,000 Europeans living in Tunisia. In most cases the medina/ nouvelle ville dualism was disturbed by the major influx of Moslems into the urban areas from the 1930s onwards, which resulted in the appearance of slum and shanty towns (*bidonvilles* or tin-can towns) which grew more rapidly than the authorities could rehouse or remove them. Thus the bidonvilles became an integral and steadily more significant sector of the late colonial town.

Although well developed urban systems had evolved in pre-colonial times in both Morocco and Tunisia, Algeria was comparatively poorly endowed. Thus many new centres were founded by the French to create the urban network considered necessary for the administration and commerce of the country, in the same manner as other mid-latitude colonies. New towns such as Philippeville (1838) and Sidi-bel-Abbes (1843) were designed in their entirety as French cities. In these cases the Moslem quarter was an addition to the town, more in the style of southern African cities. However, they were often ill-organised and poorly built, and in the last years of colonial rule grew into bidonvilles, in contrast with the planning and organisation of the European sector. The establishment of an urban network was an important aspect of the rural colonisation programme. New towns and villages were built in large numbers, throughout the areas of European settlement. The Mitidja Plain was transformed through the establishment of a series of small towns such as Blida and Marengo as well as the smaller villages related to the farming community.

Morocco, through its wealth and the late date of colonisation constituted possibly the most noteworthy example of French town planning in Africa, and indeed provided a model for other French possessions (Johnson, 1972). In 1913 the architect, Henri Prost, was commissioned to plan the new European sectors of the most important Moroccan towns and draw up regulations for future town planning. In all but Casablanca these plans were implemented with a high degree of state control over construction, administration and the provision of services. The extent of official supervision fluctuated, being most evident in the first and last ten years of the Protectorate. In the intervening period, especially during the depression of the 1930s, the pressures on the medinas were such that they were unable to accommodate both their own natural growth and the accelerating rural-urban migration. Only in Casablanca was the problem recognised at official levels and then more as a threat to public health and security. The result was the construction of a new medina, built on traditional Moroccan plan adjacent to the European sector. Elsewhere slums were erected and government action was limited to the control of the bidonvilles. Most were built in a haphazard plan and construction was of a rudimentary nature of metal sheets, boards, etc. The authorities in Casablanca later attempted to introduce a measure of order to the bidonvilles which were demolished and reconstructed in a series of rectangular layout suburbs (*cités*). Elsewhere sprawl continued unabated despite attempts to remove the shanties.

After the Second World War the government intervened more forcefully with the introduction of more elaborate planning machinery and the appointment of the French planner, Michel Ecochard, to draw up the guidelines for the post-war boom. A feature of this period was the breaking down of the essentially dual nature of control and planning and the institution of unified planning. Attention was particularly directed towards larger scale low cost housing projects for the Moroccan population. These projects, the cités, were designed to complement the development of industrial, commercial and governmental quarters, so that land use blocks alternated in the new town plans. In the period 1950-6 some 10,000 low cost houses and a new Jewish quarter were built in Casablanca alone. The Moroccan towns thus became highly complex structures with the pre-colonial walled medinas preserved virtually intact. Added to them were the nouvelles villes of French settlers, which although housing fewer people, sprawled over far greater areas than the medinas. However, two additional elements, the bidonvilles of 'temporary' private construction and the state-built low cost cités, both accommodated an increasing proportion of the Moroccan population.

The Italians similarly encountered the Islamic city in their colonies. A dual African-European settlement emerged in the main towns as the Italian new city was laid out and developed adjacent to the high density old city (Tripoli, 1938). The Italian additions to the Moslem city of Tripoli for example were designed according to contemporary planning principles in the metropole, with high density housing in the centre and villas on the periphery. It was remarkable for the irregularity of plan and the inclusion of numerous piazzas and public buildings reflecting Italian urban design. The Roman heritage of the city was emphasised with the Arch of Marcus Aurelius given prominence in the plan. Indeed Roman remains throughout North Africa were restored and studied as a measure of affirming the continuity between classical and modern colonisation.

South Africa

The largest group of European settler towns on the continent was established in southern Africa (Davies, R.J., 1972). They were mostly planned entities akin to those founded in other mid-latitude European settlements of the same era. However, the same dualism between African and European towns evident in North Africa became apparent in the southern part of the continent in the late nineteenth and early twentieth centuries, as the indigenous population was drawn into the colonial urban economy. An added complication was the imposition of two European traditions, Dutch and British with their derivatives. Particular attention will be directed towards Cape Town as the first major town which exhibits in its fabric the complex evolution of colonialism, segregation and latterly apartheid.

The fort and garden at Cape Town were laid out in 1652 and five years later the first free settlers were allowed to build their own houses outside the fort. The town was planned with a grid of small blocks separated by broad streets at right angles to the sea and narrow cross-streets. Water-furrows were dug to provide a water supply down the main streets and trees planted to give an enclosed urban atmosphere. Strict control over building encouraged high density construction and as a result of the fire hazard, thatch and timber were banned at an early stage. As local bricks were of a poor quality and the Dutch products expensive to import, resort was made to plaster in order to protect walls. The distinctive whitewashed flat roofed Cape variant of Dutch urban architecture thus dominated the townscapes of Cape Town and other southern African towns until the mid-nineteenth century (Lewcock, 1963; Pearse, 1968).

Although the town was the administrative, commercial, ecclesiastical and military capital of southern Africa, for the first 200 years of its existence it remained comparatively small (Picard, 1968). Even in 1806 at the end of the Dutch period the total population was only 16,400 of whom 6,400 were Europeans. By 1855 the population stood at 25,000 of whom approximately 15,500 were Europeans. It is scarcely surprising that given the tight control over urban development the town covered little more than 100 ha until the nineteenth century. It did however exhibit some degree of functional zoning by this stage. Trade was the *raison d'être* for the town and this was reflected in the warehouses, stores and hotels, etc., erected adjacent to the beach and pier, in the era before the harbour was constructed in the 1860s. The second, government, function was maintained in the castle, but this became increasingly cramped and new areas adjacent to the government gardens were set aside for the church, slave lodge, government house and other offices, leaving the castle to its military function. It was the government and its officials which provided the most noticeable evidence of conspicuous spending in the town and thereby contributed to its embellishment in progressively larger structures. However, within the remainder of the town the residential function remained dominant until the 1840s, with businesses, trades and processing industries carried on within the residential areas. Differentiation and the emergence of the Central Business District was a product of the second half of the nineteenth century.

As a result of substantial industrial and trade expansion and the technical innovations of the Victorian era, Cape Town experienced rapid growth between 1855 and 1904. At the latter date the population totalled 179,000 of whom 107,000 were Europeans. This more than sixfold increase in population was expressed in a substantial sprawl of the built-up area and a redevelopment of the central core of the city. Possibly the most significant aspects were the construction of the docks and the railway. Cape Town's sea links were improved through the construction of the Alfred and Victoria Basins, begun in 1860, which allowed vessels to use protected quays instead of the open roadstead. A graving dock was also built, and with coaling, later oil bunker, facilities and specialised handling sheds for cold storage the port was able to maintain itself as a major point on the trade routes of the world. The railway, opened in the same year as the docks were begun, provided cheaper transportation and finally solved the problem of crossing the shifting sands of the Cape Flats. The railway and its workshops at Salt River, to the east of the city, gave a major impetus to the shift in population and industry. Within the city the trams and suburban railway line to Simonstown facilitated residential sprawl.

Thus by the first decade of the twentieth century a modern city had been created (Picard, 1969). The central core had lost its essentially residential function and a series of business streets, devoid of trees, waterfurrows and gardens had emerged. The major banks, and stores vied with one another to construct prestigious edifices, with buildings rising six to ten stories in height by the First World War. The main street, Adderley Street (initially the Heerengracht) also acquired a new General Post Office and railway station, and together with the offices and shops had taken on a distinctively British Imperial architectural style, in marked contrast to the earlier Cape-Dutch appearance. The government sector had been extended by encroaching upon the gardens, now converted into a public park, where the Houses of Parliament, Cathedral, Museum, Art Gallery, University, Public Library and other offices were erected. The industrial sector was transformed through the construction of the docks and the railway which cut the wholesale district off from the beach and forced relocations adjacent to the docks and the railway line. Processing and repair industries and some basic import substitution such as the Woodstock glassworks were established prior to the First World War.

It was the sprawl and differentiation of the residential areas which were particularly noticeable as the constraints of early town planning were broken and private developers and speculators laid out streets and plots with little regard to a general plan. Individual estates were laid out within the confines of each owner's property, usually in a grid form, but with little linkage between adjacent properties. The result was the construction of a mixed landscape of houses, shops, schools, churches and factories. A gradation in housing class from the upper mountain slopes to the Cape Flats was evident, with class and elevation closely related. On the higher elevations large plots of several hectares apiece were laid out with substantial villas and houses in exotic architect-designed styles ranging from Victorian Gothic to English Arts and Crafts. These gave way to double-storied terraces and semi-detached villas and finally single-story terraces at the lowest levels. The earlier farmsteads were largely removed, although some such as Leeuwenhof and Zonnebloem survived. Within the residential areas a degree of racial segregation became apparent, reflecting in large measure the lower socio-economic status of the non-European groups. They therefore occupied the poorer parts of the town, adjacent to the industrial areas and in other concentrated areas such as the Malay Quarter. Legislative segregation had not been enforced until African labourers were introduced to the city to work in the docks in the 1890s (Saunders, 1978). The first separate location for Africans, Ndabeni, was established in 1901 on the Cape Flats, 8 km from the city centre, introducing a new element into the urban system and a forerunner of the major feature of the Southern African town in the present century.

South Africa, unlike North Africa, possessed no stock of precolonial towns to be adapted by the colonial powers to their needs, so that foundation was usually the conscious selection of a new site devoid of any structure. The resultant towns, until the late nineteenth century, were thus closely related to other frontier towns established in zones of mid-latitude European settlement. Over 600 towns were founded in South Africa in the colonial period for the exercise of administrative, commercial, ecclesiastical and later industrial functions. Their distinguishing feature was the presence of permanent settlers exercising these functions within a substantial colonial population.

Town foundation was usually on an *ad hoc* basis as the need for additional centres was perceived, and the state, church or private individual attempted to satisfy the need through the laying out of a town which might or might not fulfil the plans of the promoters. Most towns were established as a result of the European colonisation of new areas and the development of the economy and expansion of population within existing areas. There was little systematic planning of the urban network, as opposed to the towns themselves. The 1848 Town Commission of Natal which selected sites for an urban network for the colony, and the Orange Free State prohibition after 1856 on the siting of new towns within 32 km of an existing town, were rare examples of state intervention in this field (Moll, 1977; Natal, 1848). The general pattern was of excessive town foundation and competition between foundations, often to the ultimate simplification of the urban hierarchy. Certain towns, after initial periods of growth, shrank as their functions were taken away from them. For example, Weenen was progressively replaced by Estcourt except in basic services. Other towns such as Harrismith were physically moved to new sites when the inadequacy of the original sites was demonstrated.

The majority of towns were established to serve rural communities, and predated the integration of an industrial economy in southern Africa. The towns thus had a substantial component with large plots of up to one hectare and extensive townlands of often several thousand hectares for common grazing and the supply of materials for building. The large plots were irrigated in the case of many early towns, so that the plotholder could feed himself and his family. In addition each community had to be largely self-sufficient prior to the transport revolution of the late nineteenth and early twentieth centuries, so that processing and basic manufacturing industries were widespread with mills, forges and handicraft industries. The establishment of a magistracy with drostdy buildings, church and parsonage, shops and warehouses led to a degree of differentiation which increased with time from the simple village form of the early Dutch towns to the complex functioning of the twentieth-century urban economy.

In plan the towns were almost invariably laid out on a rigid gridiron pattern with streets intersecting at right angles (Christopher, 1976a; Haswell, 1979). Blocks were set aside for open spaces or squares, usually a market square and church square, and in late foundations for public gardens. The former often provided the site for government offices, markets and more recently parking lots, replacing the open air nature of the original periodic markets. In towns built prior to the mid-nineteenth century, houses were usually placed adjacent to the road to maximise the use of the plot for agricultural purposes. In the late Victorian period plots were increasingly viewed as gardens, reflecting increased English influence, and houses were sited in the centre of the plots. Housing styles changed at the same time, as Cape Dutch façades were replaced by the ornate Victorian and Edwardian structures of the 1860-1914 period, followed by contemporary European and American styles (Kearney, 1973). The town plans were often focused upon a major structure so that vistas focusing upon the church, drostdy, parsonage, prison, or other significant building introduced an urban characteristic to the townscape. Uniformity within the towns in terms of plot size and usage was rare. Many nineteenth-century foundations included not only agricultural smallholdings but also small plots for the townhouses of neighbouring farmers. These were used for the season of periodic markets, quarterly communion services and later, retirement homes. Also the introduction of traders, usually English as opposed to the mainly Afrikaans-speaking plotholders, was reflected in a dichotomy of landscapes, one English and commercial, the other Cape-Dutch and horticultural (Smith, 1976). Disparities increased in the course of the nineteenth century with zoning on usage and class lines within settler society.

South African towns prior to the First World War were still small. In 1911 only 1.5 million persons lived in the 362 listed towns, of whom 667,000 were White and 494,000 were African. Half the listed towns enumerated under 1,000 inhabitants and only 9 per cent exceeded 5,000 inhabitants. These largely included the mining towns and the port cities. In the following 50 years there was a fivefold increase in urban population, but the main expansion took place in the Witwatersrand conurbation and the port cities (Davies, 1963). The majority of the smaller towns experienced only limited growth and even decline in the same period, with decline becoming more significant afterwards (Van der Merwe, 1982). It was the increasing concentration of economic activity in the southern Transvaal and the generation of wealth in the interior of the country which resulted in the transformation of the space economy and the emergence of a structured urban hierarchy (Davies, 1967; Davies and Cook, 1968).

Three major features may be distinguished in the post-First World War era, namely redevelopment of the Central Business District, the sprawl of residential and industrial areas, and the introduction of legislated segregation of the various racial groups. Each represented an acceleration of processes at work beforehand. The Central Business Districts of South African cities followed not the example of Cape Town as in the nineteenth century, but the innovations of Johannesburg, which assumed a dominant role in the financial life of the subcontinent (Shorten, 1970). The development of old structures and the construction of high-rise office buildings occurred in all the main centres, although the skyscraper was not the essential status symbol of a growing town. Redevelopment was selective, as the major financial and commercial houses together with the rapidly expanding bureaucracy and state corporations located their national and regional offices in a comparatively re-stricted number of towns. Vertical expansion was accompanied by a slower outward movement across zones of transition and occasional outbursts of activity on newly reclaimed land adjacent to the original Central Business District such as the foreshore in Cape Town and the railway lands in Johannesburg (Davies, 1965; Davies and Beavon, 1973). In commercial terms two Central Business Districts evolved, one catering essentially to the European trade and the other to the more basic African and Coloured trade (Davies and Rajah, 1965; Wills and Schulze, 1976). The latter, in the case of the majority of the Natal and Transvaal towns, was usually in the hands of Indian traders, thus constituting a distinctive cultural enclave within the 'European' sector of the towns.

Sprawl was one of the noticeable features of South African towns after the First World War, when the rural-urban migration to the medium and large centres assumed ever more significant propor-tions and the transport revolution permitted more affluent Euro-peans to move to more distant suburbs (Hart, 1976). Expansion took three major forms, paralleling the North African town fairly closely. The first was the evolution of the classic American rural-urban fringe, conditioned by the private land market which passed through progressive stages of subdivision from farmland to the construction of housing estates. Subdivision in the Transvaal was aided in 1920 by the introduction of legislation easing the costs of the process (South Africa, 1957). Thus by the mid-1950s some 300,000 ha had been divided into approximately 60,000 small-holdings of 1–20 ha apiece on the fringe of Transvaal towns and smaller areas were present in the other Provinces. At the same time suburban expansion through the division of smallholdings into residential and industrial areas reflected the provision of space for the growing European population and increasing demands for space by manufacturing industry (Young, 1973). The latter increased its production value from £8.9 million to £525.5 million between 1911 and 1960 when it contributed almost as much to the South African Gross Domestic Product as agriculture and mining combined. Half this production was concentrated in the southern Transvaal, where the Witwatersrand conurbation housed some 2.2 million people, including 0.8 million Whites by 1960 (Davies and Young, 1970a).

The second form of sprawl was the construction of the informal shanty towns, built of tin, iron, wood and cardboard, which were formed on the margins of the towns (Beavon, 1982). Governmental control and planning for these areas were minimal and interest was only sporadic, so that it was not until the late 1950s that a concerted effort was made to remove them by rehousing some of their inhabitants and by sending the remainder back whence they had come. Although the vast majority of such settlements housed Africans, Europeans particularly in the depression, flocked to the cities and took up temporary squatter quarters. Industrialisation during the Second World War solved the European squatter problem but aggravated that of the Africans, as an accelerated flow of work-seekers entered the settlements (Smit and Booysen, 1981). The third form of sprawl was the result of increasing state and municipal intervention in the housing market. City governments regarded the shanty towns as a health hazard, giving rise to the 'sanitary syndrome' whereby the local authorities sought to remove them and establish separate segregated African residential areas at some distance from the European town. The result was the construction of the location, regularly laid out and physically isolated from the town it served. As a result of outbreaks of bubonic plague in 1904 both Johannesburg and Port Elizabeth municipalities established locations, the former at Pimville, 20 km from the city centre and the latter at New Brighton some 8 km distant. State housing for other groups of the population was limited until the 1950s as they were expected to find their accommodation on the private market.

Although restriction and often *de facto* segregation, particularly of the African population, was evident in the early South African city, legislated segregation was at most ineffective until the 1920s. Two strands in an increasing European racial intolerance may be detected in the twentieth century, leading to enforced segregation. The one sought to keep the towns European in character in the face of an accelerating African inward migration and the other sought to segregate the immigrant groups to reduce competition for the available urban resources which were viewed as a European monopoly.

Urban segregation of the African population was enforced under the Natives (Urban Areas) Act of 1923 which enshrined the settler doctrine that 'the town is a European area in which there is no place for the redundant Native' (Davenport, 1971). As far as possible the African migration to the towns was to be slowed and if possible reversed. Despite the legal requirement for all towns to establish locations, segregation between African and non-African was not strictly enforced until 1948 when the National Party was returned to power; after which extensive new locations were constructed on the margins of the towns (Davenport, 1972). The shanty towns on the urban fringe were removed and the African occupied areas within the major towns were similarly demolished. The resulting locations became major features of the South African townscape in the form of dormitory appendages. They ranged in size from a few dozen houses adjacent to the small towns to the scale of Soweto, south-west of Johannesburg, where 100,000 houses were built (Morris, 1980). In appearance it was the depressing uniformity of design and layout which was the most noticeable feature, as government agencies and municipalites erected a standard form of low cost housing.

The second thread in the imposition of legal segregation upon the colonial city was a legislative programme directed against the Indian and Coloured population. Indian migration to South Africa increased markedly between 1880 and 1900 and many established trading enterprises, thus encountering the opposition of entrenched European traders, who were able to exercise their control of the government to combat Indian competition. Natal, particularly after the granting of responsible government in 1893, enacted a series of restrictive measures, even attempting to remove the Indian right to trade at all (Huttenback, 1976). In the Orange Free State the government barred access completely, while in the Transvaal separate 'bazaars' were established for the Indian traders on the edge of the European town. Nevertheless, particularly in Natal, Indians prospered and moved into previously recognised European sectors of towns both in the inner suburbs and in the rural-urban fringe. Competition for housing led Europeans in Natal, especially in Durban, to demand enforced segregation and an end to Indian 'penetration' of business and residential areas. This goal was achieved in 1943 under the Trading and Occupation of Land (Transvaal and Natal) Restriction Act which halted inter-racial transactions, and after 1950 the Group Areas Act sought to remove all non-European people from areas deemed desirable for European occupation. Under the latter Act, Indian traders were removed from the centres of the majority of South African towns and Indian and Coloured people were removed to new housing estates on the edges of the towns, paralleling the removal of the African population (Davies, 1971; Scott, 1955). The racially mixed residential and trading areas, together with inner areas belonging to the Indian and Coloured population, were expropriated and in most cases the structures were demolished and the land redeveloped for the expansion of the Central Business District and for middle-class European housing.

The result was the emergence of the Apartheid city, a distinct variant of the colonial city (Davies, 1981; Western, 1981). Although the core of both was held by Europeans, such Indian presence in the Central Business District as had occurred in the colonial city was largely removed. Outside the original European core town, the new pattern was sectoral, with the largest sectors held by Europeans and smaller sectors assigned to each of the other racial groups present within the city (Figure 6.7). Each group was separated by buffer strips of open land and by stategically situated industrial sites. This was in marked contrast to the colonial city with its concentric rings of European core, locations, smallholdings and squatter townships, often highly interdigitated, reflecting a much lower degree of state intervention in the affairs of the indigenous population.

The South African variant of the colonial city was emulated in colonies to the north, particularly in Northern and Southern Rhodesia, South West Africa and Kenya, where substantial numbers of permanent European urban settlers resided, in contrast to the transitory staffs of tropical Africa. Despite restrictions on

Figure 6.7: Port Elizabeth, 1960

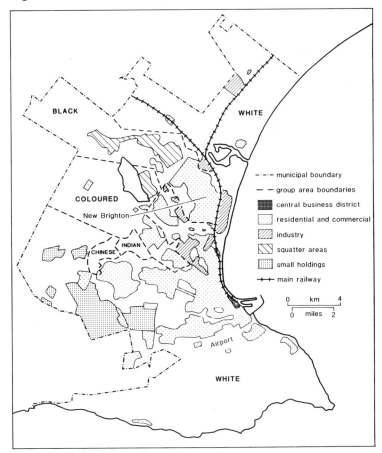

African landownership in several colonies, no attempt was made to convert the colonial city into the Apartheid city, except in South West Africa. Segregation was in evidence as the spacious residential layouts of the European suburbs constrasted with the more crowded African working-class townships. Interestingly in Nairobi the Central Business District was controlled by Asians who in 1962 constituted three-quarters of its population, while the European and African populations were housed predominantly in Upper Nairobi at 15 persons per residential hectare, and Eastlands at 311 persons per hectare respectively (Morgan, 1967). The dominant feature, however, was the sheer amount of space available for the layout of colonial cities, on a scale often unimaginable in Europe. Within the British and German colonies no attempt was made to create a close urban environment akin to the urban view of society and town planning evident in the French and Portuguese colonies. It was the garden city movement with essentially middle-class connotations which dominated the British colonial town in the twentieth century. Southern Rhodesian towns were particularly extensive in form (Christopher, 1976a; Kay and Smout, 1977). Bulawayo with a population of only 11,000 persons in 1911 enjoyed townlands of over 11,000 ha as well as urban plots often exceeding 0.6 ha in extent. Within the colonial cities the imprint of the government was particularly significant as extensive reserves were set aside for police and army camps, experimental farms as well as parks, racecourses, golf-courses and polo grounds for the benefit of the officials and their families. Such facilities were usually located close to the centre of the city reflecting the priorities of colonial society.

7 THE IMPRINT

Although the colonial era was of short duration over much of the African continent, the European powers shattered the majority of pre-existing societies or at least held them in subservence for long enough to impose many alien ideas (Rodney, 1972). In most cases the pre-colonial states were destroyed and the fragments were incorporated into the new colonial states. The economies of the pre-existing societies were similarly integrated into the world economy with often disastrous immediate and long-term results for indigenous agriculturalists. Particularly significant were the large numbers of Europeans who came to Africa either to settle permanently or to exploit the opportunities offered in the continent. Inevitably this led to competition for resources, in particular the land resources. New European societies were formed which were able to impress their ideas upon the landscape and create an image of France or England overseas. When decolonisation finally took place the African peoples were inextricably entangled in the world economy and decolonisation generally meant the indigenisation of the colonial state, which remained intact. Breaks with the past were few in the post-colonial period. The sudden exodus of French settlers from Algeria and Portuguese settlers from Angola and Moçambique were the most spectacular breaches with the colonial era, resulting in a large-scale redistribution of resources and permitting radical reorganisation of the economy. In general as Europeans departed, their positions were filled by Africans with few discontinuities. Only in South Africa did the colonial state remain in European hands as a result of the strength of the immigrant population. Throughout the continent there has thus been a remarkable degree of continuity from colonial to post-colonial times and this is reflected in the present landscape of Africa.

The Colonial Heritage

In macro-geographic terms the state pattern of the colonial period has survived remarkably in the post-colonial era, following the adherence of political leaders, through the Organisation of African Unity, to the colonial states' boundaries. At decolonisation some redrawing took place including the uniting of British and Italian Somaliland and the British and French Cameroon, but the problems of linking states with different colonial experiences are often insuperable (Gambia, 1968). The major attempts at redrawing boundaries through secessionist movements such as those for separate Katangan or Biafran states were unsuccessful. Similarly the various unification plans devised by political leaders have come to nought as state bureaucracies and structures have been fundamentally resistant to change. The major problem areas, Ethiopia-Eritrea and Morocco-Western Sahara, illustrate the moves made by countries to re-establish the extent of the pre-colonial state, where colonial boundaries had partitioned it — as opposed to demands for the separate states to maintain the colonial structure. As a result, the difficulties of nation building have been severe but nowhere insurmountable in the post-colonial era.

Although state boundaries have been more stable than the corresponding colonial boundaries prior to independence, the same has not been true of internal administrative boundaries. The administrative structures of the colonial state have generally been radically altered to meet the changed methods of administration and adjusted to internal pressures ignored during the colonial period. The repeated redrawing of Nigeria's internal boundaries is a case in point (Barbour, 1982). The number of provinces has been steadily increased and their strength *vis-à-vis* the central government decreased, in an effort to promote national unity. Such a concept was meaningless in the colonial period when indirect rule left much of the power of the government in the hands of the local rulers and no attempt was made to foster a Nigerian national awareness. The same pattern of fragmenting powerful and potentially dissident provinces within the colonial state has been particularly evident in the ex-British colonies, because of the degree of local autonomy afforded within the state structure. This has not however been true of the ex-French and ex-Portuguese colonies, where centralisation was the key to administration both before and after independence. Thus colonial administrative structures have survived, as they were more readily attuned to the political ideas of African rulers.

Many symbols of nationhood reside within the capital city. The majority of African capitals at independence were small. All were under one million inhabitants in size and most housed fewer than 100,000 people. (Egypt is excluded from consideration as direct colonial rule was a brief eight-year interlude.) Hence the majority of capitals, being small and situated on the margins of national territory in the headlink position with the colonising power, were capable of being moved to more central sites at independence; but few transfers were effected. Indeed, the birth and demise of capitals has been less noticeable than in the colonial period. Apart from the special cases of Mauritania and Botswana, only three countries — Malawi, Nigeria and Tanzania — have chosen to move their capitals. In each case the new cities have been centrally located in the national territory and the move has been prompted by the apparent overcrowding of, and colonial nature of, the pre-existing capital. Thus not only has the state inherited the colonial territory but its most important element, the capital, and with it the basic infrastructure of the state usually focused on the capital. It is scarcely surprising that independent governments have sought to modify and Africanise the image of the colonial capitals, with new parliament buildings, conference centres, etc., but the basic colonial structures have remained intact (Davies, D.H., 1972).

The colonial period profoundly changed the economy of the African continent by linking it firmly to the World System. The connection had taken place in some regions prior to the imposition of direct colonial rule, but claims have been made that as late as the 1880s parts of West Africa were still unincorporated (Jones, 1979). Change was rapid and Africa through its late incorporation was placed on the periphery of the World System in a markedly dependent state, parallel to its political position. The controversy over development and undevelopment has undergone a number of marked changes in the decades since decolonisation, as a fuller appreciation of the processes of economic change has been obtained. However, the physical, structural results of the process may be clearly seen. These were related to the realignment of the economic and political systems towards an export trade in primary products, the construction of an infrastructure to effect that export, and direct intervention into the African economic system through demands for labour, products and land. The whole was backed by the degree of coercion necessary to maintain the system.

The products which Africa had to offer in the colonial period may be divided into three major groupings: human, agricultural and mineral. The first, in the form of slaves, was the primary African export until the mid-nineteenth century. The internal trade was under African control and it was only at the coast that European traders were directly involved. The extent and nature of the internal trade is still a matter of dispute but the weakening of indigenous society preparatory to European conquest was significant. The external trade was probably no more profitable for its investors than other trades at the same time (Rawley, 1981). It was certainly more costly in European lives and generated an image for European consumption of Africa and the Africans which was anything but congenial and complimentary. The longevity of the slave trade for four centuries provided the contact, the beginning of new trade alignments and the preparation for the opening up of the continent for European products of the industrial age. It also provided one of the spurs to later action in the form of the humanitarian impulse of the nineteenth century which involved missionaries and politicians seeking to alleviate the sufferings caused by slavery and the slave trade through direct intervention.

European penetration of the interior, however, was slow because of the problems of disease and the apparent strength of African political entities. Conquest on the pattern of the sixteenth-century Spanish intervention in America proved to be impossible and it was more on the Asian model that European relations with Africa initially developed. Full-scale penetration did not take place until late in the nineteenth century when, as a result of a number of major medical and technological innovations, the European states achieved such a disparity of power *vis-à-vis* the African states that their conquest became not only possible but easy and even desirable in European eyes. The medical and transport revolutions were the two most vital elements in this process, allied to overwhelming military power. Quinine and other such medicines enabled Europeans to live in Africa with a reasonable chance of survival. Steam-ships enabled the rivers to be navigated and regular shipping links to be maintained with Europe, while steam trains enabled products to be moved in areas devoid of beasts of burden and so previously limited by human porterage. These revolutions were prerequisites for the exploitation of the agricultural and mineral wealth of the continent.

The coastal holdings, whether obtained for trade, evangelisation or provisioning on the route to India, became the points from where lines of communications and trade were developed. The coastal and interior infrastructure was constructed rapidly from the 1860s onwards as railways were built inland by each colonial power, parallel to its neighbours. The major ports were built at considerable expense to serve not only the local needs of the individual colonies but the global strategies of the colonial powers. These became the foci of railway and road networks which were designed in simplest terms to facilitate the export of primary products and the import and distribution of manufactured goods. These basic networks of differing railway gauges, overseas shipping links and information flows, have proved to be particularly resistant to change. Inter-African transport links were neglected, even the major Trans-Sahara and Cape-Cairo railways were never built and attempts at continental transport integration since independence have had only limited success.

The African continent possessed considerable agricultural wealth, although through most of the colonial era it proved to be largely illusory. It is perhaps significant that the major plantation developments took place first in the Americas in the seventeenth and eighteenth centuries and then in South and South-east Asia in the late nineteenth and twentieth centuries. African agricultural prospects were not inviting for European investors and only the off-shore islands such as Sao Tomé, Réunion and Mauritius developed plantations prior to the present century. The products sent to Europe were therefore largely of two types, those which could be gathered and those which could be grown as an integral part of the African economic system. The gathering phases for products such as palm-oil and rubber were component parts of the early exploitation and depletion of the continent's resources. The exhaustion of the latter, particularly in the French and Belgian Congos, provoked crises for the entire tropical colonial system. Both products, however, were amenable to plantation production and were later produced as such. Groundnuts and cocoa were produced by African cultivators in West Africa as a means of raising money to buy the new industrial products and to pay a rising tax burden. Apart from the export marketing, Europeans were little involved in these crops. Increased African production during the colonial period in order to pay taxes is well documented and the exactions of colonial governments played an important role in the fostering of new crops both directly through production quotas and indirectly through the introduction of a monetary economy. However, taxation when levied at ever increasing rates was designed not to increase production but to obtain a supply of cheap labour and ultimately the collapse of the indigenous economy. The deliberate destruction of the African rural economy was most marked in areas with large numbers of European settlers and attained its most advanced phase in South Africa and Algeria. In these colonies the settlers replaced the Africans as the producers of primary products and no competition was permitted.

It was the mineral wealth of the continent which attracted large-scale investment. The gold mines of West Africa remained exclusively in African control until the 1870s. Other minerals likewise were only exploited by Europeans in the post-1850 era. The major discoveries of diamonds at Kimberley, gold on the Witwatersrand and finally copper on the Rhodesia-Congo border created wealth and a significance for African ventures which had been unthinkable for a purely agricultural economy. In each case the discoveries were located in a region peripheral to existing European interests, thereby providing the incentive for the colonial powers to extend their lines of communication into central Africa. Because of the sequence of events it was the Cape of Good Hope base which benefited and extended its economic and political influence as a sub-metropole in the World System. The region was one of the few areas where transport competition and intercolonial integration took place, as the mineral strikes were of such value that several ports could share the wealth generated. The mines also attracted investment not only in basic infrastructure but in other enterprises ranging from agriculture to banking in the territories involved, in the expectation of general economic development according to the diffusion model. Mineral discoveries in other parts of Africa were generally either too small to warrant such investment or occurred too late in the colonial period to affect its course.

European Settlement

Although Europeans viewed African colonialism primarily in terms of exploitation through trade and the direct gathering and mining of its resources, a small number of colonies of settlement were established and developed on modified mid-latitude models. The two major cores of North and South Africa were dissimilar in their origins and patterns of expansion, yet there were similarities in the small scale of the settlement and the continued numerical preponderance of the indigenous population. The dissimilarities of origin, as a metropolitan extension by conquest for settlement and as a supply base for ships bound for the East Indies, respectively, were striking. The one was highly regulated and with few exceptions the government prepared the ground for the settlers, while the other was unregulated as settlers moved on to new lands and the government followed. Hence in the Southern African case it was not a new Netherlands or a new England which emerged, but a new entity of European origin though African outlook. Indeed it was the only settler government to obtain international recognition of its independence. In the French case the European colony remained dependent upon France economically, culturally and militarily, even to the extent of demanding and obtaining incorporation into the administrative structure of metropolitan France. The outcome was its complete removal at the time of decolonisation.

The colonies of settlement were the most spectacular manifestations of colonialism for they involved the expropriation of land from the indigenous population and their displacement, and the settlement and redistribution of land to immigrants from another continent. The process of expropriation was pursued with varying degrees of determination depending upon the period and government concerned. The metropolitan humanitarian movements which campaigned against land confiscation and the exploitation of colonial peoples only became effective in the first decade of the present century, after a number of major crises in tropical Africa. In that decade the future of the French, Belgian and German colonies was reassessed while the British colonies came under the control of the Liberal government which wanted no additional problems with settlers in the tropics. The colonies of settlement established prior to the rise of this movement were therefore able to acquire all the land they could militarily conquer and hold, without any severe check from the metropolis. Rural reserves for the indigenous population were established to preserve the indigenes from European influences in the humanitarian view, or to provide pools of cheap labour from the settler viewpoint. Finally the paramountcy of indigenous rights was recognised and a number of colonies were closed to European settlement. Thus in the earliest colony of settlement, the Cape of Good Hope, some 81.1 per cent of the land had been granted to European settlers by 1914, compared with 37.0 per cent in Southern Rhodesia then a quarter of a century old, and only 5.4 per cent in Kenya where settlers were more restricted by the metropolitan government in a settlement only one decade of age.

Colonial governments, having acquired the land, sought to attract European settlers usually with the offer of free land grants in the initial phases and later by offering land on reasonable terms. Agriculture was officially viewed as the basis of the settler economy and the aim was to transfer the perceived better features of a rural agrarian society in the metropolis to Africa, even if it no longer existed and probably never had existed in Europe. Hence the obsession with grouped village settlement by colonial governors virtually throughout the period. The philosophy behind grouped settlement remained remarkably constant whether it was the Dutch at Stellenbosch in the Cape of Good Hope (1679), the French at Boufarik in Algeria (1837), the British at Winterton in Natal (1904) or the Portuguese at Vila Trigo de Morais in Moçambique (1956). Community settlement making use of shared facilities and services was viewed as the essential manner of maintaining civilisation upon the frontier. Schools, churches, stores, magistracies and prisons were all deemed integral parts of European overseas settlement. This attitude was particularly marked in Algeria where farms were grouped as a part of a village virtually from the beginning of the planning of rural colonisation. Direct state intervention was clearly highly important as it was usually government officers who planned, organised, and sometimes built the settlements. The contrast between domestic free enterprise in the metropoles and state control in the colonies is highly noticeable in this as in many other spheres of activity.

Land was distributed in parcels which by European standards were large, and hence highly attractive to those who viewed Africa in terms of agricultural systems in Europe. However, conditions were not the same and the intensive agricultural practices evolved in Europe either could not be transferred to Africa or took a long time to be built up. Thus there was paradoxically a constant demand for an increased farming area to accommodate the more extensive systems developed in the colonies. Schemes throughout Africa suffered from the discontent of settlers who perceived their farms to be too small. Farms were thus frequently abandoned and settlers moved on, either to new areas or to the towns or to other colonies and continents. The planned and even the more informal agricultural settlements were occupied by people who generally sought to recreate the landscape or perceived more desirable features of the landscape of the regions from whence they had come. Thus the villages and farms were organised and often consciously built in styles reminiscent of Europe, introducing a new element to the African landscape.

The exception to this rule was to be found in South Africa where the lack of metropolitan control over the colonists in the Cape of Good Hope in the eighteenth century led to the emergence of a distinctive people of European origin, but with little emotional attachment to Europe. Here rural settlement came to be viewed largely in terms of pastoralism based on large, dispersed farms of 2,500 ha or more where local adaptation to circumstances afforded. The pastoral frontier was thus highly extensive and marked by only low density settlement which influenced a wide area of the continent south of the equator. The Afrikaners, as the Cape settlers became, were welcome as pioneers outside their core region until the early twentieth century, when the colonial powers sought to control their frontiers more carefully, and impress their own national imprint upon the continent. The South African pastoral farm with its distinctive economy and building styles was a particular feature of the colonial landscape from the south-western Cape to the vicinity of Eldoret in Kenya.

The process of decolonisation has profoundly affected the rural areas which were occupied and settled by the Europeans (Fowler, 1973; Muntin, 1977; Schulze, 1978). With the exception of the extreme south of the continent, the majority of the rural European population has left the land, and even in the south the process of abandonment and sale is in progress (South Africa, 1982). However, only in rare occurrences does the land revert to its previous character. The imprint of the colonial system has in some degree been retained. The basic infrastructure of roads, farm buildings, fences and other improvements survive as post-colonial governments seek to reorganise their countries within the framework they inherited (Kassab, 1981; Le Coz, 1968; Popp, 1982). Thus farm boundaries established by European farmers may be maintained, although the farm may be divided into a closer-settlement scheme. The basic concepts of property have been retained and the colonial units are inherited and documented in the land registries. Only where large-scale simultaneous abandonment and expropriation have taken place have such boundaries been deleted from the record and the landscape. Other elements in the landscape, such as the farmsteads have been more ephemeral as indigenous architectural styles have been favoured and the European houses either modified or destroyed altogether.

The Colonial City

The majority of European settlers came to the towns and established a markedly extensive and distinctive form of urban settlement (Mabogunje, 1970; Vennetier, 1969). The colonial town reflected the ideas and ideals of the various European powers as on a virtually clear site the latest ideas in urban design could be effected without the constant need to consider the restrictions imposed by the inheritance from the past, nor the cost of acquiring the land. Urban design therefore varied from the close urban settlements of French North Africa and Dutch Cape Town to the garden cities of the later colonial period. It was often in the towns and more especially in the public buildings that the particular national imprint of the colonial powers was to be seen. Moreover, because land was freely available the resultant structures could be set in grander surroundings than was possible in the metropolis. Again the state played the dominant role in the siting and layout of towns and it was thus not surprising that plans should have emphasised the role of the state on the model of Paris or Lisbon, rather than London. The provision of parks, squares and monuments, together with boulevards indicate planning on a grand scale according to ideas prevalent in Europe, as modified by the essentially middle-class rulers of the colonial states. Space permitted members of colonial society to build on a more extensive scale and live in more generous style than was possible in the metropolis. Houses and gardens, and even apartments exhibited a spaciousness for most classes of settler society which indicated the emulation of the lifestyle of the upper echelons of metropolitan society rather than their social equals.

The colonial town, although built by Europeans to house Europeans, also had to accommodate other peoples. A dual character ensued as Europeans attempted to segregate themselves from the indigenous population and to emphasise class distinctions within their own societies (Abu-Lughod, 1980). The colonial city was thus an immensely complex structure which was reflected in the landscape in a wide variety of patterns. In view of the high degree of government contol exercised over their form and occupation, and the dualism of the population, it would seem unlikely that many of the free enterprise Western urban features would be found within them. The settler towns were of two basic types, the North African and the South African. The North African town consisted of a pre-existing Islamic town and a colonial appendage (Figure 7.1).

Figure 7.1: The North African Colonial City

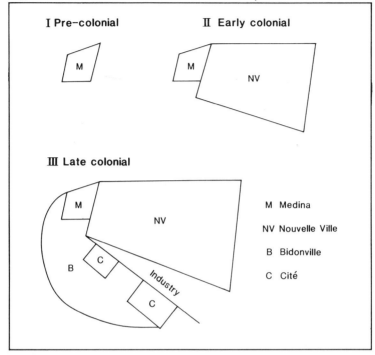

The two contrasted markedly in layout and style with often a high degree of residential segregation between them. The orderly layout of wide streets in geometrical patterns lined with multistorey terraces characterised the centre of the European town. On the outskirts, once security had been achieved, villas on large individual plots spread in a marked sprawl similar to the Mediterranean villas on the Côte d'Azur, as settler society emulated the wealthy of metropolitan society. In certain cities the European additions overwhelmed the pre-existing medinas surrounding them and destroying their economy, but in others, particularly in Morocco, the medina remained the core of the indigenous city operating a separate economy from the European city. Attempts at integrating the two (as for example in Algiers and Tripoli) represented the Haussmann approach of physical integration by driving boulevards through the medina, rather than social integration, whereby the

Moslems were displaced to even more crowded conditions as the poor of Paris had been before them.

In contrast the Southern African city evolved from the European foundation, usually in the form of a rigid grid pattern and growth took place by the extension of the grid and by the layout of new European suburban areas beyond it (Figure 7.2). The various immigrant groups lived within the one town in areas effectively segregated and often distinguishable by the architectural styles. The Southern African city presented a lower profile than the North African city with a preponderance of single storey buildings. Multistorey structures were only built in the city centres as land prices rose. The detached bungalow on Indian lines characterised the British South African residential area, distinguishable with its corrugated iron roofs and verandahs. The older Cape-Dutch tradition of architecture with gables and thatched roofs and smaller flat roofed structures with parapets remained, often producing a great variety of styles. Apartment blocks only made their appearance on any scale after the Second World War, whereas in the North African city they were an accepted part of urban living from the early stages of the colonial period.

It was in the field of often institutionalised segregation that the colonial city was most distinctive and that the North and South African variants grew closer together in the twentieth century. The rural-urban migration of the indigenous people set up stresses which the imported structure could not bear. The reaction of the authorities was to separate Europeans and Africans and allow areas beyond the margin of the European town to be used either for organised government townships or squatter camps. The resulting indigenous settlements were of various styles ranging from organised government constructed houses laid out on a grid pattern; through site and service schemes where the basic infrastructure of streets and plots were laid out and water taps and sewerage provided, but housing was left to the individual family; to the completely unorganised squatter camp, built and laid out entirely on indigenous lines. The two extremes, the organised location and the informal squatter camp were present in most African cities. Often organisation into a location resulted from settler pressures arising from the perceived hazards of the squatter settlements and hence the proportion of the indigenous urban population housed within them varied both from town to town and period to period. The economic changes of the post-Second World War era were

Figure 7.2: The South African Colonial City

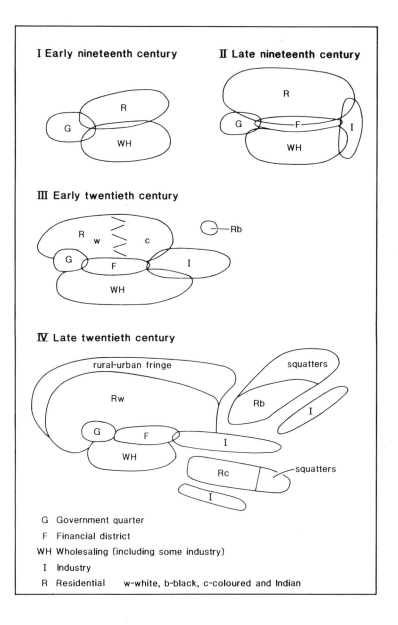

I Early nineteenth century

II Late nineteenth century

III Early twentieth century

IV Late twentieth century

G Government quarter
F Financial district
WH Wholesaling (including some industry)
I Industry
R Residential   w-white, b-black, c-coloured and Indian

particularly critical for the increased attraction of the towns as a result of industrialisation. The rate of rural-urban migration was such that the squatter camp on the edge of the urban area was a permanent feature of the late colonial town. Attempts to remove it through enforced rustication or rehousing were successful only in part. In South Africa by the mid-1960s squatters had all but disappeared from the margins of the towns, only to reappear in the following decade. In neighbouring Moçambique few houses were built in planned locations and the squatter towns occupied areas as large or larger than the organised town. The same history was apparent in the North African towns where the Moslem influx resulted in extensive squatter towns on the edge of the European towns by the end of the colonial period. The situation was aggravated in states such as Rhodesia and Algeria where in the late colonial period refugees fleeing from the military actions of the wars of independence streamed into the major cities.

The four elements of the colonial town, namely the pre-industrial indigenous town, the European town, the organised location and the squatter camp varied in importance and in geographical extent. The pre-colonial indigenous town was largely Islamic in character, as few non-Islamic societies had developed an urban-based civilisation. It was therefore a characteristic of the northern regions of the continent and largely absent elsewhere. The European town was most clearly developed in the North and South African sectors where substantial numbers of colonists settled permanently. However, government, military and other posts were laid out on similar lines even though the European population was small. The planned locations were a constant characteristic, if a limited one, of colonial cities, but it was the squatter camps which became one of the major features of the late colonial period, although they were present in some form throughout the era.

The colonial city within the tropics exhibited many of the characteristics of the settler towns in the North and South, with a marked, often enforced segregation between the European and indigenous population. Dakar was progressively segregated as health and building regulations displaced Africans into a planned medina in 1918, paralleling developments elsewhere (Seck, 1970). Lagos was subjected to pressures from rural-urban migration which were such as to lead the authorities to attempt to clear the squatter settlements by reversing the flow in 1946, complementing an earlier proposal to move the capital to Yaba (Gale, 1979; Nigeria, 1946). All the elements of the colonial town were present despite the existence of only a transient European population in most tropical regions (De Blij, 1962, 1963, 1968).

Apart from very extensive physical characteristics, the African colonial city was not large in terms of the population it housed. Only Johannesburg had attained 'million-city' status by 1960 and less than half were Europeans. Indeed in the colonial period no town housed a population of 500,000 Europeans. The contrast with other continents or with Egypt, where both Cairo and Alexandria achieved million-status earlier in the century, is most marked and reflects the low level of economic activity during the colonial era. It is also a measure of the small number of Europeans who came to settle in Africa compared with the other continents and hence comparability with the Americas and Australasia is limited; while the indigenous cities were unable to follow the Asian model owing to the restricted nature of their economies.

The colonial towns and cities, because of their capital investment and size have witnessed little physical destruction or abandonment in the manner of the rural areas, although deterioration, 'gourbisation', is evident as services have declined from the levels demanded by the European settlers (Blake, 1971). The towns have continued to attract people from the rural areas and as a result the colonial city has often been overwhelmed by sheer numbers. Rebuilding and extension have simply tended to perpetuate the patterns of the colonial period. The new indigenous elites have occupied the European sectors of towns as have an often growing number of non-African contract workers. However, much of the increase has been accommodated in the growing squatter camps, transforming African cities into relatives of contemporary Latin American and Asian cities. The European imprint of the styles in the city centre remains, if the extension is more African in character. Just as many of the pre-colonial cities were able to resist radical change in the colonial era, so the colonial city is now resisting rapid physical transformation in the post-independence era.

Postcript

The colonial period in Africa has undergone significant re-evaluation in the years since 1960, as European and African ethno-centric interpretations of the era have been modified. Yet the divergence of opinion evident at independence is still apparent. The complementary and illuminating views of King Baudouin of the Belgians and Patrice Lumumba, Prime Minister of the Congo Republic, expressed at the independence celebrations in Leopold-ville, with regard to the disposition of land and the creation of towns in the colonial period, are still relevant:

> *King Baudouin:* Agriculture has been improved and modern-ized. Large towns have been built, and across the whole country there has been remarkable progress in housing.
> *Patrice Lumumba:* All the time our lands were being despoiled in the name of texts claiming to be legal, which, only, however, recognized the right of the strongest . . . in the towns there were magnificent houses for the whites and ramshackle straw huts for the blacks. (Emmer and Wesseling, 1979, pp. 171-3)

These opposed interpretations of landrights, seizures, and urban growth inevitably colour the perceptions of the geography of the continent as they do of its history or political systems, for their outcomes are concrete and tangible reminders of the colonial era. The colonial governors, even a great many of the settlers, have returned to Europe, but the physical structures of colonialism, which still evoke such mixed responses, are highly visible in the African landscape. The details of that landscape may be rejected and erased as far as possible, but the main lineaments of the colonial era are indelibly stamped upon the continent.

To return to the idea expressed in *The Go-Between*, alluded to in the introduction: the Congo Free State and the Belgian Congo portray the past, another country, while the Republic of Zaire is the present. Patrice Lumumba concluded his independence list of colo-nial evils with the words 'but all this . . . all of it, has now ended'. Independence marked the demise of the colonial state and the new emancipated state took its place. Different ideas, different priori-ties, different rulers began to shape the geography of Africa. Colonial Africa in a sense is becoming another continent as each colony is relegated to the past, yet the transformation can not be complete as past and present are merged in the African landscape.

Regrettably little of the debate on the nature and impact of the colonial period and even less of the research, has been of a geogra-phical nature, reflecting the prime concern of the discipline with the problems of national development. However, the colonial period was of profound significance for the landscape of Africa, not only in the economic and political forces which it unleashed upon the indigenous peoples, but also in terms of the physical imprint of the colonisers themselves. In the reinterpretation of African historiography it is natural that the search for indigenous history should be of paramount importance and this priority has been transferred to geographical enquiry. Yet through the exercise of political, military and economic power, the colonisers were able to impose a major transformation upon the continent such that any late-twentieth-century interpretation of the African landscape can no more disregard the colonial than the indigene.

BIBLIOGRAPHY

Abu-Lughod, J.L. (1980) *Rabat: Urban Apartheid in Morocco*, Princeton University Press, Princeton

Ageron, C.R. (1979) *Histoire de l'Algérie contemporaine*, Presses Universitaires de France, Paris

Akpan, M.K. (1978) 'The Return to Africa — Sierra Leone and Liberia', *Tarikh*, *5(4)*, 92-116

Ardener, E. (1960) *Plantation and Village in the Cameroons*, Oxford University Press, London

Atger, P. (1960) 'Les comptoirs fortifiés de la Côte d'Ivoire (1843-1871)', *Revue Française d'Histoire d'Outre-Mer*, *47*, 427-74

Baker, C. (1980) 'The Chinde Concession 1891-1923', *Society of Malawi Journal*, *33*, 6-18

Baker, H. (1944) *Architecture and Personalities*, Country Life, London

Barbour, K.M. (1982) *Nigeria in Maps*, Hodder and Stoughton, London

Barnard, W.S. (1982) 'Die geografie van 'n revolusionere oorlog: SWAPO in Suidwes-Afrika', *South African Geographer*, *10*, 157-74

Beavon, K.S.O. and Rogerson, C.M. (1980) 'The persistence of the casual poor in Johannesburg', *Contree*, *7*, 15-21

Beavon, K.S.O. (1982) 'Black Townships in South Africa: Terra Incognita for Urban Geographers', *South African Geographical Journal*, *64*, 1-20

Bechuanaland Protectorate (1963) *Gaberones*, Bechuanaland Press, Mafeking

Bender, G.J. (1978) *Angola Under the Portuguese: the Myth and the Reality*, Heinemann, London

Bening, R.B. (1979) 'The Location of Administrative Capitals in Ashanti, Ghana 1896-1911', *International Journal of African Historical Studies*, *12*, 210-34

Bernard, A. (1932) 'Rural Colonization in North Africa' in W.L.G. Joerg (ed.), *Pioneer Settlement*, American Geographical Society, New York, pp. 221-35

— (1937a) *Afrique septentrionale et occidentale (Géographie Universelle; tome 11)*, Armand Colin, Paris

— (1937b) 'Le recensement de 1936 dans l'Afrique du Nord', *Annales de Géographie*, *46*, 84-8

Best, A.C.G. (1970) 'Gaberone: Problems and Prospects of a New Capital', *Geographical Review*, *60*, 1-14

— (1976) 'Angola: Geographic Background of an Insurgent State', *Focus*, *26(5)*, 1-8

Billington, R.A. (1961) *Frontier and Section*, Prentice Hall, Englewood Cliffs

Blake, G.H. (1971) 'Urbanization in North Africa', *Tijdschrift voor Economische en Sociale Goegrafie*, *62*, 190-6

Blusse, L. and Gaastra, F. (1981) *Companies and Trade: Essays on Overseas Trading Companies during the Ancien Régime*, Leiden University Press, Leiden

Boateng, E.A. (1978) *A Political Geography of Africa*, Cambridge University Press, Cambridge

Bowman, I. (1931) *The Pioneer Fringe*, American Geographical Society, New York

Boxer, C.R. (1969) *The Portuguese Seaborne Empire 1415-1825*, Knopf, New York

211

— and De Azevedo, C. (1960) *Fort Jesus and the Portuguese in Mombasa 1593-1729*, Hollis and Carter, London

Brant, E.D. (1971) *Railways of North Africa*, David and Charles, Newton Abbot

Braudel, F. (1976) *The Mediterranean and the Mediterranean World in the Age of Philip II*, Harper & Row, New York

Breil, J. (1957) *La population en Algérie: étude de démographie quantitative*, La Documentation Française, Paris

British East Africa (1919) *Final Report of the Economic Commission*, Government Printer, Nairobi

British South Africa Company (1897) *Report on the Company's Proceedings and the Condition of the Territories Within its Sphere of Operations*, British South Africa Company, London

Browett, J.G. and Fair, T.J.D. (1974) 'South Africa 1870-1970: A View of the Spatial System', *South African Geographical Journal, 56*, 111-20

Brownlie, I. (1978) *African Boundaries*, Hurst, London

Brunschwig, H. (1967) 'Note sur les technocrates de l'impérialisme francais en Afrique noire', *Revue Francaise d'Histoire d'Outre-Mer, 54*, 171-87

Bundy, C. (1979) *The Rise and Fall of the South African Peasantry*, Heinemann, London

Cameron, I. (1980) *To the Farthest Ends of the Earth*, Macdonald, London

Cape of Good Hope (1876) *Report of the Surveyor-General for the year 1875*, G. 30-76

— (1892) *Report of the Commission on the Van Wyks Vley Estate*, G. 31-92

Christopher, A.J. (1970) 'The Closer-settlement Movement in Natal 1875-1910', *Journal for Geography, 3*, 569-78

— (1971a) 'Land Tenure in Rhodesia', *South African Geographical Journal, 53*, 39-52

— (1971b) 'Colonial Land Policy in Natal', *Annals of the Association of American Geographers, 61*, 560-75

— (1976a) *Southern Africa: Studies in Historical Geography*, Dawson, Folkestone

— (1976b) 'The Variability of the Southern African Standard Farm', *South African Geographical Journal, 58*, 107-17

— (1982a) 'Towards a Definition of the Nineteenth Century South African Frontier', *South African Geographical Journal, 64*, 97-113

— (1982b) *South Africa*, Longman, London

— (1983) 'Official Land Disposal Policies and European Settlement in Southern Africa 1860-1960', *Journal of Historical Geography, 9*

Clarence-Smith, W.G. (1976) 'The Thirstland Trekkers in Angola – some Reflections on a Frontier Society', University of London, Institute of Commonwealth Studies, *Collected Seminar Papers, 20*, 42-51

Cohen, W.B. (1971) *Rulers of Empire: the French Colonial Service in Africa*, Hoover Institution Press, Stanford

Collins, R.O. (1971) *Land beyond the Rivers: the Southern Sudan 1898-1918*, Yale University Press, New Haven

Cooper, F. (1981) 'Peasants, Capitalists and Historians: a review article', *Journal of Southern African Studies, 7*, 283-314

Coquery-Vidrovitch, C. (1972) *Le Congo au temps des grandes compagnies concessionaires 1898-1930*, Mouton, Paris

Cornaton, M. (1967) *Les regroupments de la décolonisation en Algérie*, Editions

Ouvrières, Paris

Cornet, R.J. (1965) *Les phares verts*, Editions Cuypers, Brussels

Crush, J.S. (1980a) 'The Genesis of Colonial Land Policy in Swaziland', *South African Geographical Journal, 62,* 73-88

— (1980b) 'The Colonial Division of Space: the Significance of the Swaziland Land Partition', *International Journal of African Historical Studies, 13,* 71-86

— (1982) 'The Southern African Regional Formation: a Geographical Perspective', *Tijdschrift voor Economische en Social Geografie, 73,* 200-12

Cumming, R.C.G. (1850) *Five Years of a Hunter's Life in the Interior of South Africa*, Murray, London

Curtin, P.D. (1961) 'The White Man's Grave' Image and Reality, 1780-1850', *Journal of British Studies, 1,* 94-110

— (1964) *The Image of Africa: British ideas and action 1780-1850*, University of Wisconsin Press, Madison

— (1969) *The Atlantic Slave Trade: a Census*, University of Wisconsin Press, Madison

— Anstey, R. and Inikori, J.E. (1976) 'Measuring the Atlantic Slave-trade: a Discussion', *Journal of African History, 17,* 595-627

— (1981) 'Recent trends in African historiography and contribution to history in general', in Ki-Zerbo, J. (ed.) *General History of Africa, Vol 1 – Methodology and African Prehistory*, Heinemann, London, pp.54-71

Davenport, T.R.H. (1971) *The Beginnings of Urban Segregation in South Africa, the Natives (Urban Areas) Act of 1923 and its Background*, Rhodes University, Institute of Social and Economic Research, Grahamstown

— (1972) 'Rhodesian and South African policies for Urban Africans', *Rhodesian History, 3,* 63-76

— (1977) *South Africa: A Modern History*, Macmillan, London

Davies, D.H. (1965) *Land Use in Central Cape Town, a Study in Urban Geography*, Longman, Cape Town

— (1972) 'Lusaka: from Colonial to Independent Capital', *Proceedings of the Geographical Association of Rhodesia, 5,* 14-21

— and Beavon, K.S.O. (1973) *Changes in Land-use Patterns in Central Cape Town 1957-1964*, University of the Witwatersrand, Department of Geography, Johannesburg

Davies, R.J. (1963) 'The Growth of the Durban Metropolitan Area', *South African Geographical Journal, 45,* 15-44

— (1967) 'The South African Urban Hierarchy', *South African Geographical Journal, 49,* 9-19

— (1972) *The Urban Geography of South Africa*, University of Natal, Institute for Social Research, Durban

— (1981) 'The Spatial Formation of the South African City', *GeoJournal Supp. Issue, 2,* 59-72

— and Cook, G.P. (1968) 'Reappraisal of the South African Urban Hierarchy', *South African Geographical Journal, 50,* 116-32

— and Rajah, D.S. (1965) 'The Durban CBD: Boundary Delimitation and Racial Dualism', *South African Geographical Journal, 47,* 45-58

— and Young, B.S. (1970a) 'Manufacturing in South African Cities', *Journal for Geography, 3,* 595-605

— (1970b) 'Manufacturing and Size of Place in the South African Urban System',

Journal for Geography, 3, 699-713

Davies, W.J. (1971) *Patterns of Non-White Population Distribution in Port Elizabeth with Special Reference to the Application of the Group Areas Act*, University of Port Elizabeth, Institute for Planning Research, Port Elizabeth

De Blij, H.J. (1962) 'The Functional Structure and Central Business District of Lourenço Marques, Moçambique', *Economic Geography, 38*, 56-77

— (1963) *Dar es Salaam, a Study in Urban Geography*, Northwestern University Press, Evanston

— (1968) *Mombasa: an African City*, Northwestern University Press, Evanston

De Peyerimhoff, M. (1906) *Enquete sur les resultats de la colonisation officielle de 1871 à 1895*, Imprimierie Torrent, Algiers

Delcourt, J. (1981) *L'Ile de Gorée*, Editions Clairafrique, Dakar

Denoon, D. (1973) *A Grand Illusion: the Failure of Imperial Policy in the Transvaal Colony during the Period of Reconstruction 1900–1905*, Longman, London

Dickson, K.B. (1965) 'Evolution of Seaports in Ghana 1800-1928', *Annals of the Association of American Geographers, 55*, 98-111

— (1969) *A Historical Geography of Ghana*, Cambridge University Press, Cambridge

— (1972) 'Historical Geography in Africa', in A.R.H. Baker (ed.), *Progress in Historical Geography*, David and Charles, Newton Abbot, pp. 187-206

Duly, L.C. (1968) *British Land Policy at the Cape 1795-1844: a Study in Administrative Procedures in the Empire*, Duke University Press, Durham

Dunbar, G.S. (1970) 'African Ranches Ltd., 1914-1931: an Ill-fated Stockraising Enterprise in Northern Nigeria', *Annals of the Association of American Geographers, 60*, 102-23

Dunlop, H. (1971) *The Development of European Agriculture in Rhodesia 1945-1965*, University of Rhodesia, Department of Economics, Salisbury

Ehrlich, C. (1973) 'Building and Caretaking: Economic Policy in British Tropical Africa 1890-1960', *Economic History Review,26*, 649-67

Eichler, G. (1977) 'From Colonialism to National Independence: Algiers' Social Ecology', *GeoJournal, 1(5)*, 5-12

Elphick, R. and Giliomee, H. (1979) *The Shaping of South African Society 1652-1820*, Longman, Cape Town

Els, W.C. (1968) 'Die besproeiingsakie in die Groot-Vis-Rivierbesproeiings Distrik tot 1925', *Journal for Geography, 3*, 115-26

Emmer, P.C. and Wesseling, H.L. (1979) *Reappraisals in Overseas History*, Leiden University Press, Leiden

Ettinger, N., Huxley, E. and Hamilton, P. (1973) *Africa and Asia: Mapping Two Continents*, Jupiter, London

Fage, J.D. (1978) *A History of Africa*, Hutchinson, London

Fetter, B. (1976) *The Creation of Elisabethville 1910-1940*, Hoover Institution Press, Stanford

Fieldhouse, D.K. (1978) *Unilever Overseas; the Anatomy of a Multinational*, Croom Helm, London

Foltz, W.J. (1965) *From French West Africa to the Mali Federation*, Yale University Press, New Haven

Forbes, V.S. (1965) *Pioneer Travellers in South Africa*, Balkema, Cape Town

Fowler, G.L. (1972) 'Italian Colonization of Tripolitania', *Annals of the Association of American Geographers, 62*, 627-40

— (1973) 'Decolonization of Rural Libya', *Annals of the Association of American Geographers*, 63, 490-506

Fox, H.W. (1913) *Notes and Information Concerning Land Policy*, British South Africa Company, London

Franc, J. (1928) *La colonisation de la Mitidja*, Librairie Ancienne Honoré Campion, Paris

Frankel, S.H. (1938) *Capital Investment in Africa: its Course and Effects*, Oxford University Press, London

Fransen, H. and Cook, M.A. (1980) *The Old Buildings of the Cape*, Balkema, Cape Town

Fredrickson, G.M. (1981) *White Supremacy: a Comparative Study in American and South African history*, Oxford University Press, New York

Gale, T.S. (1979) 'Lagos: the History of British Colonial Neglect of Traditional African Cities', *African Urban Studies*, 5, 11-24

Gambia (1968) *Report on the Alternatives for Association Between the Gambia and Senegal*, Sessional Paper 13/1964

Gann, L.H. and Duignan, P. (1969) *Colonialism in Africa 1870-1960*, Cambridge University Press, Cambridge

— (1978) *The Rulers of British Africa 1870-1914*, Stanford University Press, Stanford

— (1979a) *African Proconsuls: European governors in Africa*, Hoover Institution Press, Stanford

— (1979b) *The Rulers of Belgian Africa 1884-1914*, Princeton University Press, Princeton

Gautier, E.F. (1930) *Un siècle de colonisation*, Librarie Felix Alcan, Paris

Gerteiny, A.G. (1967) *Mauritania*, Praeger, New York

Ghaidan, U. (1976) *Lamu: a Study in Conservation*, East African Literature Bureau, Nairobi

Giese, E. (1979) 'Transformation of Islamic cities in Soviet Central Asia into Socialist cities' in R.A. French and F.E.I. Hamilton (eds.), *The Socialist City: spatial structure and urban policy*, Wiley, Chichester, pp. 145-66

Goffin, L. (1907) *Le Chemin de Fer du Congo (Matadi-Stanley Pool)*, M. Weissenbruch, Brussels

Great Britain (1896) *Matabeleland: Report of the Land Commission of 1894 and Correspondence Relating Thereto*, C8130

— (1898) *Africa: Correspondence Relating to the Preservation of Wild Animals in Africa*, C8683

— (1906) *Correspondence Relating to the Preservation of Wild Animals in Africa*, Cd3189

— (1934) *Report of the Kenya Land Commission*, Cmd4556

— (1949) *Report on Preliminary Reconnaissance for a Survey of a Link Between the East African and Rhodesian Railway Systems*, Colonial Office, London

Guelke, L. (1976) 'Frontier Settlement in Early Dutch South Africa', *Annals of the Association of American Geographers*, 66, 25-42

Haefele, E.T. and Steinberg, E.B. (1965) *Government Controls on Transport: an African Case*, Brookings Institution, Washington

Hailey, Lord (1938) *An African Survey*, Oxford University Press, London

Haines, E.S. (1933) 'The Transkei Trader', *South African Journal of Economics*, 1, 201-16

Hance, W.A. (1954) 'The Gezira: an Example in Development', *Geographical*

Review, *44*, 253-70

— (1964) *The Geography of Modern Africa*, Columbia University Press, New York

Hardy, G. (1933) *Géographie et Colonisation*, Librarie Gallimard, Paris

Harms, R. (1975) 'The End of Red Rubber: A Reassessment', *Journal of African History*, *16*, 73-88

Harris, R.C. and Guelke, L. (1977) 'Land and Society in Early Canada and South Africa', *Journal of Historical Geography*, *3*, 135-53

Harrison-Church, R.J. (1948) 'The Case for Colonial Geography', *Transactions of the Institute of British Geographers*, *14*, 17-25

Hart, T. (1976) 'The Evolving pattern of Elite White Residential Areas in Johannesburg 1911-1970', *South African Geographical Journal*, *58*, 68-75

Haswell, R.F. (1979) 'South African Towns on European Plans', *Geographical Magazine*, *51*, 686-94

Headrick, D.R. (1981) *The Tools of Empire: Technology and European Imperialism in the Nineteenth Century*, Oxford University Press, New York

Henderson, R.D.A. (1976) 'Two Aspects of Land Settlement Policy in Moçambique 1900-1961', University of London, Institute of Commonwealth Studies, *Collected Seminar Papers*, *20*, 142-50

Hennessy, A. (1978) *The Frontier in Latin American History*, Edward Arnold, London

Hertslet, E. (1909) *The Map of Africa by Treaty, Revised and Completed to the end of 1908*, HMSO, London

Hess, R.L. (1966) *Italian Colonialism in Somalia*, University of Chicago Press, Chicago

Hill, M.F. (1950) *Permanent Way*, East African Railways and Harbours, Nairobi

Hodder-Williams, R. (1981) 'The British South Africa Company and the Search for "suitable" White Immigrants', University of Cape Town, Centre for African Studies, *Africa Seminar Collected Papers*, *2*, 195-234

Hoyle, B.S. and Hilling, D. (1970) *Seaports and Development in Tropical Africa*, Macmillan, London

Husson, P. (1960) *La question des frontières terrestres du Maroc*, CIB, Paris

Huttenback, R.A. (1971) *Ghandi in South Africa*, Cornell University Press, Ithaca

— (1976) *Racism and Empire: White Settlers and Colored Immigrants in the British Self-governing Colonies 1830-1910*, Cornell University Press, Ithaca

Huxley, E. (1935) *White Man's Country*, Chatto and Windus, London

Huybrechts, A. (1970) *Transports et structures de developpement au Congo*, Mouton, Paris

Hyam, R. (1968) *Elgin and Churchill at the Colonial Office*, Macmillan, London

— (1972) *The Failure of South African Expansion 1908÷1948*, Macmillan London

Ibrahim, H.A. (1979) 'Mahdist Risings against the Condominium Government in the Sudan, 1900/1927', *International Journal of African Historical Studies*, *12*, 440-71

Iliffe, J. (1969) *Tanganyika under German Rule*, Cambridge University Press, Cambridge

Inikori, J.E. (1978) 'The Origins of the Diaspora: the Slave Trade from Africa', *Tarikh*, *5(4)*, 1-19

Isnard, H. (1939) *La réorganisation de la propriété rurale dans la Mitidja*, A. Joyeux, Algiers

— (1949) 'Vigne et colonisation en Algérie', *Annales de Géographie*, *58*, 212-9

— (1954) *Algérie*, B. Arthaud, Paris

— *(1971) Géographie de la Décolonisation*, Presses Universitaires de France, Paris

Issacman, A. (1972) *Mocambique: the Africanization of a European Institution, the Zambesi Prazos 1750-1902*, University of Wisconsin Press, Madison

Istituto Agricolo Coloniale Italiano (1940) *Ente per la colonizzazione della Libia*, Istituto Agricolo Coloniale, Florence

— (1945) *Some Data on Italian Activity in the Colonies*, Istituto Agricolo Coloniale, Florence

— (1947) *La colonizzazione della Tripolitania*, Tipografia del Senato, Rome

Jewsiewichi, B. (1979) 'Le colonat agricole europeen au Congo Belge 1910-1960: questions politiques et économiques', *Journal of African History, 20*, 559-71

Johnson, H.B. (1967) 'The Location of Christian Missions in Africa', *Geographical Review, 57*, 168-202

Johnson, K.M. (1972) *Urbanization in Morocco*, Ford Foundation, New York

Jones, C. (1978) 'British Investment in the Later Nineteenth Century: Argentina and South Africa', University of London, Institute of Commonwealth Studies, *Collected Seminar Papers, 22*, 42-9

Jones, W.O. (1979) 'Review of the Cambridge History of Africa', *African Economic History, 8*, 225-38

Jorgensen, J.J. (1981) *Uganda: a Modern History*, Croom Helm, London

Katzenellenbogen, S.E. (1973) *Railways and the Copper Mines of Katanga*, Clarendon Press, Oxford

Kassab, A. (1981) 'L'agriculture tunisienne sur la voie de l'intensification', *Annales de Géographie, 90*, 55,86

Kay, G. (1967) *A Social Geography of Zambia*, University of London Press, London

— (1970) *Rhodesia: a Human Geography*, University of London Press, London

— and Smout, M. (1977) *Salisbury: a Geographical Survey of the Capital of Rhodesia*, Hodder and Stoughton, London

Kay, G.B. (1972) *The Political Economy of Colonialism in Ghana*, Cambridge University Press, Cambridge

Kearney, B. (1973) *Architecture in Natal 1824-1893*, Balkema, Cape Town

Kenya (1959) *A Game Policy for Kenya*, Sessional Paper 1/1959-60

Kibulya, H.M. and Langlands, B.W. (1967) *The Political Geography of the Uganda-Congo boundary*, Makerere University College, Department of Geography, Kampala

King, A.D. (1976) *Colonial Urban Development*, Routledge and Kegan Paul, London

Kirkman, J. (1975) *Fort Jesus, Mombasa*, Museum Trustees of Kenya, Mombasa

Koerner, F. (1969) 'Décolonisation et économie de plantation (Madagascar)', *Annales de Géographie, 78*, 654-79

Kubicek, R.V. (1979) *Economic Imperialism in Theory and Practice: the Case of South African Gold Mining Finance, 1886-1914*, Duke University Press, Durham

Lamar, H. and Thompson, L. (1981) *The Frontier in History: North America and South Africa Compared*, Yale University Press, New Haven

Langlands, B.W. and Namirembe, G. (1967) *Studies in the Geography of Religion in Uganda*, Makerere University College, Department of Geography, Kampala

Lanning, G. and Mueller, M. (1979) *Africa Undermined: Mining Companies and the Underdevelopment of Africa*, Penguin, London

Latham, A.J.H. (1978) *The International Economy and the Underdeveloped World*,

1865-1914, Croom Helm, London

Lawrence, T.W. (1963) *Trade Castles and Forts of West Africa*, Jonathan Cape, London

Le Coz, J. (1968) 'Le troisième age agraire du Maroc', *Annales de Géographie, 77*, 385-413

Lederer, A. (1965) *Histoire de la Navigation au Congo*, Musée Royal de L'Afrique Central, Tervuren

Lefevre, D. (1974) 'La situation economique de la Réunion au debut du VIe Plan', *Annales de Géographie, 83*, 319-49

Lemon, A. (1976) *Apartheid: A Geography of Separation*, Saxon House, London

Leubuscher, C. (1963) *The West African shipping trade 1909-1959*, A.W. Sijthoff, Leiden

Lewcock, R. (1963) *Early Nineteenth Century Architecture in South Africa, a Study of the Interaction of Two Cultures 1795-1837*, Balkema, Cape Town

Lobato, A. (1967) *Ilha de Moçambique: Panorama Historico*, Agencia-Geral do Ultramar, Lisbon

Lock, M. and Theis, M. (1967) *Kaduna 1917-1967-2017*, Faber and Faber, London

Lucas, C. (1922) *The Partition and Colonization of Africa*, Oxford University Press, Oxford

Lugard, Lord (1965) *The Dual Mandate in British Tropical Africa*, Frank Cass, London

Mabogunje, A.L. (1968) *Urbanization in Nigeria*, University of London Press, London

— (1970) 'Urbanization and Change' in J.N. Paden and E.W. Soja (eds.), *The African Experience, Vol. 1: Essays*, Northwestern University Press, Evanston, pp. 331-58

Mackenzie, J.M. (1974) 'Red Soils in Mashonaland: A Reassessment', *Rhodesian History, 5*, 80-8

Magubane, B.M. (1979) *The Political Economy of Race and Class in South Africa*, Monthly Review Press, New York

Maurette, F. (1939) *Afrique équatoriale, orientale et australe (Géographie Universelle: tome 12)*, Armand Colin, Paris

Mbaeyi, P.M. (1978) *British Military and Naval Forces in West African History*, Nok, New York

McIntyre, W.D. (1967) *The Imperial Frontier in the Tropics 1865-75*, Macmillan, London

Meinig, D.W. (1982) 'Geographical Analysis of Imperial Expansion' in A.R.H. Baker and M. Billinge (eds.), *Period and Place: Research Methods in Historical Geography*, Cambridge University Press, Cambridge, pp. 71-8

Meredith, M. (1979) *The Past Is Another Country: Rhodesia 1890-1979*, Deutsch, London

Mettam, R.W.M. (1937) 'A Short History of Rinderpest with Special Reference to Africa', *Uganda Journal, 5*, 22-6

Middlemas, K. (1979) 'Twentieth Century White Society in Moçambique', *Tarikh, 6(2)*, 30-45

Mikesell, M.W. (1961) *Northern Morocco: A Cultural Geography*, University of California Press, Berkeley

Miller, C. (1971) *The Lunatic Express: an Entertainment in Imperialism*, Macmillan, New York

Moll, J.C. (1977) 'Dorpstigting in die Oranje-Vrystaat: 1854-1864', *Contree*, 2, 23-8

Moodie, D.W. and Lehr, J.C. (1976) 'Fact and Theory in Historical Geography', *Professional Geographer*, 28, 132-5

— (1981) 'Macro-historical Geography and the Great Chartered Companies: the Case of the Hudson's Bay Company', *Canadian Geographer*, 25, 267-71

Morais, A.T. (1964) 'O Colonato do Limpopo', *Estudos Politicos e Sociais*, 2, 477-98

Morgan, D.J. (1980) *The Official History of Colonial Development*, HMSO, London

Morgan, W.B. (1959) 'The Influence of European Contacts on the Landscape of Southern Nigeria', *Geographical Journal*, 125, 48–64

— and Pugh, J.C. (1969) *West Africa*, Methuen, London

Morgan, W.T.W. (1963) 'The White Highlands of Kenya', *Geographical Journal*, 129, 140-55

— (1967) *Nairobi: City and Region*, Oxford University Press, Nairobi

Morocco (1956) *Annuaire Statistique du Maroc*, Government of Morocco, Rabat

Morris, P. (1980) *Soweto: a Review of Existing Conditions and Some Guidelines for Change*, Urban Foundation, Johannesburg

Munro, J.F. (1981) 'Monopolists and Speculators: British Investment in West African Rubber 1905-1914', *Journal of African History*, 22, 263-78

Muntin, G. (1977) *La Mitidja: décolonisation et éspace géographique*, Centre National de la Recherche Scientifique, Paris

Murray, M. (1953) *Union Castle Chronicle 1853-1953*, Longman, London

Nash, M.D. (1982) *Bailie's Party of 1820 Settlers*, Balkema, Cape Town

Natal (1848) *Report on the Division of Natal into Separate Magistracies and Selection of Sites for Towns*, Colony of Natal, Pietermaritzburg

Neil-Tomlinson, B. (1977) 'The Nyassa Chartered Company 1891-1929', *Journal of African History*, 18, 109-28

Neumark, S.D. (1957) *Economic Influences on the South African Frontier*, Stanford University Press, Stanford

Nigeria (1946) *Report with Recommendations on the Planning and Development of Greater Lagos*, Sessional Paper 24/1946

Norregard, G. (1966) *Danish Settlements in West Africa, 1658-1850*, Boston University Press, Boston

Northern Rhodesia (1960) *First Report on a Regional Survey of the Copper Belt*, Government Printer, Lusaka

Ogundana, B. (1972) 'Oscillating Seaport Location in Nigeria', *Annals of the Association of American Geographers*, 62, 110-21

Olivier, S.P. (1943) *Die Pioniertrekke na Gazaland*, Unie Volkspers, Cape Town

Osborn, R.F. (1964) *Valiant Harvest, the Founding of the South African Sugar Industry 1848-1926*, South African Sugar Association, Durban

Pachai, B. (1977) *Land and Politics in Malawi c. 1875-1975*, Limestone Press, Kingston

Palmer, R. (1976) *Land and Racial Domination in Rhodesia*, Heinemann, London

— and Parsons, N. (1977) *The Roots of Rural Poverty in Central and Southern Africa*, Heinemann, London

Pankhurst, R. (1964) 'Italian Settlement Policy in Eritrea and its Repercussions 1889-1896', *Boston University Papers in African History*, 1, 119-56

Pasquier, R. (1960) 'Villes du Sénégal au XIXe siècle', *Revue Francaise d'Histoire d'Outre-Mer*, 47, 387-426

Patterson, K.D. (1980) 'The Veterinary Department and the Animal Industry in the

Gold Coast 1909-1955', *International Journal of African Historical Studies, 13*, 457-91

Pearse, G.E. (1968) *Eighteenth Century Architecture in South Africa*, Balkema, Cape Town

Pechoux, P.V. (1975) 'Mostaganem, ou la mutation d'une région coloniale en Algérie', *Annales de Géographie, 84*, 698-713

Pedler, F. (1974) *The Lion and Unicorn in Africa*, Heinemann, London

Pehaut, Y. (1978) 'L'évolution des structures de commercialisation des produits agricole en Afrique noire', *Cahiers d'Outre-Mer,31*, 313-24

Pelissier, R. (1974) 'Conséquences démographiques des revoltes en Afrique portugaise (1961-1970), essai d'interprétation', *Revue Française d'Histoire d'Outre-Mer, 61*, 34-73

Phimister, I.R. (1978) 'Meat and Monopolies: Beef Cattle in Southern Rhodesia 1890-1938', *Journal of African History, 19*, 391-414

Picard, H.W.J. (1968) *Gentleman's Walk*, Struik, Cape Town

— (1969) *Grand Parade: the Birth of Greater Cape Town 1850-1913*, Struik, Cape Town

Picton-Seymour, D. (1977) *Victorian Buildings in South Africa*, Balkema, Cape Town

Pirie, G.H. (1982) *Aspects of the Political Economy of Railways in Southern Africa*, University of the Witwatersrand, Department of Geography, Johannesburg

Poncet, J. (1962) *La colonisation et l'agriculture européennes en Tunisie depuis 1881*, Mouton, Paris

Pool, G. (1982) *Pionierspoorwee in Duits-Suidwes-Afrika 1897-1915*, Butterworth, Durban

Popp, H. (1982) 'Land Reform and Cooperatives in Morocco', *Applied Geography and Development, 20*, 112-27

Porter, A. (1981) 'Britain, the Cape Colony, and Natal 1870-1915: Capital, Shipping and the Imperial Connection', *Economic History Review, 34*, 554-77

Prescott, J.R.V. (1961) 'Overpopulation and Overstocking in the Native Areas of Matabeleland', *Geographical Journal, 127*, 212-25

— (1971) *The Evolution of Nigeria's International and Regional Boundaries, 1861-1971*, Tantalus Research, Vancouver

Prickett, B. (1969) *Island Base; a History of the Methodist Church in the Gambia 1821-1969*, Methodist Church of Gambia, Bathust

Pringle, J.A. (1982) *The Conservationists and the Killers*, Bulpin, Cape Town

Raven-Hart, R. (1967) *Before van Riebeeck: Callers at South Africa from 1488 to 1652*, Struik, Cape Town

Rawley, J.A. (1981) *The Transatlantic Slave Trade*, Norton, New York

Rea, W.F. (1976) *The Economics of the Zambezi Missions 1580-1759*, Institutum Historicum SI, Rome

Ricard, R. (1936) 'Le problème de l'occupation restreinte dans l'Afrique du Nord (XVe-XVIIIe siecles)', *Annales d'Histoire Economique et Sociale, 8*, 426-37

Roberts, B. (1976) *Kimberley: Turbulent City*, David Philip, Cape Town

Roberts, S.H. (1929) *History of French Colonial Policy 1870-1925*, P.S. King, London

Rodney, W. (1972) *How Europe Underdeveloped Africa*, Bogle–L'Ouverture Publications, London

Ross, R. (1982) *Racism and Colonialism*, Martinus Nijhoff, The Hague

Rossi, G. (1973a) 'Le colonie italiane alla conferenza di Potsdam', *Africa, 28*, 507-44
— (1973b) 'Une ville de colonisation française dans l'Océan Indien', *Cahiers d'Outre-Mer, 26,* 410-26
Rossouw, P.J. (1951) 'Die Arbeidskolonie Kakamas', *Archives Yearbook for South African History, 14(2),* 347-450
Rotberg, R.I. (1970) *Africa and its Explorers: Motives, Methods and Impact,* Harvard University Press, Cambridge
Samuel, R. (1981) *People's History and Socialist Theory,* Routledge and Kegan Paul, London
Saunders, C. (1978) 'Segregation in Cape Town: the Creation of Ndabeni', University of Cape Town, Centre for African Studies, *Africa Seminar Collected Papers, 1,* 43-63
Sbacchi, A. (1977) 'Italian Colonization in Ethiopia: Plans and Projects 1936-1940', *Africa, 32,* 503-16
Scassellati-Sforzolini, G. (1926) *La Societa Agricola Italo-Somala in Somalia,* Istituto Agricolo Coloniale Italiano, Florence
Scham, A. (1970) *Lyautey in Morocco: Protectorate Administration 1912-1925,* University of California Press, Berkeley
Schulze, G. (1978) 'Die Mitidja-Ebene bei Algier: Probleme der Dekolonisation, am Beispiel agrargeographischer Wandlungen', *Geographische Rundschau, 30,* 242-51
Scott, P. (1951) 'The Witwatersrand Goldfield', *Geographical Review, 41,* 561-89
— (1955) 'Cape Town: a Multi-racial City', *Geographical Journal, 121,* 149-57
Seck, A. (1970) *Dakar, Métropole Ouest-Africaine,* Institut Fondamental d'Afrique Noire, Dakar
Segrè, C.G. (1974) *Fourth Shore: the Italian Colonization of Libya,* University of Chicago Press, Chicago
Shorten, J.R. (1970) *The Johannesburg Saga,* Shorten, Johannesburg
Sidikou, A.H. (1975) 'Niamey', *Cahiers d'Outre-Mer, 28,* 201-17
Silver, J. (1981) 'The Failure of European Mining Companies in the Nineteenth Century Gold Coast', *Journal of African History, 22,* 511-29
Slater, H. (1975) 'Land, Labour and Capital in Natal: the Natal Land and Colonisation Company 1860-1948', *Journal of African History, 16,* 257-83
Smalberger, J.M. (1974) 'IDB and the mining compound system in the 1880s', *South African Journal of Economics, 42,* 398-414
— (1975) *A History of Copper Mining in Namaqualand,* Struik, Cape Town
Smit, P. (1973) *Die ontvolking van die blanke platteland: onlangse tendense,* University of Pretoria, Pretoria
— and Booysen, J.J. (1981) *Swart verstedeliking – proses, patroon en strategie,* Tafelberg, Cape Town
Smith, K.W. (1976) *From Frontier to Midlands: a History of the Graaff-Reinet District, 1786-1910,* Institute of Social and Economic Research, Rhodes University, Grahamstown
Smith, T. (1978) *The French Stake in Algeria, 1945-1962,* Cornell University Press, Ithaca
Smuts, F. (1979) *Stellenbosch: Three Hundred Years,* Town Council, Stellenbosch
Société des fermes francaises de Tunisie (1925) *Vingt-cinq ans de colonisation Nord-Africaine,* Société d'Edition Géographie maritimes et coloniales, Paris
Solomon, V.E. (1982) *The South African Shipping Question 1886-1914,*

Historical Publication Society, Cape Town

Sorrenson, M.P.K. (1967) *Land Reform in the Kikuyu Country: a Study of Government Policy*, Oxford University Press, Nairobi

— (1968) *Origins of European Settlement in Kenya*, Oxford University Press, Nairobi

South Africa (1913) *Annual Report of the Department of Lands, 1912*, UG 62-1913

— (1957) *Report of the Commission on Smallholdings in the Peri-urban Areas of the Union of South Africa*, UG 37-1957

— (1960) *Report of the Commission of Inquiry into the European Occupancy of the Rural Areas*, Government Printer, Pretoria

— (1982) *Abstract of Agricultural Statistics*, Department of Agriculture, Pretoria

Southern Rhodesia (1915) *Land Settlement Department: Report for the Year ended 31/3/1915*

Stamp, L.D. (1953) *Africa: a Study in Tropical Development*, Wiley, New York

Stephenson, G.V. (1975) 'The Impact of International Economic Sanctions on the Internal Viability of Rhodesia', *Geographical Review*, *65*, 377-89

Stewart, C.F. (1964) *The Economy of Morocco 1912-62*, Harvard University Press, Cambridge

Strage, M. (1977) *Cape to Cairo*, Jonathan Cape, London

Strandes, J. (1961) *The Portuguese Period in East Africa*, East African Literature Bureau, Nairobi

Streak, M. (1970) *Lord Milner's Immigration Policy for the Transvaal 1897-1905*, Rand Afrikaans University, Johannesburg

Strydom, C.J.S. (1976) *Afrikaners in die vreemde*, Tafelberg, Cape Town

Suret-Canale, J. (1971) *French Colonialism in Tropical Africa 1900-1945*, Pica Press, New York

Sutton, K. (1981) 'The Influence of Military Policy on Algerian Rural Settlement', *Geographical Review*, *71*, 379-94

— and Lawless, R.I. (1978) 'Population Regroupings in Algeria: Traumatic Change and the Rural Settlement Pattern', *Transactions of the Institute of British Geographers, New Series*, *3*, 331-50

Taieb, M. (1971) 'La structure urbaine d'Alger', *Annales de Géographie*, *80*, 33-44

Tanser, G.H. (1965) *A Scantling of Time*, Stuart Manning, Salisbury

Tatz, C.M. (1962) *Shadow and Substance in South Africa: a Study in Land and Franchise Policies Affecting Africans 1910-1960*, University of Natal Press, Pietermaritzburg

Taylor, J. (1982) 'Changing Patterns of Labour Supply to the South African Gold Mines', *Tijdschrift voor Economische en Sociale Geografie*, *73*, 213-20

Temu, A. and Swai, B. (1982) *Historians and Africanist History: A Critique*, Zed Press, London

Tenreiro, F. (1953) 'Descricao da ilha de S. Tomé no século XVI', *Garcia de Orta*, *1*, 219-27

— (1961) 'A floresta e a ocupacao humana na ilha de Sao Tomé', *Garcia de Orta*, *9*, 651-5

Thompson, V. and Adloff, R. (1958) *French West Africa*, Allen and Unwin, London

Touval, S. (1967) 'The Organisation of African Unity and African Borders', *International Organisation*, *21*, 102-27

Transvaal (1900) *Lists of Farms and Owners in the Twenty Districts and Mapock's Ground*, Transvaal Government, Pretoria

— (1908) *Report of the Transvaal Indigency Commission*, TG 13-08

Tripoli (1938) *Pianta di Tripoli*, Unione Coloniale Italiana Publicita e Informazioni, Tripoli

Tunisia (1914a) *Statistique Générale de la Tunisie*, Regence de la Tunisie, Tunis

— (1914b) *Notice sur la Tunisie à l'usage des émigrants*, Société Anonyme de l'Imprimerie Rapide, Tunis

Vail, L. (1975) 'The Making of an Imperial Slum: Nyasaland and its Railways 1895-1935', *Journal of African History*, *16*, 89-112

— (1976) 'Moçambique's Chartered Companies: the Rule of the Feeble', *Journal of African History*, *17*, 389-416

Van Dantzig, A. (1980) *Forts and Castles of Ghana*, Sedco Publications, Accra

Van der Merwe, I.J. (1982) 'Die klein dorp in verval', *Contree*, *12*, 15-22

Van der Merwe, P.J. (1938) *Die trekboer in die geskiedenis van die Kaap Kolonie*, Nasionale Pers, Cape Town

— (1945) *Trek, studies oor die mobiliteit van die pioniersbevolking aan die Kaap*, Nasionale Pers, Cape Town

— (1962) *Nog verder noord*, Nasionale Boekhandel, Cape Town

Van Dongen, I.S. (1954) *The British East African Transport Complex*, University of Chicago, Department of Geography, Chicago

Van Onselen, C. (1982) *Studies in the Social and Economic History of the Witwatersrand 1886-1914*, 2 vols., Longman, London

Van Rensburg, J.I.J. (1954) 'Die geskiedenis van die wingerdkultuur in Suid-Afrika tydens die eerste eeu', *Archives Yearbook for South African History*, *17(2)*, 1-96

Van Zyl, J.A. (1967) 'Aspekte van Blanke landelike vestiging in die Orange-Vrystaat tot 1910', in R.J. Davies, R.A. Preston-Whyte and B.S. Young (eds.), *Jubilee Conference Proceedings*, South African Geographical Society, Durban, pp. 221-50

Vance, J.E. (1970) *The Merchant's World: the Geography of Wholesaling*, Prentice Hall, Englewood Cliffs

Vansina, J. (1966) *Kingdoms of the Savanna*, University of Wisconsin Press, Madison

Vennetier, P. (1969) 'Le développement urbain en Afrique tropicale, considérations générales', *Cahiers d'Outre-Mer*, *22*, 5-62

— (1978) 'Expériences de développement en Afrique tropicale, difficultés et échecs', *Cahiers d'Outre-Mer*, *31*, 314-42

Wallerstein, I. (1974) *The Modern World System, I — Capitalist Agriculture and the Origins of the European World Economy in the Sixteenth Century*, Academic Press, New York

— (1976) 'The Three Stages of African Involvement in the World Economy', in P.C.W. Gutkind and I. Wallerstein (eds.), *The Political Economy of Contemporary Africa*, Sage Publications, London, pp. 30-57

Webb, W.P. (1952) *The Great Frontier*, Houghton Mifflin, Boston

Weinmann, H. (1972) *Agricultural Research and Development in Rhodesia Under the Rule of the British South Africa Company, 1890-1923*, University of Rhodesia, Department of Agriculture, Salisbury

Western, J. (1981) *Outcast Cape Town*, University of Minnesota Press, Minneapolis

White, L.W.T., Silberman, L. and Anderson, P.R. (1948) *Nairobi: Master Plan for a Colonial Capital*, HMSO, London

Whittlesey, D. (1935) 'The Impress of Effective Central Authority upon the Landscape', *Annals of the Association of American Geographers*, *25*, 85-97

Widstrand, C.G. (1969) *African Boundary Problems*, Scandinavian Institute of African Studies, Uppsala

Wiese, B. (1981) *Seaports and Port Cities of Southern Africa*, Franz Steiner Verlag, Wiesbaden

Wills, T.M. and Schulze, R.E. (1976) 'Segregated Business Districts in a South African City' in D.M. Smith (ed.), *Separation in South Africa: Volume 2*, Queen Mary College, Department of Geography, London, pp. 67-84

Wilson, D. and Ayerst, P. (1976) *White Gold: the Story of African Ivory*, Heinemann, London

Wilson, F. (1972) *Labour in the South African Gold Mines 1911-1969*, Cambridge University Press, Cambridge

Wilson, R.T. (1979) 'The Incidence and Control of Livestock Diseases in Darfur, Anglo-Egyptian Sudan, during the Period of the Condominium 1916-1956', *International Journal of African Historical Studies, 12*, 62-82

Winters, C. (1982) 'Urban Morphogenesis in Francophone Black Africa', *Geographical Review, 72*, 139-54

Wolff, R.D. (1974) *The Economics of Colonialism: Britain and Kenya 1870_1930*, Yale University Press, New Haven

Wood, R. (1976) 'Siting the Capital of the Central African Federation' in J.A. Benyon (ed.), *Studies in Local History*, Oxford University Press, Cape Town, pp. 71-9

Wright, H.M. (1977) *The Burden of the Present: Liberal-Radical Controversy over Southern African History*, David Philip, Cape Town

Young, B.S. (1973) 'Two Intra-metropolitan Industrial Models', *South African Geographer, 4*, 131-8

Zeederberg, H. (1971) *Veld Express*, Howard Timmins, Cape Town

Zidouemba, D.H. (1977) 'Les sources de l'histoire des frontières de l'Ouest africain', *Bulletin de l'Institut Fondamental d'Afrique Noire, 39B*, 695-835

INDEX

Abidjan 48
Accra 70
Aden 71
administrative units 54, 194
administrators, 3, 46-63, 126, 140, 144,
    182-4, 188, 194
Adowa 33
African Association 11, 12
African Inland Association 72
African Ranches 106
Africanisation 195
Africans 5, 188-9
Afrikaners 4, 124-9, 143, 149, 159, 201
agricultural assistance 57, 147, 165,
    172
agriculture: European 99-102, 110,
    124, 150-76, 182-4; indigenous
    56-7, 62, 102
Akassa 66
Albany 153-4
Alcazarquivir 14
Alexandria 49, 70, 72, 75, 207
Algeria 5, 14, 41, 43-5, 56, 71, 76, 81,
    120, 130-2, 162-6, 177-9, 206
Algiers 47, 76, 130, 177-9
American methodists 86
Anglo-American Corporation 118
Anglo-Belgian Rubber Company 92-3
Anglo-Boer War 111-12, 127, 129,
    136, 149
Anglo-Egyptian Sudan 32, 34, 48, 62,
    89
Angola 16-17, 41, 43, 45, 47, 83, 110,
    121, 128, 132-4, 137, 149, 151, 175
Antananarivo 72
'any port' model 70
Apartheid city 190-1
architecture 20, 51-4, 147-8, 152, 179,
    186, 203-4
Arguim 15, 17
armies, 4, 40-1, 130
asbestos 117
Ascension 71
Ashanti 41
Asians 68, 122, 129, 134-6
Asmara 47, 171
Assab 32, 40

Australia 101, 104, 139
Azores 10

Baker, S. 12, 13, 73
Bamako 48
Bancroft 118
Bangassou 95
Bangui 48, 73
Banque d'Algérie 165
Barberton 111-12
Barotseland 58, 149
Barth, H. 13
Basakusu 92-3
Basutoland 35-6, 61
Bathurst 47
Baudouin, King 208
bauxite 121
Bechuanaland 35, 48, 58, 77, 128
Beira 78, 106
Belgian Congo 67, 87, 97, 103, 110,
    197, 208
Belgium 34, 174
Benghazi 169
Benin 18
Berlin (Cape) 156
Berlin Conference 1, 31, 87, 91
Berlin Geographical Society 11
Biafra 194
bidonvilles 179-81
bilharzia 25
Bingerville 48
Bismarck, Count 27
Bizerte 40
Blida 181
Bloemfontein 43, 48, 53
Boksburg 115
Boma 48
Botswana 195
Boufarik 163-4, 200
boundaries 33-9, 41, 54, 194
Bowman, I. 133
Brandenburg 16
Brazzaville 35, 49, 73, 76
British East Africa 38, 47, 128, 135-6,
    173
British German Legion 43
British Kaffraria 38, 43, 49, 127, 154-5

225

Salisbury 49, 51, 74, 77
Salsibury, Lord 27
sanctions 117, 173
Sansanding 62
Sao Salvador 22
Sao Tomé (e Principe) 10, 16-17, 23, 98, 197
secessionism 194
segregation 86, 117, 129, 177, 184, 188-91, 203-7
self-government 144, 189
Selukwe 117
semi-subsistence 138-41
Senegal 17, 38, 48, 74, 76-7, 87, 98
Senegambia 18, 36
Sennar dam 62
settlement schemes 24, 79, 119, 172
settlers 4, 29, 35, 44, 48, 101, 122-92, 198-201
Sfax 167
Shabani 117
sheep 145-9
Shela 20
shipping 68-71
Sidi-bel-Abbes 180
Sierra Leone 18, 24-5, 31, 110, 120
Sierra Leone Company 24
Sierra Leone Selection Trust 120
Simonstown 40, 183
sisal 102, 104-5, 174
slave trade 5, 15, 17-19, 22, 64
slaves 17-18, 24, 84, 134-5, 195
sleeping sickness 25
smallholdings 100, 185-8
smallpox 125
Societa Agricola Italo-Somala 103-4
Société Anversoise 93-4
Société du Haute-Ogooué 94
Société Franco-Africaine 167
Sofala 22
Sokoto 33, 66
soldiers 3, 14-22, 39-46
Somalia 35, 36, 98-9, 103-4, 194
Songhay Empire 10
Sousse 167
South Africa 34-6, 41, 43, 49, 53, 60, 71, 75-8, 108-16, 123-30, 137-60, 181-92, 201, 204-6
South African Iron and Steel Corporation 115
South African Railways 77, 80
South West Africa 34, 47, 61, 77, 79, 90, 110-11, 120-1, 128, 145, 148, 190-1
Southern Nigeria 36, 38

Southern Rhodesia 36, 44, 59-60, 90, 107, 116-17, 129, 145, 155, 171-3, 176, 190, 192
Soweto 189
space-economy 77, 114, 187
Spain 14-15, 18, 41, 131, 196
speculation 94, 100
Speke, J. 12-13
spheres of influence 31
squatters 141, 144, 147, 188, 204
stage coaches 74
Stanley, H. 13, 73
steam ships 66, 69, 72-3, 196
Stellaland 143
Stellenbosch 81, 152, 200
submarine cables 71
Sudan 32, 41, 107
Suez Canal 40, 70, 76
sugar 23, 98-101, 135, 155, 159, 174
sunflowers 173
survey 141, 144
Swahili towns 19, 134, 176
Swaziland 35, 58, 120
Swakopmund 47, 79
Sweden 16, 87
Swift, J. 10
Swynnerton Plan 45

Tanganyika 36, 63, 87, 133, 136, 195
Tanganyika Concessions 117
Takoradi 70
Tangier 14, 35, 72
Tarkwa 119
taxation 46, 55-7, 92-3, 162, 197
Tazara line 80
Tchad 94
tea 97, 101, 174
technology 65-6, 76
telegraphs 71
territorial claims 28
Thabong 114
timber 98
Timbuktu 10, 12
tobacco 155, 173-4
Togo 34, 82
Tongaat Estates 100
town planning 51, 114, 117-19, 177-92, 202-7
trade routes 3, 11, 67, 89
traders 3, 14-22, 29, 64-8, 95, 141, 149, 182-3, 195-6
Trading and Occupation of Land Restriction Act 190
Transkei 68
transporters 68-82, 96-7, 196